ILLUSTRATIONS OF
CHAUCER'S ENGLAND

ILLUSTRATIONS OF CHAUCER'S ENGLAND

EDITED BY

DOROTHY HUGHES, M.A.

AUTHOR OF " THE EARLY YEARS OF EDWARD III "

WITH A PREFACE BY

A. F. POLLARD, M.A., Litt.D.

FELLOW OF ALL SOULS, AND PROFESSOR OF ENGLISH HISTORY IN THE
UNIVERSITY OF LONDON

[UNIVERSITY OF LONDON INTERMEDIATE SOURCE-BOOKS
OF HISTORY, No. I]

FOLCROFT LIBRARY EDITIONS / 1972

Library of Congress Cataloging in Publication Data

Hughes, Dorothy, ed.
    Illustrations of Chaucer's England.

    Original ed. issued as no. 1 of University of
London intermediate source-books of history.
    Bibliography: p.
    1. Great Britain--History--Edward III, 1327-1377--
Sources. 2. Great Britain--History--Richard II, 1377-
1399--Sources. 3. Chaucer, Geoffrey, d. 1400-
Contemporary England. I. Title. II. Series: London.
University. University of London intermediate source
-books of history, no. 1.
DA220.H8 1972   942.03'7   72-5333
ISBN 0-8414-0037-7 (lib. bdg.)

ILLUSTRATIONS OF CHAUCER'S ENGLAND

EDITED BY

DOROTHY HUGHES, M.A.

AUTHOR OF "THE EARLY YEARS OF EDWARD III"

WITH A PREFACE BY

A. F. POLLARD, M.A., Litt.D.

FELLOW OF ALL SOULS, AND PROFESSOR OF ENGLISH HISTORY IN THE
UNIVERSITY OF LONDON

[UNIVERSITY OF LONDON INTERMEDIATE SOURCE-BOOKS
OF HISTORY, No. I]

NEW IMPRESSION

LONGMANS, GREEN AND CO.
39 PATERNOSTER ROW, LONDON
FOURTH AVENUE & 30TH STREET, NEW YORK
BOMBAY, CALCUTTA, AND MADRAS
1919

PREFACE.

THE immediate object of this volume, and of the
series which it inaugurates, is of a practical character. It is to remove some of the difficulties
which beset students, teachers, and examiners in
connection with the original texts prescribed as
part of the Intermediate course and examination
in history in the University of London. That
students, even in their intermediate stage, should
have occasion to study something in the nature of
original sources is nowadays a principle so well
recognized as to need no defence. But there is
a considerable difference between the recognition
of a principle and the provision of means for its
application; and the authorities which prescribe
these original texts have hitherto been compelled
to rely on a market that is not supplied on any
definite plan or from any educational source. The
printed documentary evidences for English history
consist of shreds and patches produced by individual enterprise and interest in particular epochs
or aspects of history, and generally unavailable in
sufficient quantity for students in schools and universities; and when any design other than that

of producing a saleable book has stimulated their publication, it has seldom been that of meeting the needs of university students.

Even the rare exceptions have suffered from at least one serious defect. Nothing, for instance, could be more admirable in their way as historical sources or illustrations than Horace Walpole's "Letters" or the "Paston Letters," Fortescue's "Governance of England" or Burke's "Reflections on the French Revolution". But such works almost invariably illustrate no more than one aspect of a period or exemplify but one kind of historical source; and the numerous students, who cease to study history after their intermediate examination, stand in particular need of source-books, which will illustrate the various aspects of their respective periods and provide some means for comparing different kinds of historical evidence. A political pamphlet or a ballad has not the same kind of value as a contemporary letter; and the weight to be attached to a chronicle differs from that which an official record will carry. The student loses many opportunities of historical education if his source-book is restricted to one type of evidence and provides him with no means of comparing the multitudinous material of which the temple of historical truth is built. The absence of source-books selected and arranged according to recognized principles of historical science has constrained the Board of Studies in History in the University of London to embark on the experiment of which the present volume is the beginning.

It is hoped, however, that the series will serve other purposes than those for which it has been primarily designed. Others than professed students of history are interested in historical studies ; and in particular there is an increasing weight of opinion in favour of the view that the language and literature of a country or of a period cannot be satisfactorily studied apart from its history. Readers of Chaucer can hardly be indifferent to these authentic illustrations of the age in which he lived ; and while not every volume in this series can be expected to make so direct an appeal to the student of English literature, few of them are likely to be devoid of interest and instruction for the historian of letters.

Apart from the general outlines and supervision of the scheme, this volume is the work of Miss Dorothy Hughes, whose "Early Years of Edward III"[1] has borne witness to her knowledge of the sources for the history of the period. These documents will not, of course, enable the student to dispense with further reading on the subject, and Miss Hughes has provided the following notes to guide the reader ; her own previous volume should be added to her list of authorities.

A. F. POLLARD.

[1] Published for the University of London Press by Messrs. Hodder & Stoughton, 1915.

CONTENTS.

NOTES.

A. NOTE ON AUTHORITIES.

For the general history of the period, "The Political History of England," ed. Hunt and Poole, vol. iii. (T. F. Tout) and vol. iv. (C. Oman); "A History of England," ed. Oman, vol. iii. (K. H. Vickers, "England in the Later Middle Ages"); the "Constitutional History of England," Stubbs, vols. ii. and iii. For Edward III's reign, "The Life and Times of Edward III," W. Longman; "The History of Edward III," J. Mackinnon (more recent, but devotes attention mainly to military affairs). Of Richard II's reign the only account is the "Histoire de Richard II," by Henri Wallon; cf. also "John of Gaunt," S. Armitage Smith; "England in the Age of Wycliffe," G. M. Trevelyan. For special subjects, "The Black Death of 1348-49," F. A. Gasquet; "The Enforcement of the Statute of Labourers," B. H. Putnam. "Le Soulèvement des Travailleurs d'Angleterre," A. Réville; "The Great Revolt of 1381," C. Oman. For ecclesiastical history, the "History of the English Church," ed. Stephens and Hunt, vol. iii. ("The English Church in the Fourteenth and Fifteenth Centuries," W. W. Capes); "Wycliffe and Movements for Reform," R. L. Poole; "Wyclif and his English Precursors," P. Lorimer (translated from J. Lechler). For naval and military affairs, the "History of the Royal Navy," Sir H. Nicolas, vol. ii.; "History of the Art of War in the Middle Ages," Oman. Valuable notes and commentaries upon matters connected with the French War are to be found in M. Luce's notes to the First Book of Froissart's "Chronicles" (Société de l'Histoire de France, ed.

Luce and Raynouart), and in Kervyn de Lettenhove's indexes to his "Froissart". Taxation is dealt with in the "History of Taxation," S. Dowell; cf. also, "Taxes on Movables in the Reign of Edward III," J. S. Willard, "English Historical Review," xxx.

Valuable articles and references may be found in the "Dictionary of National Biography". Bibliographies of the period are given in the volumes of the "Political History of England" mentioned above; full and detailed references are given in the standard bibliography, "Sources and Literature of English History," C. Gross, 2nd ed., 1915.

B. NOTES ON THE CHRONICLERS PRINCIPALLY QUOTED.

ADAM OF MURIMUTH. A Doctor of Civil Law and Canon of St. Paul's, frequently employed in diplomatic and other business by the governments of Edward II and Edward III. He accepted the rectory of Wraysbury in Buckinghamshire in 1337, and died in 1347 at the age of seventy-two. In compiling his "Continuatio Chronicorum" he "had access to documents and private information of which he freely availed himself".

ROBERT OF AVESBURY. A canon lawyer, Registrar of the Court of the Archbishop of Canterbury. His chronicle "De mirabilibus gestis Edwardi III," extending to 1356, devotes especial attention to military affairs; "holding a public position, he had access to some of the material of which Murimuth also makes use".

GEOFFREY LE BAKER OF SWINBROOK, a secular clerk, was to some extent indebted to the work of Murimuth, with whom he was probably acquainted; for his "Chronicon," begun possibly about 1350, he "obtained most of his information from living sources".

HENRY OF KNIGHTON, a Canon of Leicester, is responsible for a "Chronicon" containing important accounts of domestic affairs especially, to about 1366. His anonymous "Continuator," also closely connected with Leicester, resumed a full narrative of events from the death of Edward III.

The "Chronicon" of WALTER OF HEMINGBURGH was completed by a continuation from 1326 to 1346.

THOMAS WALSINGHAM was closely connected with St. Albans Abbey, presiding over the Scriptorium for many years. His death occurred in c. 1422. His literary activities began about 1380, the "Chronicon Angliae" being an early work, while the "Historia Anglicana" represents a final history, much rewritten and revised. From the St. Alban's Scriptorium proceed also the "Annales Ricardi II," contributing, like the above, original and contemporary accounts of the events which they describe.

JEAN FROISSART came to England in 1361, and was for some years attached to the household of Queen Philippa. In 1369, after her death, he left the country; the first edition of the First Book of his "Chronicles" was probably written between this time and 1373, being perhaps compiled from material already carefully collected. After 1376, when under the influence of the Court of Brabant, he produced a second version of this Book, his English bias appearing much weakened; this version is represented by the "MS. d'Amiens". The third and latest edition (represented by the "MS. de Rome") was written after Richard II's deposition, covers the period to 1350 only, and exhibits strong anti-English feeling.

JEAN LE BEL, Canon of Liège, probably compiled the first portion of his "Chronicle" (to 1346) between 1352 and 1356, the portion 1346-58 in the latter year, and the remainder from time to time until 1361. He may have obtained much information from John of Hainault, but we are told that he spared no pains and expense to secure authentic information from all sources. He died in 1370. Froissart borrowed lavishly, often word-for-word, from this "Chronicle" for the first edition of his book.

C. NOTE ON THE TRANSLATIONS.

In the translations from Froissart, use has been made of Lord Berners' Tudor Translations and of the version by Johnes, but careful comparison has been made with the original (ed. Luce and Raynouard). For Nos. 53 and 59 (Book I), Lord Berners' translation is used with little modification; No. 39 is based mainly on his version, but some changes, more closely following the original, have been made. For No. 55 (*b*), not included in Berners' translation, use has been made of Johnes' version, freely modified with reference to Froissart. No. 23 has been carefully compiled and translated from Froissart's various narratives, with some reference to Johne's version.

The French letters and despatches quoted by Murimuth and Avesbury[1] have been newly translated from the originals, but reference has in all cases been made to the renderings given by Sir E. M. Thompson in his edition of these writers for the Rolls Series; his translations have been adopted for No. 2 (Book I), with some modifications, and for No. 2 (Book III) completely.

For extracts from the Statutes, the translations printed in the "Statutes of the Realm" have been compared with the originals, and in some cases new renderings are given.

For other translations, unless otherwise indicated, the Editor is responsible.

[1] Book I, Nos. 7, 17, 18, 19, 22, 27-30, 35, 36.

BOOK I. THE FRENCH WAR.

A. The War on the Continent.

1.

[Schedule to be read by influential persons commissioned to explain
the King's business before meetings to be held in all counties.
(French.) "Foedera," II, ii. 994.   28 August, 1337.]

THESE are the offers made to the King of France by
the King of England to avoid war.

First, the King of England sent solemn messengers to the
King of France, begging him to restore the lands that he
is arbitrarily and unreasonably withholding from him in
the Duchy of Guienne; at whose request the King of
France did nothing; but at last he promised that if the
King of England would come to him in his own person,
he would do him justice, grace, and favour.

Trusting in which promise, the King of England
crossed secretly into France, and came to him humbly
requesting the delivery of his aforesaid lands, offering and
performing to the said King whatever he ought, and more;
but the King of France put him off always with words
and treaty, and in reality did nothing; and moreover,
during these same discussions, he wrongfully drew to
himself more and more the King of England's rights in
the aforesaid duchy.

Item, the King of England, seeing the stubbornness of
the King of France, to have his goodwill, and that which
he wrongfully detains from him, held out to him the
following great offers, that is to say, when one was refused,
he put forward another :—

1

First, the marriage of his eldest son, now Duke of Cornwall, for the said King of France's daughter, taking nothing with him for the marriage ;

Item, the marriage of his sister, now Countess of Gelders, for his son, with a very great sum of money ;

Item, the marriage of his brother, the Earl of Cornwall, whom God assoil, for some demoiselle of his royal blood.

Item, to make recompense for the inconvenience, he offered him money, as much as he might reasonably wish to ask. Item, because the King of England was given to understand that the King of France wished to undertake the blessed voyage to the Holy Land, and desired greatly to have the King of England in his company, and therefore he would show him grace and favour, the King of England, so that no hindrance of the said voyage might be charged upon him, made offer to the King of France to pass over with him with great force on the said voyage; on condition, however, that before his going he should make him full restitution of the aforesaid lands.

Item, then he offered to go with him on the said voyage, on condition that before his going, he should make restitution of the half, or of a certain part, of the said lands.

Item, afterwards he made him more ample offers, namely, that he would go with him, so that on his return from the Holy Land the King of France should make him such restitution.

Item, then to arrest the malice of the King of France, who was striving to charge the hindrance of the said voyage upon the King of England, he proffered his readiness to undertake the voyage with him, so that, upon his return, he should accomplish justice towards him.

But the King of France, who was striving by all means in his power to undo the King of England and his people, so that he might retain what he wrongfully withheld, and conquer more from him, would accept none of the aforesaid offers; but seeking occasion, he busied himself in aid and maintenance of the Scots, the King of England's enemies, striving so to delay him by the Scottish war, that he would have no power to pursue his rights elsewhere.

Item, then, in deference to the King of France, and at the request of his envoys, the King of England granted the Scots respite of war, and truce, in the hope of parley concerning peace; during the which respite, the Scots slew the Earl of Athol and others, and seized many great men of the King of England's allegiance, and besieged and took castles and other places of the King and his people. And nevertheless, at the request of the said envoys, he offered the Scots a truce for four or five years, on condition that they would make restitution of the things which they had seized during the first truce, so that in the meantime, the aforesaid voyage might have been undertaken. But to this restitution the King of France would not assent, but maintained the Scots in their malice with all his might; and moved open war upon the King of England without just cause, and has sent to sea his galleys and his fleet, which he caused to be prepared under feigned colour of the said voyage, with great number of men-at-arms, to destroy the fleet and the subjects of the King of England. And these men have in warlike manner seized and carried off many English ships, capturing and killing those on board; and they have come to England, and to the King of England's islands, burning, slaying, robbing, and committing other horrible mischiefs, according to their power.

Item, then the King of England, by the counsel and advice of the great men and sages of his realm, wishing to avoid war so far as he could, sent solemn messengers to the King of France, to offer him whatever he could, without great disherison, in order to have peace with him. But the King of France, hardened in his malice, would not suffer the said messengers to come to him, nor agree to peace, or talk of peace; but sent his host, great and strong, to take into his hands by force, the whole of the aforesaid Duchy, saying untruly, that the Duchy is forfeit to him; the which host is doing very great mischiefs in the Duchy, besieging and taking castles and towns.

Item, the King of France, to cover his malice, etc., is striving falsely to inform the Pope, and other great persons of Christendom, against the King of England, compassing with all his might to win not only the said Duchy, but all the lands of the King of England.

These things and others, as many as the King and his Council can think of, have been offered to the King of France in order to have peace; and if any man may know other fitting way, he will be glad and ready to accept it.

2.

[During 1337 Edward III obtained the alliance of many princes of the Netherlands, including his brother-in-law the Count of Gelderland, and John, Duke of Brabant; he also secured promises of support from the Emperor Louis of Bavaria. In October of that year his relations with France became hopeless, and some fighting began in Flanders. But truces were arranged, as the result of Papal diplomacy, and it was not until July, 1338, that his first expedition set sail. After waiting at Antwerp until late in August, he set out on his expedition up the Rhine, where he met the Emperor on 5 September and was created Imperial Vicar. But various delays occurred after his return to Brabant, and no serious expedition was undertaken until the summer of 1339. Letter inserted by Robert of Avesbury in his "Chronicle". (French.)]

Edward, etc., to our dear son, and to the honourable fathers in God, John, by the same grace, Archbishop of Canterbury, Richard, Bishop of London, William de la Zouche, our Treasurer, and others of our Council in England, greeting. The cause of our long sojourn in Brabant we have often made known to you before now, and well is it known to each one of you. But because lately scarcely any aid has come to us from our realm, and the delay was so grievous to us, our people in such straits, and our allies all too tardy about the business; and also our ambassadors, who had tarried so long with the Cardinals and the Council of France to treat of peace, brought us no other offers but that we should have not one hand's breadth of land in the realm of France; and moreover, as we had tidings, our cousin Philip of Valois had always sworn that we should not be a single day in France with our host without that he would give us battle—we, always trusting in God and our right, caused our allies to come to us, and had it certainly shown to them that we would on no account wait longer, but would advance in pursuit of our right, taking the grace that God should give us. And seeing the dishonour that would have fallen upon them if they had stayed behind, they agreed to follow us. A date was appointed for us to be on the marches within France on a certain day, at which day and place we were all ready, and our allies came after, as well as they could. The Monday on the eve of St. Matthew we went out from Valenciennes,[1] and the same day there began burning in the Cambrécis, and we were burning the country there all the following week, so that that district is full clean laid waste, the corn and cattle, and other goods. On the following Saturday we came to Marcoing, which lies between Cambrai and France, and that same day we began to burn in France.[2] And we had heard that the said lord Philip was coming towards us at Péronne, on his way to Noyon. So we still held on our march, our people burning and devastating the country commonly for the space of twelve or fourteen leagues. The Saturday[3] next before the Feast of St. Luke we crossed the water of Oise, and camped and tarried there on the Sunday; on which day we had our allies with us, who

[1] 20 September.   [2] 9 October.   [3] 16 October.

showed us that their victuals were nearly spent, and that winter was coming hard upon us; and that they could not stay with us, but when their victuals were spent they must set out on their return march. Truly, they had the shorter supplies by reason that they expected our said cousin would have given us speedy battle. On the Monday morning there came letters to my lord Hugh of Geneva from the master cross-bowman of France, making mention that he wished to say to the King of England, from the King of France,—let him take up a field not protected by wood, marsh, or water, and he would give him battle before the Thursday next following. The next day we moved on, so as always to do what damage we could. The Wednesday after there came a messenger to the said lord Hugh, bringing letters from the King of Bohemia and the Duke of Lorraine, with their seals hanging, containing that as to whatever the said master cross-bowman had sent on behalf of the King of France, he would keep covenant. We, seeing the said letters, at once drew towards Flamangerie, where we stayed all day on Friday. At vespers three spies were taken, and were examined, each one separately, and they all agreed that the said Philip would give us battle on Saturday,[1] and that he was a league and a half from us. On the Saturday we were on the field a full quarter before daybreak, and took up our position to fight, in a place fitting for us and for him. In the early morning some of his scouts were taken, who told us that his advanced guard was in front of the field in battle array, and coming out towards us. When the news came to our host, our allies, although they had before borne themselves sluggishly towards us, were truly of such loyal intent that never were men of such good will to fight. In the meantime, one of our scouts, a knight of Germany, was taken, who perchance showed all that he had seen of our array to

[1] 23 October.

the enemy; so that he at once withdrew his vanguard, and gave orders to encamp. And they made trenches around them, and cut down the big trees, to prevent our approach. We stayed all that day on foot, drawn up for battle, until towards vespers, when it seemed to our allies that we had tarried long enough. And at vespers we mounted our horses, and went near to Avesnes, a league and a half from our said cousin, and made known to him that we would await him there all the Sunday; and thus we did. And we can send no other news of him, save that on the Saturday, when we mounted our horses, in departing from our ground, he thought that we should have come against him, and he was in such haste to take stronger ground, that in his crossing, a thousand horsemen foundered in the marsh, coming down one over another. On Sunday, the lord of Faniels was taken by our people. On the Monday morning we had news that the lord Philip and all his allies were scattered and withdrawn in great haste; so that our allies would not afterwards stay longer. And as to what is to be done further, we shall hold a Council with them at Antwerp on the morrow of St. Martin. And afterwards we will send you tidings thence speedily as to what shall in the meantime have been done. Given under our Privy Seal at Brussels, the first day of November.

3.

[Protest addressed to Edward III, on his assumption of the title of King of France, by the Pope, Benedict XII. (Latin.) "Foedera," II, ii. 1117. Edward formally assumed the title of King of France in January, 1340, in accordance with his agreement with the Flemings, made in the previous autumn.]

Benedict, Bishop, and servant of the servants of God, to his dearest son in Christ, Edward, the illustrious King of England, greeting, and the Apostolic benediction. Letters of the King's excellency were lately presented to us, wherein, their contents being understood, a new title, and the impression of a seal engraved, as it appeared, with the arms of both France and England, afforded us matter of great amazement. Verily, most dear son, insomuch as we bear great affection towards thee, we are the more seriously disturbed, in perceiving thee to be led by perverse and knavish counsel into courses neither expedient nor seemly. Nevertheless, our affection suffers us not to pass these over in silence, without exposing them before thy mental view, that thou mayst more profitably take thought for thyself in these matters.

Since the assertion admits of no doubt, that a certain custom, hitherto unbrokenly observed, does not permit succession to the throne of France in the female line, the succession does not belong, it is said, to thee, who art descended in that line from the race of the house of France. And albeit even that a successor in such line were not debarred by custom, there are indeed daughters and daughters' children of the Kings of France who in turn succeeded Philip, thy grandfather of famous memory, who, in respect of the succession are, as is shown, nearer to the Kings their fathers than art thou and our dear daughter Isabel, thine illustrious mother, the child of the said Philip. . . . But to think that thou couldst seize upon that realm by force—of a truth, considering the greatness and might of the King of France, for that thy strength is held by no means sufficient ; indeed, this calling of thyself King of France, and this assumption of his arms, albeit thou dost possess nothing in that kingdom, we hold to proceed, beyond all doubt, from evil and iniquitous counsel. If indeed, they who have urged thee to such steps strive to assert, in excuse, that thou art lord in Flanders, which is known to be a fief of the King and realm of France, yet thy royal prudence should diligently consider who, and of what character, are they who there have introduced thee.

Hitherto they have been by no means distinguished for their constancy, for often have they, at their arbitrary pleasure, expelled their natural lords, to whom they were bound by the obligation of fealty ; and if they have dealt thus with those whom they were naturally bound to revere, consider, my son, what is to be expected in thy case, and what manner of title may thence be construed. Observe also, whether it is the result of good and just counsel that thou dost cause thyself to be called King of France while our beloved son in Christ, Philip, is reigning, who has for many years peacefully possessed that kingdom —and didst thou not, by doing fealty and liege homage to him as such, for the lands pertaining to thee within that realm, recognise him as King of France, and thy liege lord ? Verily, these who hear it are amazed ! ascribing it not to judgment, but rather to foolish vaingloriousness. Moreover, we think thou shouldst more discerningly take heed how it is feared that such title, lacking both profit and reason, may prove a poisonous root, which if care be not had, will in all likelihood send forth fruits of sorrow and bitterness ;—and it is said that they suggested it who love not thee, but are busied about seeking their own gain at thy expense, believing they can attain it when they have procured thee to be entangled in deep toils and parlous difficulties. Furthermore, we think that thou shouldst diligently take thought as to what number and manner of kings, princes, and magnates, sprung from the stock of the house of France, or joined thereto by marriage and alliance, who hitherto have not opposed thee, thou wouldst provoke by this title, and wouldst expressly incense, shouldst thou persist. It might set up such argument as would render peace between thee and the said King of France, so far as human judgment is concerned, for ever impossible ; and by it these same princes and others of that Kingdom—who, as the common saying runs, would sooner risk death and loss of all their goods than suffer these things—will be made the more valiant and ready in defence of the same Philip and his kingdom.

Nor shouldst thou, dearest son, place much confidence in the Teutons and Flemings, for thou wilt find them courteous and kindly while they may consume thy fortune, but otherwise thou mayst not depend upon their assistance. If also thou wilt reflect upon the deeds of thy forefathers—how these same Flemings and Teutons have behaved to them in times past, thou wilt plainly find what manner of trust thou mayst put in them. Therefore do we entreat thy royal highness, earnestly exhorting thee in God to receive in friendly spirit the foregoing matters, which we have written of our fatherly goodwill and sincere affection, examining them, and other points which may occur to thee touching them, with due consideration ; and, laying aside the aforesaid title, to turn thy heart into the way of peace and concord, whereby, when mutual accord is established between thee and the said King, thou mayst peaceably attain and hold those things which shall be thine of right.

And as ye are united in truth by blood and affinity, so may ye be bound by the lasting bond of mutual alliance and affection. Given at Avignon on the 5th of March, in the sixth year of our Pontificate.

4.

[Memorandum of the King's passage, 1340. (Latin.) "Foedera," II, ii. 1129, from the Close Roll. Edward remained on the Continent until February, 1340, when he at last returned to England. Preparations were soon made for another expedition, supplies being obtained from Parliament. Shortly before he sailed, news arrived of the presence of a French fleet off the Flemish coast, but, in spite of the opposition of some of the Council, he set out.]

Be it remembered that on the Thursday next before the Feast of St. John Baptist, to wit, on the 22nd day

of the month of June, in the 14th year of the reign of
our lord King Edward III in England, and the first year
of his reign in France, the King, with certain magnates
and others of his realm of England, with his great fleet
assembled in the port of Orwell for his passage to parts
beyond the sea, set sail from that port to the same parts,
about the hour of prime.

5.

[The account given to Parliament of Edward's victory at Sluys, and
his intention to besiege Tournai. (French.) "Rolls of Parliament,"
ii. 118.]

And upon this came the Earls of Arundel and Gloucester,
and Sir William Trussel, with letters of credence under our
lord the King's Privy Seal, addressed to the Prelates, Earls,
and other great men assembled in the Parliament, making
mention of the said victory, and of our lord the King's
great necessity, so that he must be speedily succoured, or
lose his friends and allies ;—the tenor of which letters is as
follows :—Edward, by the Grace of God King of England
and France, and Lord of Ireland, to the Duke, and the
Archbishops, Bishops, Earls, Barons, and others who shall
be assembled in this our next Parliament at Westminster, Greeting.   After our last coming into England, our
Parliament being summoned, and on the appointed day
assembled in the above place, and our business over here,
with the great need in which we stood of having aid for
its favourable execution being shown to those who were
present, the great men and others, we found them of right
goodwill, which they plainly proved by the great subsidy
granted to us.[1]   But because such an aid cannot at once
be converted into money, and we, and other great men
with us were bound to return to Flanders, and keep our
faith with those to whom we had pledged ourselves in that

[1] The aid of "the ninth sheep, fleece and lamb".

country and elsewhere (for to hold to this we were determined) ; and also because the great men of our Council
who were there counselled us to do so, we resolved to cross
over at this time with a certain number of men-at-arms,
and that afterwards other great men should come with the
other fleet, that was ordained to be ready at Midsummer,
with all the great men and others who were appointed to
come then. And as we were on the point of crossing,
with great part of our horses shipped, news came that our
enemy of Valois had arrayed a great fleet of ships, that
was before us in the water of Zwyn. Having heard this,
and having considered the perils that might befall if they
had set out to injure our realm of England, or our people
elsewhere—and also what comfort it would have been to
our enemies, and especially to Scotland, if such a force
had come to them—we determined at once to seek them
out wherever we might find them, as is well known to
those of our Council who were present at our departure
from England. And we found them on St. John's day,[1] in
the aforesaid port, and our Lord Jesus Christ showed us
such mercy touching them that day, that the victory
rested with us, as we think, indeed, has fully been made
known to you by those who were present. For which
mercy we praise God, and entreat you all to give thanks
unto Him. After this same St. John's day, the people of
Flanders, and also other great men our allies came to us,
and showed us how our said enemy was on the border,
ready to invade our allies in Flanders or elsewhere, where
he could most injure them, and force them to withdraw
from our alliance. We, having regard to the pursuit of
our right, and above all, the keeping our faith and resisting his malice, resolved with the consent of our said allies,
and of the great men of our realm of England and of the
country of Flanders, who were with us, to disembark,

[1] 24 June.

and to divide our army ; ourselves with the one part going towards Tournai, where there will be a hundred thousand armed men of Flanders, and Sir Robert of Artois to St. Omer with fifty thousand men, besides all our allies and their power. For the managing and conducting of the which host, a full great sum of money is wanted, besides the debts which we must needs pay before our going. We pray you earnestly, and each one of you, that before all things you will consider the claim we have, in consequence of the great peril that will ensue if we be not shortly succoured with money and supplies, to satisfy the said country and our allies, as well as the soldiers who have before been retained with us, who will withdraw if they be not paid. And moreover, if our allies themselves be not paid, they will peradventure go over to the enemy, and with his malice, and their power drawn unto him, consider that our land, ourselves, our children, and all the great men and others would be on the verge of destruction. And if we be speedily aided, we hope to find him in ill plight, and ourselves ever henceforth at an advantage. We beg you then to make provision that we may be succoured in all haste with money or supplies, in such manner, and at such time, that we may make satisfaction there where we are pledged, and retain our forces. And the Earls of Arundel, Huntingdon, and Gloucester, and Sir William Trussel, who have borne themselves very loyally and nobly towards us in this business, and come to you in order to explain the state of our affairs, can show you our intent more fully by word of mouth. Please to give full faith and credence to them and each one of them, in what they shall tell you from us. Given under our Privy Seal at Bruges, the 9th day of July.

6.

[The Siege of Tournai was begun on 23 July. Philip of France had an army of some 70,000 men in the neighbourhood of Arras; he came to Bouvines early in September, but did not attempt to attack the English. On 25 September the Truce of Esplechin was signed. (Latin.) Adam of Murimuth.]

The siege of the city of Tournai lasted until the Feast of St. Cosmo and St. Damian; on which day, after much treaty about the setting afoot of an armistice contrived by the French, agreement was come to for the making of a truce, at their request, until the Feast of St. John the Baptist next following, so that in the meantime there might be discussion as to the making of peace. Prisoners were restored on both sides, under a sworn agreement that they would return at the said Feast of St. John in case a final peace should not be made. And thus the siege was raised, and some English noblemen returned home. But there was much talk concerning this truce, since the King of England lay at Tournai, besieging the city, and Philip of Valois with his whole army was within four leagues of him, yet dared not come near to raise the siege, but there was much treaty through the King of Bohemia who was with him, about the offering of a truce. At last the Duke of Brabant, the Count of Hainault, the Marquis of Juliers, the Duke of Guelders, and others of the King of England's allies agreed that an honourable, though unprofitable truce should be made—unprofitable, I say, to the King and his people, not to the aforesaid allies, whose towns and castles, which the King of France had seized some time before were restored. The King of England long delayed his consent to the truce, hoping for money from England, which did not come; and therefore, on account of his want of money, and because he had only a few Englishmen with him, he was obliged to fall in with the wishes of his allies, and to agree at last to the truce. He did so unwillingly, and also against the wishes of the men of Flanders, but he could do nothing else at that time.

7

[The French Government having undertaken to enforce the decision of the Parlement of Paris in favour of the claim of Charles of Blois to the Duchy of Brittany, Edward III agreed in 1342 to support the claim of Charles's rival, John de Montfort. In June an English fleet was sent to relieve Hennebont, then besieged by the French, and in October of the same year Edward himself set out with an expedition to Brittany. Edward's letter to his son from Brittany. (French.) Preserved in Robert of Avesbury's " Chronicle ".]

Right dear and well-beloved son, we know well that you desire greatly to hear good news of us and of our estate. We do you to wit that on the departing of these letters we were well and of good cheer praised be God, desiring also to hear and know this of you. Right dear son, as for how things have passed with us since our leaving England, we do you to wit that we have made a long raid through the Duchy of Brittany, the which country is yielded to our obedience, with many good towns and strongholds, namely, the town of Ploermel, the castle and town of Malestroit, and the castle and town of Redon, which are good towns and well enclosed. And know that the lord of Clisson, who is one of the greatest men of Poitou, and four other barons, namely, the lord of Loyat, the lord of Machecoul, the lord of Retz, and the lord of Rieux, and other knights of the said country, and their towns and strongholds, which are right on the borders of France, and of our Duchy of Gascony, are surrendered to our peace ; the which is thought a great achievement for our war. And before the writing of these letters, we sent into the parts of Nantes our cousin of Northampton, the Earl of Warwick, and Sir Hugh le Despenser, with great number of other bannerets and 300 men-at-arms, to achieve what success they may. And since their departing, we

have news that the Lord of Clisson and the aforesaid barons
have gone to the support of our cousin and his company,
with a good number of men-at-arms; but at the sending
of these letters we have yet no news of their doings.
Nevertheless, we hope speedily to have good tidings, with
God's help. Right dear son, know that, with the advice of
the wisest men in our host, we have laid siege to the city
of Vannes, which is the best town of Brittany, after the
town of Nantes, and can best hold down and constrain the
country to our obedience; for we thought that if we advanced further without being sure of the said city, the
country which has yielded to us could not in any manner
keep holding for us. And moreover, this town is on the
sea, and is well enclosed, so that if we can have it, it will
be a great exploit for our war. And know, right dear son,
that Sir Louis of Poitiers, Count of Valentinois, is captain of the town, and they say that there are good men
with him; but we hope, by God's puissance, to have a
good issue. For since our coming into these parts, He
has given us a good beginning, and success enough for the
time, for the which may He be praised. The country is
full abundant in corn and flesh; none the less, dear son,
you must needs urge our Chancellor and Treasurer to send
us money, for they well know our condition. Dear son,
know that on the third day that we were encamped at the
aforesaid siege, there came to us an abbot and a clerk
from the Cardinals with their letters asking us to send them
safe-conduct to come to us: and they told us that if they
had safe-conduct, they could be with us in about eight
days. We caused our council to answer the messengers,
and to deliver them our letters of conduct for the Cardinals to come to the town of Malestroit, thirty leagues from
us, which was lately surrendered to our peace. For it is
not our intent that they should approach nearer to our
army than the said town, for several reasons. And know

that in whatever case we are, with God's help our intent is always to incline to reason, at what time soever it shall be offered us. Howbeit that the Cardinals must needs come to us in this manner, we do not mean to hinder our purpose for one day, for we have well in mind the delays we have suffered before this time through parleys with them and others. Dear son, as soon as we shall have any issue of our siege or of other business touching us, we will at all times send you news as speedily as the messengers may cross.

Dear son, cause these letters to be shown to the Archbishop of Canterbury, and to those of our council with you. Dear son, God have you in His keeping. Given under our secret seal at the siege of Vannes, on the eve of St. Nicholas.[1]

Right dear son, after the writing of these letters, there came news that our cousin of Northampton and the Earl of Warwick, Sir Hugh le Despenser and the other bannerets of their company have laid siege to the town of Nantes, for they hope, with God's help, to have speedy issue.

8.

[The Truce of Malestroit, signed on 19 January, 1343. (Latin.) "Chronicle" of Henry Knighton.]

And King Edward was planning to make an assault upon the said town;[2] but when he had prepared the engines and other contrivances that were needed in so great a business, and he was ready with his people to attack the place, forthwith there came two Cardinals, sent expressly from the Pope, and these so importuned him with their entreaties that he granted them a truce for three years, that is, between the Kings of England, France, and Scotland.

[1] 5 December.   [2] Vannes.

9.

[Proceedings in the Parliament held at Westminster on the quinzaine
of Easter, 1343. The business opened on 30 April, when the
causes of summons were explained by the Chancellor. (French.)
" Rolls of Parliament," ii. 136.]

In the first place it was explained that the sovereign and
principal cause is to treat and take counsel with the great
men and Commons of the realm about the matters touching our lord the King in regard to the truce made in
Brittany between him and his adversary of France. And
then afterwards to deal with matters concerning the estate
of our lord the King, and the government and safe-keeping
of his realm of England and of his people, and the relief
of their estate. But because Sir Bartholomew Burghersh,
who was with the King in Brittany at the making of the
last truce, can set forth how matters have occurred there
better than the Chancellor, he was commanded by the
King to describe the manner of the making the said
truce.

And Sir Bartholomew began to relate how, after our
lord the King had undertaken his war against France,
with the consent of the Prelates, great men, and commons
of his realm of England, to win his rights and his inheritance there, he had crossed the sea several times with his
host ;—and showed what success he had had, and how
that after his last passage into Brittany he had traversed
great part of the Duchy, and with God's help had taken
towns, castles, and strong places, until he came to the city
of Vannes, whereto he laid seige, by the advice of the great
men with him ; when request was made to him by our
Holy Father the Pope, for the reverence of God and Holy
Church, and at the prayer of the Holy Father (who sent
two Cardinals to him for the sake of peace, and to put
before him the matters with which they were charged by
the court of Rome touching this business) ; and to avoid

the evils that have happened, and happen daily, through the war, that he would agree to peace, or to a truce, during which discussion might be had concerning peace. And how our lord the King, seeing that the form of this truce was honourable and profitable to himself and his people, gave his consent to the said truce, so that while it lasted, treaty about peace might be held before the Pope but as common friend, and not as judge or arbitrator. And that, in case he could have a good peace, and one· honourable to himself, he would accept it; and if not, he would pursue his quarrel as before. And Sir Bartholomew said further from our lord the King, that because this war was undertaken by the common consent of the prelates, great men, and Commons, the King did not wish to hold consultation about peace, or to make peace, without their common consent.

Wherefore the prelates and great men were charged to assemble by themselves in the White Chamber on Thursday, the first day of May, to treat, take counsel, and agree among themselves as to whether or not the King should send envoys to the court of Rome, to show and put forward his right before our Holy Father the Pope, as has been said. And in the same way the knights of the shires and the Commons were charged to assemble in the Painted Chamber, to treat, take counsel, and agree among themselves about the said business; and to report their answer and their agreement in Parliament on the same Thursday.

On which day, the prelates and great men assembled in the White Chamber answered, that it was their opinion that the said truce was honourable and profitable to the King and to all his people; and that every Christian ought to wish that the war, that is so great and so hurtful to all Christians should be stilled and ended in good and fitting manner. Wherefore they were agreed and consented that

2 *

the truce be held, according to its form and effect.   And
that certain solemn messengers be sent to the Court of
Rome, to set forth the King's rights concerning his claims
before the Holy Father as common friend, and not as
judge or arbitrator; and to treat further about the making
of peace, according to the form of the truce.

And afterwards the knights of the shires and the Commons came, and made answer in the White Chamber by
Sir William Trussel (who spoke for the knights and Commons in presence of the King, and of the Prelates and
great men)—that they fully agreed to the keeping of the
truce, so that good and honourable peace might be had.
And the Commons prayed further that our lord the King
would send solemn messengers to set forth his rights and
treat of peace, as is aforesaid; and in case that he should
be able to have an honourable peace, profitable for him
self and his people, that he would deign to accept it.   And
in case that he could not have it, the Commons granted
that they would aid him to maintain his quarrel with all
their might.

10.

[Proceedings in Parliament, 1344. (French.)   "Rolls of Parliament,"
   ii. 147. Speech by the Chancellor, rehearsing the main points
   of the recent truce, and continuing :—]

"And against the above-mentioned points attacks have
been made in the following manner, from what those of
the Council have heard from certain persons of Boulogne.
—In the first place, that some of the allies of him who
calls himself King of France have seized and imprisoned
many men-at-arms of our lord the King's allies, and have
put them to death in presence of the Legate; and some
have been sent to France, to remain in prison there at the
pleasure of the King's adversary.   Also, his adversary has
caused many knights, squires, and other persons (who

were well known to be of the King's allegiance and obedience in the parts of Brittany before and after the making of the truce, and who notoriously were, and ought to be included in it and protected by it) to be seized; and many of them he caused to be taken to Paris, and shamefully put to death, contrary to the assent and decree of the great men and others of his Council in his Parliament.[1] And he has had some of them wrongfully and maliciously murdered in their own country, contrary to the said truce, and his oath. Beyond this, the said foe has sent great number of men-at-arms and foot-soldiers into the parts of Gascony and Brittany, who, since the making of the truce, have notoriously seized castles, towns, manors, and strong places, and occupied lands and property in the obedience of our lord the King when the truce was made —(wherein is contained, among other matters, that nothing fresh should be attempted during the same truce). Further, the said foe is striving by all means in his power, to seize upon all the lands and possessions of our lord the King beyond the sea, and to take from him his allies, as well in Brabant and Flanders as in Germany. And from what the King and his Council have heard for certain, he is of firm purpose, if remedy be not had by force against his malice, to destroy the English tongue, and to seize the land of England, which God forbid! On the other hand, the Scots, who are allies of the said foe, say openly, that whenever he shall make known to them that he is unwilling to keep the truce, they will by no means keep it, but they will raid the land of England, and do what harm they can."

[1] On 2 August, 1343, Olivier de Clisson was executed in Paris, on a charge of treason. In November of the same year, six Breton lords and ten squires suffered in the same manner; in April, 1344, proceedings were taken against three Norman lords. (Luce, "Froissart," note.)

Wherefore our lord the King prayed and charged the Prelates, Earls, and Barons, and the Commons, the above matters being considered, to apply fitting aid and counsel, in salvation of his rights and honour, and of themselves.

When these matters related by the Archbishop had been heard, the Prelates, Earls, Barons, and the others of the Commons begged that they might have deliberation thereon until the Monday next following;—and also from that same Monday, because they had not yet taken full consideration, from day to day, until Wednesday, the eve of St. John. On that day, the Archbishop, the Bishops of London, Chester, Chichester, Bath, Ely, Salisbury, Lincoln, Carlisle, and the Bishop-elect of Hereford; . . . [1] the Earls of Northampton, Warwick, Huntingdon, Suffolk, Oxford, Pembroke, Devonshire, and Angus; the lords Wake, Percy, Berkeley; Sir Ralph Neville, Sir Hugh le Despenser, and Sir Nicholas de Cantilupe; and the Commons of the Realm, being assembled in the White Chamber, in the King's presence—entreated him, all with one accord, and each of the great men separately that he would make an end of this war, either by battle or by a suitable peace if he could have it; considering the great mischiefs and perils that may happen to him and all his subjects and allies, if the malice of his said foe be not checked; and having regard to the heavy charges that the great men and Commons of England have suffered by reason of the war, that has endured so long, through feigned truces hitherto made; and perceiving clearly that if an end of this war were to be had, it could only be with great forces of men, and great power.

And they entreated further, that when our lord the King should be ready and equipped to cross the sea, to take what God should send him in the carrying out of this

---

[1] And seven abbots and priors.

business, he would not abandon his voyage, for letters or other charges or prayers from the Pope or others, until he had made an end in one way or another. This prayer the King fully granted.

But because this cannot be done without a great and appropriate aid, the Archbishop, Bishops, prelates, and procurators for the clergy of the Province of Canterbury granted the King a triennial tenth, to be paid according to a certain form . . . and on the following Saturday, for the same cause, the Commons granted two " fifteenths " from the community of the land, and two " tenths " from the cities and boroughs, on the conditions contained in a schedule which they handed in before the King in Parliament, whose tenor is as follows :—

Because our lord the King's necessity has been shown to his Commons by his Council, who have asked an aid of them, with the purpose of ending his war, with God's help, in one way or another ; they, considering his hardships and those of the great men, and the great peril of their lives that they are willing to suffer for the safety of his people, have granted, of their goodwill, for the great affection that they bear to their liege lord, and although they have suffered mischief through many aids and charges before this time, the fifteenth penny of their goods, and the tenth from the city and boroughs, the said sum to be raised in the same manner as the " fifteenth " last granted him, and not otherwise ;—understanding, most dread Lord, that this sum is more burdensome to your poor people than four " fifteenths " were in times past. Saving to your said Commons in all points their franchises granted them by your charters in your Parliaments ; Your Commons make you this on such conditions, that the money raised from it be expended on the business put before them in this Parliament, by the advice of the great men ; that the petitions which they put forward in this Parliament be granted ; and that the whole aid beyond Trent be used in defence of the North; and that that the Prince, Sir Edward of Balliol, or some other near in blood to the King be in this march, to act there as may best be ordained in salvation of the land.

And afterwards the Commons, seeing their liege lord's good intent to make a complete end of the said business, granted another fifteenth upon the conditions shown to them; namely that if the King himself cross the sea, and bring matters to an end, then it shall be raised, and if not, the Commons shall be relieved from it.

And they requested that the aforesaid " fifteenths and tenths " be paid in two years, under the above condition, namely, at the Feast of All Saints and at Easter, so always that the Commons be relieved of all manner of aids hence-forth . . .; and that passage of the sea be open to all manner of merchants and merchandise ; and that none who have come to this Parliament by writ be put on a commission to raise the said " fifteenth and tenth ".

11.

[The renewal of war was delayed until 1345. Then, in May, Edward addressed to the Pope a formal denunciation of the French King's action, and in July he issued a general manifesto in similar terms ("Foedera," III, i. 41). The Earl of Derby was sent to Gascony, and another expedition was sent to Brittany under the Earl of Northampton. The King himself interviewed James van Artevelde at Sluys, but the Flemish alliance was not renewed. His financial position was extremely critical, and in this year his indebtedness to the Florentine bankers involved their complete financial ruin. But early in 1346 he was preparing another expedition, and on 6 May he announced his intention of joining the Earl of Lancaster in Gascony ("Foedera," III, i. 181). No Parliament had met in 1345. Letters, requesting the loan of various sums of money, were sent out at this time to certain bishops, abbots, priors, and other ecclesiastics, and to some laymen. (French.) "Foedera," III, i. 68. 13 February, 1346.]

Edward, by the Grace of God King of England and France, and Lord of Ireland, to the honourable Father in God John, by the same grace Bishop of Hereford, greeting. Since by the deliberation and advice of the great men of our realm and the sages of our Council we have made fixed resolve to cross the sea in as great force as we can, for the necessary defence of our realm, and to check the malice of our adversary of France, who is trying with all his might to subdue us, and bring harm and destruction to our said realm, and to destroy the English tongue, if he can, which God forbid!—And because to make this crossing and defence we must incur very heavy expenses (for although great aids were granted us for this cause as well by the clergy as the Commons of our realm, nevertheless, the terms of payment of great part of these aids are not yet come, and for this cause we must needs be aided elsewhere, by way of loan or advance, to bear such great costs), we, considering that you and all our subjects are bound, each according to his power, to help in such urgent business, that concerns the common profit and the estate and salvation of our realm, do earnestly beg that making no excuse or pretence, you will be willing to lend us at this time three hundred marks, for the above cause, and to send the money to London at once, to be delivered to our Treasurer. And upon the delivery of the money, we will cause you to have sufficient security for your repayment; and we shall be for ever most beholding to you, and most gracious in all matters in which you shall have dealings with us in time to come.

As to what you are willing to do in this matter, certify us distinctly by the bearer of this, and by your letters. Given under our Great Seal at Westminster, the 13th day of February.

12.

[The Bishop of Hereford's reply. (French.) From the "Register" of John de Trillek, Bishop of Hereford. Ed. J. H. Parry for the Canterbury and York Society.]

To the right excellent and right puissant prince, and his well-beloved lord Edward, by the Grace of God King of England and France, his devout chaplain John, by the sufferance of God, Bishop of Hereford with humble recommendations, whatsoever he can and may, duty and reverence, and ready service. Most dread lord, I have received your honourable letters sent by my dear friend sir Henry Haydok, bearer of this, making mention of a certain sum of money that you desire to have by way of loan for the despatch of your urgent business touching the defence of your realm. Right dear lord, deign to know that I am of right goodwill to accomplish your desires and commands by all the ways and manners that I know, so far as my small power may extend; as I am indeed bound more especially than any other, by divers favours and benefits that you have often bestowed on me without my deserving, for the which I pray that Almighty God may repay you. And I pray and entreat your highness, as devoutly with all my heart as I can and may, that you will kindly hold me excused, for that I send no money forthwith by the said sir Henry; for may God be my witness that I have none at the present wherewith I could do so, and know not where to borrow in such haste. But truly, right dear lord, I will use loyal and diligent endeavour to do so, without pretence, and will certify your gracious lordship at this quinzaine of Easter next coming.

Right dread lord, the Holy Ghost give you prosperous life and long, increase your honours, and send you grace always to do his will.

13.

On 27 March, 1346, Edward, with the consent of the Archbishops
and some of the Bishops, asked that the clergy would agree to
anticipate the terms of payment of the tax that they had granted.
The Bishop of Hereford replied as follows to the royal letters addressed to him. (French.) From the "Register" of John de
Trillek of Hereford, ed. Parry.]

Right puissant lord, deign to know that, having received
and understood your honourable letters, I at once caused
the clergy of my diocese, as well the religious as the seculars, to assemble at as early date as I well could. On
which day I was present, and explained fully and expressly
to them all the matters contained in your said letters; and
God be my witness, I prayed them, stirred them up, and
urged them so far as I could and knew how, that considering the said matters, they would agree in good part to the
anticipation, as touching themselves. And having had
treaty and deliberation among themselves for a while apart,
they answered that, howsoever they were all of entire goodwill to aid you in this need and in all others according to
their power, they were so poor, and brought to such great
mischief by divers charges that they had, and by the great
murrain of their beasts, and destruction of their corn
through this bad year, that they could in no way agree to
the said anticipation; and upon this they begged that I
would kindly make their excuses to your highness, for the
above causes. And other answer I could get none from
them, for all the pains and diligence that I could put into
the business. But, right honoured lord, deign to know
that although I must needs raise a loan, as for my own
person, I assent to the anticipation, and am, and always
shall be, ready to fulfil your wishes and commands as I
am bound to do, after my small power.

14.

[(*a*) Proclamation that rumours are not to be repeated. Writ to the Sheriffs of London, 5 March, 1346. (Latin.) "Foedera," III, i. 72.]

Whereas among other statutes ordained at Westminster in the time of Edward our grandfather, lately King of England, . . . there is contained, that none shall be so bold as to assert or repeat false rumours or fictions, whereby discord or dissension, or grounds of scandal might arise between ourself and the people and magnates of our realm; and that if any person shall do so, he shall at once be seized and detained in prison until he shall produce in court the person by whom such rumours were contrived— And now we understand that some persons are inventing divers false rumours, and repeating and uttering them publicly in various places, and do not cease daily to do so, whereby matter of dissension and discord might easily arise between us and the magnates of our realm and our people; we, desiring the said statute to be strictly observed, and to guard against these perils, do command you, immediately upon receipt of this present order, to proclaim publicly in the City, in such places as you shall deem expedient, that none shall presume to invent or repeat such rumours in public or in private. And if, after this proclamation, you shall find any persons doing so, you shall cause them to be arrested without delay, and safely kept in our prison.

[(*b*) To the Provincial of the Order of Friars Preachers in London, 15 March, 1346. (Latin.) "Foedera," *ibid.*]

In order to inform and quicken the minds and hearts of our faithful lieges, and to check the tongues of those who are slandering us, we have thought well, by these present letters to intimate to you the cause of the war that we have against Philip of Valois, particularly requesting that you will openly set forth the same cause to the clergy and people in public and private sermons and congregations, wherein it shall seem expedient, instructing them very clearly with regard to it, as your prudence is best able; and that you will enjoin the same to be done by the brothers of your obedience.

15.

[The military preparations of 1346.   (Latin.)   Adam of Murimuth.]

In Lent the lord King of England caused inquiry to be made in each county as to the value of every man's lands and revenues, in order that from every person who had a hundred shillings in rent he might have one archer to go abroad with him, and from those having ten marks, a hobeler, and from those having twenty marks, one man-at-arms; which seemed excessively burdensome to the whole realm, and a thing never seen hitherto, especially for going out of the country.   He also made inquiry concerning all persons who were between sixteen and sixty years old, and the number of them, so that they might be ready for the defence of the realm, if foreign enemies should chance to invade it. . . .   Afterwards the King allowed those who were charged with men-at-arms, hobelers, and archers to make payment in money; and desiring to please the community, he caused it to be publicly proclaimed in the city of London and in all counties that he did not intend to subject lands and tenements to service by the aforesaid burdens, nor to draw such burdens into a consequence in future.

During the whole summer he caused ships to be assembled at the harbour of Portsmouth, and the neighbouring places, so that at the end of the month of June he had there, as was estimated, seven hundred and fifty ships, great and small.   And calling together all the knights, men-at-arms, and bowmen, both English and Welsh, he paid them wages in arrears and for the next fifteen days, charging them to go on board the ships assigned to them with all speed. To set an example, he himself went on board ship with his friends, and sailed as far as the Isle of Wight, there awaiting the whole fleet of ships ; and afterwards all those who were willing, and could have ships, followed him quickly with one accord, and with him awaited a favourable wind. But as yet none could know for certain towards what parts he meant to sail, or where he wished to invade the foreign shore.

16.

[The English invasion of Normandy, 1346. (French.) Jean le Bel, ii. 70. Edward set sail on 2 July, and landed at La Hogue on 12 July.]

The noble King Edward resolved to betake himself into Normandy, and first of all into the good country called Cotentin. This was by the advice and persuasion of Sir Godfrey de Harcourt,[1] who knew all the district well, and advised that he should send the third part of his people by sea, to lay waste the country along the sea-coast. The country was wonderfully rich and abundant, and there were many good towns. The noble King and his young son the Prince of Wales, who had never before borne arms, were to go by land, and lay waste the country of Normandy, and they were to go as far as Paris, to greet King Philip.

Then the noble King Edward appointed as marshal of his host the said Sir Godfrey de Harcourt, who willingly undertook the office; and he appointed another, the Earl of Stafford. . . .

The Earl of Warwick and the Earl of Stafford went off

[1] Lord of St. Sauveur-le-Vicomte in Normandy. He was banished by Philip of France in 1343, and in 1345 was received by Edward in England.

by sea along the coast, and they took all the ships they found and carried them along with them. Archers and men on foot went along the shore at the same time, burning, laying waste, and pillaging everything. They went on until they came to a fine seaport called Barfleur, and they won it, for the burgesses surrendered to them for fear of death. But for all that, the whole town was pillaged, and they took gold, silver, and jewels which they found in such plenty that the very grooms cared nothing for furred cloths or rich coverings, or any such things. They made all the men of the town come out and go on board their ships, to go with them, for they did not want these people to be able to gather together and harass them.

After the big town of Barfleur was taken and pillaged, they scattered all over the country by the sea-board, doing just as they would, for they found no men-at-arms or soldiers from King Philip to oppose them. So they went on in this way until they came to a great and rich town with a good harbour, called Cherbourg; they took this, pillaging it just as they had done at Barfleur; and in the same fashion they dealt with Montebourg and Valognes, and all the other good towns, and they found and carried off innumerable treasure. Afterwards they came to a big town, well-enclosed, and a strong castle, called Carentan, where there were a great many of King Philip's soldiers and men-at-arms. Then the lords and men-at-arms disembarked from their ships to assault the town. When the burgesses saw this, they were in fear of losing their lives and goods, and they surrendered, saving their bodies and goods, wives and children, in spite of the men-at-arms and soldiers with them; but they set their ransom at will, for they well knew that it was lost. But these lords of England would not leave the castle thus; they assaulted it for two days so fiercely that those within, expecting no succour, surrendered, saving their lives and goods;

and the English wreaked their will upon the town, and
made the men go on board the ships, carrying them off as
they had done the others. Why should I make you a
longer story? These lords of England with their company subdued, burnt, and laid waste all the country along
the coast, from the beginning of Cotentin to the border of
Normandy, working their will without opposition, and sent
all their booty and great plenty of prisoners to England;
whence there came great treasure, with which King
Edward amply paid all his soldiers. . . .

[With reference to the doings in the King's army :—]

When they had landed, Sir Godfrey de Harcourt, who
knew all the district, and all the ins and outs of the
country of Cotentin and Normandy, took two hundred
armed men and eleven hundred archers, parted from the
King, and went a good six or seven leagues ahead of the
army, burning and laying waste the country. They found
it rich and abundant in everything, the garners full of
corn, the houses stocked with all kinds of riches, rich
burgesses, horses and carts, flocks of sheep, pigs, calves,
oxen, and cows; all these they seized and carried off to
the King's host. But they kept for themselves the gold
and silver, which they found in great plenty, and did not
hand it over to him. Thus Sir Godfrey rode on as
marshal every day near the King's right flank, returning
to his company at the place where he knew the King was
to camp; and sometimes it happened that he remained
away for two days, when he found a rich district, and
enough to be gained. The other marshal marched with
five hundred armed men and two thousand archers in all,
on the other side, near the left flank of the King's army,
burning and laying waste the country. . . . The noble
King Edward and his son the Prince of Wales continued
to lead forward the rest of their host by short marches,
always camping between the third hour and midday, for

they found the country so rich that they needed not to make any purveyance, except of wine, for they found enough; because the people of the country had not taken care, and had not taken anything away. It was no wonder if they were dismayed, for they had never known war, and had not seen men-at-arms; and then they saw men killing pitilessly, burning and pillaging houses, and firing and laying waste the country.

The noble King Edward had in his host full fifteen hundred men-at-arms, and six thousand archers, with eight thousand men on foot without horses, who marched with the marshals. Thus he advanced burning and wasting the country; he found there was nothing in the city of Coutances to lead him to turn back to it, but he marched on towards the big and wonderfully busy town, called St. Lo in Cotentin, which was richer and worth three times more than the city of Coutances; and there was a great cloth trade there, and great store of merchandise, and many rich burgesses; there were in the city full eight thousand living souls, both rich burgesses and craftsmen. When the King had approached near enough, he camped outside it, for he would not camp within, for fear of fire. The big city was soon taken with little difficulty, and pillaged on all sides. There is no man living who could believe, if he were told, what riches were plundered there, or the quantity of cloths that they found; any who wanted to buy might have had them cheaply, for each man could take where he liked. But few esteemed them, since they were more eager to get gold and silver, of which they found plenty. . . .

When King Edward had worked his will with the good town of St. Lo, he departed thence to come before the town called Caen, the richest in Normandy, except the city of Rouen, full of great wealth, of rich burgesses and noble ladies, with two rich abbeys, and all kinds of merchandise.

3

17.

[Letter of Sir Bartholomew Burghersh to John Stratford, Archbishop
    of Canterbury. (French.) Inserted by Adam Murimuth in his
    " Chronicle," 1346.]

Right reverend Father in God, and my very honoured
lord, Because I well know that you will gladly hear tidings
of my lord the King and of the fleet, please you to wit
that when he had made his plans, and had caused all the
ships to be victualled for fifteen days, with the intent to
have gone towards Gascony, purposing to have sailed past
the Needles at the end of the Isle of Wight and so to have
held on a straight course towards the Channel, the wind
was so against him that he could in no way keep his
course, although he lay to for a long time, waiting to see if
God would send him weather for crossing. And since it
did not please God that he should go that way, he turned
back to make a landing where God should give him grace,
and arrived well and in good case, with all the fleet, in a
country called Cotentin in Normandy on the Wednesday
before the Feast of St. Margaret, to wit, the twelfth day
of July. And on his landing, my lord the Prince was
knighted, and Montague, Mortimer, Roos, and many
others. The town of Barfleur is taken, and my lord of
Warwick skirmished with the enemy, and carried the day
well and honourably ; my lord John of Beauchamp, and
many other knights and squires have had affair with the
enemy, in raiding and in other ways, so that, at the
making of these letters we had met with no check. But
the men-at-arms of the country have withdrawn to the
castles and strong towns, and the Commons are coming in
to our lord the King's obedience in great numbers.

Other news, my lord, I cannot send you at this time,
save that the King is advancing into the country with his

host, to win his right according as God shall give him grace.

Written at La Hogue, the 17th day of July.

18.

[Another letter from Sir Bartholomew Burghersh, describing the march from La Hogue to Caen. (French.) Adam of Murimuth's "Chronicle," 1346.]

Right reverend Father in God, and very honoured lord, because I know well that you are very desirous of hearing good news of my Lord the King, and of his success since he came into the parts of Normandy, please you to wit that from the time when he began to advance, he took his road from La Hogue, where he landed, straight to Caen, and went right by the good towns, to wit, Valognes, Carentan, St. Lo, and by many other good towns. But there was no man or woman of condition that dared wait in the towns and castles, or in the countryside where the host passed, but all fled, until the King came to Caen. And here there was the Constable of France, the Count of Eu, and the Chamberlain of Tankarville, with great number of knights and men-at-arms, and people of the countryside and townspeople, who had made ready to hold the city against my lord the King and all his power. But when the King came there with his host, and showed himself before it, the enemy withdrew beyond a bridge that is in the middle of the town, and held out there. And when we had come right up to the town, as near as we could, our archers went straight up to the bridge, and attacked them with a volley. In the meantime, some men-at-arms came up, and assaulted them fiercely, so that, for fear of the wounding of our people, because it was thought that none of our own men-at-arms were there, but only the archers of my lord of Warwick, the marshal, order was sent from the King for them to retire. And when he came

3 *

to the bridge, he found them fighting together right up at
the barriers, where himself did well and nobly ; and at last
the enemy were so hard pressed, that with the Lord's help
our people won the bridge from them, and so went into
the town and discomfited them.   Very soon the Constable
of France surrendered to Sir Thomas Holland, with many
knights and squires who were with him ; and the Chamberlain of Tankarville was taken by a batchelor of my lord
the Prince, so that he is my lord's prisoner.   Between six
and seven score brave and valiant knights were slain and
made prisoner, of whom about a hundred are still alive ; and
of squires, burgesses, and common people taken or slain
there were some five thousand.   So that, Our Lord be
praised, hitherto matters have gone as favourably as they
could.   The King will stay two days or three to refresh
his army with provisions that were found in abundance in
the town ; and he thinks of drawing straight towards his
adversary, to make such end as God has ordained for him.
The ships came to the mouth of the water that goes up to
Caen ; they have burnt and destroyed some hundred ships
along the coast, and have done great destruction on shore,
by fire and in other ways.   Other news, my lord, I cannot
send you at present.   The Holy Ghost preserve you in
your honours, and in prosperous life and long.   Written
at Caen, the 29th day of July.   My lord, it is the King's
pleasure that all the prisoners taken be sent to England,
without being delivered by ransom or otherwise, until he
shall have obtained further success in his war.

19.

[A letter from "Michael de Northburgh, a valiant clerk, one of the
council of the lord King of England, being present with him on
his march".   (French.)   Undated ; inserted in Robert of Avesbury's "Chronicle," 1346.]

Be it remembered that our lord the King and his host
landed at St. Vaast de la Hogue on the 12th day of July ;

and in order to disembark his horses, and to rest his men, and bake bread, he stayed there until the Tuesday next following. He found at La Hogue eleven ships, eight of them with castles fore and aft, which were caused to be burnt. And on Friday, while the King still abode there, some of his men went to Barfleur, expecting to have found many people, but found none to speak of. They found nine ships there, with castles fore and aft, two good craiers, and other smaller vessels, which were also burnt. The town was as fine and as large as the town of Sandwich; and after the said people had departed, the mariners burnt the town. Many of the good towns and manors in the surrounding country are also burnt. On the Tuesday, when the King moved on, he went to Valognes, where he lay all that night, and found enough store of victuals. The next day he moved forward a long day's march to the bridge over the Ouve, which the people of Carentan had broken. The King had it repaired the same night, and crossed over the next day, as far as the said town of Carentan, which is distant only about an English league from the bridge. This town is as big as Leicester. Here they found great quantity of wine and provisions; and great part of the town was burnt, in spite of anything the King could do. On the Friday the King went on, and lay in the villages on a river that was difficult to cross. The people of St. Lo broke the bridge, but the King had it made up again, and crossed the next day, himself and all his host, and lodged just beside the town. The towns-people had begun to strengthen it, and had gathered to them a great many men-at-arms to have held it, but they went away before the King's coming. And there were found there full a thousand casks of wine, and great abundance of other goods. The town is larger than Lincoln. The next day the King set out, and lay in an abbey, and his host in the villages round about. The people of the host rode along, pillaging and laying waste for five or six leagues round every day, and setting fire to many places. On the Monday the King moved on and lodged in the villages, as he did also on the Tuesday. On Wednesday he came before the City of Caen, at the hour of noon, and had news that great numbers of men-at-arms were in the city. He had his battles arrayed fair and large, and sent some men up to the city to spy it out, who found the castle fair and strong; within was the Bishop of Bayonne, with the knights and men-at-arms who were holding it. On this side of the water the city is very beautiful and very large, and at one end of it is as noble an abbey as can be, where William the Conqueror lies; it is enclosed with walls, and great and strong embattled towers. There was no man in this abbey. At the other end of the town is another noble abbey, of ladies. And no one had remained in these abbeys, or in the town on this side of the water, save in the castle, for the townspeople had withdrawn into the part that lies on the other side of the water. Here there were the Constable of France and the Chamberlain of Tankarville, who is a very great lord, and many other people, to the number of five or six hundred, with the community of the town. The men of our host, without any agreement, and without array, attacked the bridge, [1] which was strongly fortified with parapets and barriers, and they had sharp fighting, for the French defended it stoutly, and did themselves much service before it could be won from them. Then the said Constable and Chamberlain were taken, and knights to the number of a hundred, and six or seven score squires; and there were slain great number of other knights, squires, and other people of the town, in the streets, houses, and gardens. What number of men of substance were slain cannot be known, for they were at once stripped, so that they could not be recognised.

[1] The Pont St. Pierre, over an arm of the R. Orne (Luce).

No gentleman was slain of our people,[1] save a squire who was wounded, and died two days afterwards. Wines, provisions, and innumerable other goods and chattels were found in the city, which is greater than any town of England except London.

When the King moved from La Hogue, about two hundred ships remained there; these went to Rochemassé, and sailed along, firing the country for two or three leagues inland, taking much booty, and carrying it off in their ships. In this way they went to Cherbourg, where there are a good town and strong castle, and a fair and noble abbey; and they burnt the said town and the abbey. They have burnt the coast-lands everywhere, from Rochemassé as far as Ouistreham, on the haven of Caen, a distance of six-score English leagues. The number of ships which they have burnt is sixty-one ships of war, with castles fore and aft, and twenty-three craiers, and other smaller ships of twenty-one or thirty wine-tuns burden. On the Thursday after the King had come before Caen, the people of the city of Bayeux sent word to the King that they would surrender to him, themselves and their city, and do homage to him. But he would not receive them for certain reasons, and until he should be able to save them from harm.

20.

[On 3 August the Keeper of the Realm and the Council in England issued notices to all the Bishops, and to all the Sheriffs, asking them to make public the news of the King's successes, as contained in an accompanying schedule. The Sheriffs were asked also to proclaim publicly that all men-at-arms, hobelers, archers, and others who wished to come abroad to the King, should provide themselves with suitable horses and arms, to be ready when

---

[1] M. Luce points out that Northburgh makes no reference to the losses among the rank-and-file which were probably heavy; his letter was "drawn up with a view to the effect to be produced in England".

the King should give notice ; the King would prepare passage
for them.   The writs (Latin) are in the " Foedera," II, i. 88.
The copy of the schedule (French) is taken from the " Register"
of Bishop Trillek of Hereford.   The notice to the Bishops :—]

. . . Because we know that you desire to hear good
reports of ourselves and our army, now in parts beyond
the sea, for the defence of our realm, and the recovery,
with God's favour, of our rights there, we have thought
well to communicate to you, in a schedule enclosed with
these letters, for the comfort of yourself and the whole
English people, the gracious successes which the Most
High has bestowed upon us since our landing at La
Hogue in Normandy, for the dispatch of our war in these
parts.   And we earnestly request you to cause the matters
contained in the same schedule to be made known in all
places where it shall seem expedient, and prayers and
devout offerings to be made for us and for our army,
masses to be celebrated, solemn processions to be made
twice weekly, and other offices of humble intercession to
be performed daily throughout your diocese.   That God
the just Judge, by the increase of His abounding Grace
may vouchsafe to permit our glorious[1] beginning so to
prosper, that, under the guidance of His mercy, and
supported by your prayers, we may attain by our labours
an issue pleasing to him, and profitable to the Church
and the State.

[*The enclosure.*]

Our lord the King, to the honour of God and our Lady,
St. Mary, and for the comfort of all his faithful lieges of
England, makes known to them the grace and the success
that God has given him since the time of his arriving at
La Hogue near Barfleur in Normandy. . . .[2]

[1] " gratiosum " (" Foedera ") ; "gloriosum " (" Hereford Register ").
[2] Here follows a brief account of the events described in the preceding letters.

Wherefore he entreats all his liege people of England devoutly to give thanks to God, and to pray constantly that He will give him good continuance. And our lord the King has commanded his Chancellor to cause letters to be made under his Great Seal to the prelates and all the clergy of the realm, instructing them also to do this; and that the said Chancellor and others of the Council shall communicate these matters to the City of London, and to the people, for their comfort. For by the assent of all the great men, who show themselves with one accord of goodwill, he has resolved to hasten towards his adversary from day to day, wheresoever he may be, and is of firm trust that God will give him good and honourable issue of his undertaking. And as to this, our lord the King has charged the Earl of Huntingdon (whom he has caused to return to England, by reason of a severe and dangerous sickness that has overtaken him, although this return was much against his will) to explain these matters more fully to his Council in England.[1]

21.

[Extract from a letter of Richard de Wynkeley, the King's confessor, to the Prior and Convent of the Friars Preachers, London, "written between Boulogne and Witsand, on the 2nd day of September". (Latin.) The whole letter is given by Murimuth in his "Chronicle"; the following extract is also copied by Avesbury, who completes the narrative from this point by inserting another and fuller account, given by Michael de Northburgh (No. 22 below), 1346.]

It behoves us to praise the God of Heaven, and justly to acknowledge Him before all living men, because He has dealt mercifully with us. For after the conflict at Caen, wherein, after great numbers had been slain, the city was

[1] He brought back an agreement drawn up in 1338 for the invasion of England, which Edward had discovered at Caen.

taken and stripped to the bare walls, the city of Bayeux surrendered of its own accord, fearing to suffer in the same manner. Our lord the King directed his march towards Rouen, and was met by the cardinals in the city of Lisieux, who exhorted him very urgently to make peace. When they had been received in most courteous fashion, from reverence of the Apostolic See and of Holy Church, they were answered that our lord the King, always desiring peace, had sought it by all reasonable means that he knew, and had offered many ways, on account of his desire for it, although to the no small prejudice of his cause ;—and that he is still prepared to accept peace, provided only that it be offered him in a reasonable manner. The cardinals however, having spoken to the King's adversary, afterwards returned and offered the Duchy of Aquitaine as his father held it, with hope of having more by way of marriage, if peaceful discussion might be had. But because this way did not meet with approval, and the cardinals did not find the King's adversary readily yielding, they plainly withdrew, despairing of a good issue. Our lord the King nevertheless continued to advance successfully, and gained all the big towns which he passed, no resistance being made, but every man taking to flight ; for God so filled them all with terror that they seemed utterly to have lost their courage. Moreover, he took castles and fortified places, although they were very strong, with light onslaughts, only a few men attacking. His adversary had gathered together a great army at Rouen, and notwithstanding that he had very great multitude with him, he broke the bridge over the Seine, and followed our lord the King every day on the opposite side of the river, breaking down and fortifying all the bridges, lest we should cross over to him. And although there were continuously pillagings and burnings throughout the whole region, for the space of twenty miles round, and up to within a mile of him, yet he would not and dared not cross the Seine when he might have done, for the defence of his people and his kingdom. Thus our lord the King came to Poissy, where he found the bridge broken. . . .

22

[Letter from Michael de Northburgh, describing the course of events to the Battle of Crecy. (French.) Avesbury, 4 September, 1346.]

Greeting. Be pleased to know that our lord the King reached the town of Poissy on the eve of the Assumption of Our Lady, and there was a bridge there over the river Seine, which was broken; but the King stayed there until it was repaired. While it was being made up, there came a great number of men-at-arms, with the levies of the district and of Amyas, well armed. The Earl of Northampton and his men went out and attacked them, so that, thank God, more than two hundred of our enemies were slain; but the others were mounted. And another time our people crossed the water, and killed great plenty of the common levies of France and of the city of Paris, and others of the country well armed, from the host of the King of France. So that our men made another good bridge, thank·God, to reach our enemies, without loss or great damage of our people. On the morrow of the Feast of Our Lady's Assumption, our lord the King crossed the Seine and moved towards Poix, which is a strong town, enclosed with walls, with a very strong castle inside; and it was held by our enemies. And when the van-guard, and the main battle had passed the town, the rear-guard assaulted it and took it; there were slain more than three hundred men-at-arms of the enemy. On the following day the Earl of Suffolk and Sir Hugh le Despenser went out and attacked the levies of the district, which were gathered together well armed, and defeated them; they killed two hundred and more, and took over sixty prisoners of the gentlemen. Then they drew on towards Grand-villiers, and when they had lodged there, the vanguard was espied by men-at-arms of the household of the King of Bohemia. Our people went out hastily and skirmished with them, but were borne to the ground. But, thanks be to God, my lord of Northampton went out and rescued the knights and others, so that none of them were taken or slain except Thomas Talbot. They pursued the enemy up to within two leagues of Amyas, taking eight men-at-arms, and killing twelve; the rest were well horsed, and escaped to Amyas. The King of England, whom God preserve, went towards Ponthieu on St. Bartholomew's day, and came to the water of Somme, which comes into the sea from Abbéville in Ponthieu. The King of France had arrayed five hundred men-at-arms, and three hundred of the armed levies, to hold the passage; but, God be thanked, the King of England and his host took this river of Somme where man never crossed before, without any of his men being lost, and fought with the enemy, killing over two thousand men-at-arms. They pursued the rest right up to the gate of Abbéville, and took prisoner a great number of knights and squires. On the same day, Sir Hugh le Despenser took the town of Crotoy, and he and his people killed four hundred men-at-arms there; they held the town, where they found great plenty of victuals. That night the King of England lodged in the forest of Crecy, on the same river, because the King of France's host came from the other side of the town after our crossing; but he would not cross the water against us, and they returned towards Abbéville. On the next Friday, the King lodged in the same forest of Crecy. On Saturday, at morning, he moved towards Crecy, and his scouts discovered the King of France, who was coming towards us in four big battles, and there they awaited their enemies. And by the will of God, a little before the hour of Vespers, his power gathered to ours in the open field; the battle was very violent, and lasted a long time, for the enemy bore themselves right nobly, but God be praised, they were discomfited. The King our adversary took to flight, and there were slain the King of Bohemia, the Duke of Lorraine, the Count of Alençon, the Count of Flanders, the Count of Blois, the Count of Harcourt and his two sons, the Count of Aumale, the Count of Nevers, and his brother the lord of Trouard, the Archbishop of Nimes,[1] the Archbishop of Sens,[1] the Grand Prior of the Hospital of France, the Count of Savoy, the lord of Moreuil, the lord of Guise, the lord of St. Venant, the lord of Rosenberg, six counts of Germany, and a great many other counts and barons, and other lords whose names cannot yet be known.

The King of France and the Marquis called the elect of the Romans escaped wounded, as men say. The number of good men-at-arms slain in the field that day, without counting the town levies and men-on-foot amounts to fifteen hundred and forty-two accounted for. That same night the King of England with all his host remained in arms on the field where the defeat took place; and the next morning before sunrise, another great and strong battle came in front of us. My lord the Earl of Northampton and the Earls of Norfolk and Warwick went forth and overpowered them, taking prisoner a great number of knights and squires, and killing two thousand and more, and pursued them three leagues from the field. That night the King lodged at Crecy, and at daybreak he drew towards Boulogne, taking the town of Etaples on the march; whence he advanced towards Calais. From what I have heard, his purpose is to besiege the town of Calais.[2] And for this reason, my lord, the King has written to you for victuals, and that too as quickly as you can send them.

[1] Included in mistake (Luce).

[2] Preparations were being made for the siege, which was begun immediately.

For since the time when we left Caen, we have lived on the country, to the great labour and damage of our people; but, God be thanked, we have had no lack. But now we are in such plight that we must be refreshed in part with provisions. Written before Calais, the 4th day of September.

23.

[The Battle of Crecy. From Froissart's account (ed. Luce). Froissart based his narrative largely upon that given by Jean le Bel in his "Chronicle," although he considerably expanded it.]

There is no man, even though he had been present, that could exactly realise or imagine all that happened that day, especially so far as concerned the French, so great was the confusion and disorder among them. What I know I have learnt in great part from the English, who had well observed the confusion of their enemies, also from the men of Sir John of Hainault, who all that day was by the side of the King of France.[1]

The English, who were drawn up in three divisions, and were sitting down upon the ground, as soon as they saw the French approaching, rose up in good order, without any excitement, and ranged themselves in their battles, that of the Prince being the first, with the archers in front, in the form of a harrow and the men-at-arms in the rear. The Earls of Northampton and Arundel who commanded the second battle were posted in good order on the wing, to support and succour the Prince if need were. And the King of England's battle was on higher ground; the King had taken up his stand on a windmill, so as to see further all round him; he might have been then some thirty-six

[1] Here Froissart exactly follows Jean le Bel. But in the third redaction of his "Chronicle," he claims to have obtained his information from Sir John Chandos and Sir Bartholomew Burghersh; and, on the French side, from the Lord of Montmorency also.

years of age, in the flower of his youth, and greatly encouraged in his business.[1]

When King Philip came to the field near to where the English were drawn up, and saw them, his blood stirred, for he hated them exceedingly; he could not withhold from attacking them, but said to his marshal, "Let our Genoese advance and begin the battle, in the name of God and St. Denis".

There were about 15,000 of these Genoese cross-bowmen,[2] and they would fain not have begun the battle then, for they were cruelly tired and worn out with marching more than six leagues fully armed, and with carrying their crossbows. So they told their captains that they were not ready to begin any great deed of battle. These words reached the Count of Alençon, who said with fierce anger, "We should, indeed, cumber ourselves with such rascals, who fail us when we have most need of them!" Meanwhile, as the Genoese were making much trouble about getting themselves ready, there was such a violent and heavy rainfall that it was wonderful to see, with thunder and lightning very great and horrible. Before the rain began a flock of crows, so many that their flight seemed endless, had flown over the armies; whereupon some experienced knights said that it was the sign of a great battle and much bloodshed. After all this the sky began to clear and the sun shone brilliantly, so that it was full in the eyes of the French, while the English had it behind them.

When the Genoese were ranged ready to approach the enemy they began to make such loud hooting that it was wonderful to hear; they did this to dismay the English, but they kept quite still, *and let off some cannon that they*

---

[1] MS. de Rome.

[2] The number is exaggerated — there were perhaps some 6000 (Luce).

had in the battle, to daunt the Genoese.[1] The latter shouted
a second time, and then advanced a little; the English
stood quite still without moving from their places. Yet
a third time they uttered loud piercing cries, and then
advanced and drew their crossbows and began to shoot.
When the English archers saw this they advanced a little
and let fly their arrows, that came down upon the Genoese
so steadily that it seemed like snow. The Genoese had
not learned to meet such archers as these of England,
and when they felt the arrows piercing their arms and
heads, and through their armour they were soon discomfited; many of them cut the strings of their bows, others
threw them down, and so they began to retreat.

[2] But the battles of the great lords were so eager to go
forward and fight their enemies that they did not wait for
any ordinance or array, but rushed on all mingled together
until they shut in the Genoese between themselves and
the English, so that they could not escape, but the horses
fell among them, the strong stumbling over the weak who
were down. Those who were behind took no heed of the
press, so that they were thrown down among others who
were unable to rise. On the other hand the archers were
shooting so relentlessly upon those in front and on the
flanks, that the horses, feeling the sharp arrows, behaved
in an extraordinary fashion, rearing and plunging wildly;
some refused to advance, while some, in spite of their
masters, dashed towards the enemy, and those mortally
hurt were falling to the ground. The English men-at-
arms, who were drawn up on foot now advanced among
these lords and their men, carrying knives, axes, and short
spiked staves, and killed them without difficulty and with
little resistance, for they could not rise or extricate themselves. There was never before seen so great misadven-

[1] MS. d'Amiens.
[2] MS. d'Amiens, to *. Reproduced very closely from le Bel (Luce).

ture, or so many good men lost with so little fighting. In such manner this great mischief for the French lasted until nightfall, for the darkness separated them; it was already evening when the battle began, and the King of France could not get up to the fight at all, nor any of those under his banner, nor the levies from the good towns of France.*

. . . The Count Louis of Blois, nephew of King Philip, came up with the men under his banner to attack the English, and bore himself right valiantly, as did the Duke of Lorraine. And most men say that if the battle had been as well begun in the morning as it was at vespers there would have been many rallies on the French side, and many fine feats of arms. Even so, there were some lords, knights, and squires among the French, and others on their side, both Germans and Savoyards who fought their way through the archers of the Prince's battle and got right up to the men-at-arms, fighting hand to hand with their swords.

There were on the English side two gallant knights, Sir Reginald Cobham and Sir John Chandos, with many others whose names I cannot set down, for there round the Prince was the flower of English chivalry. Then the Earl of Northampton and the Earl of Arundel . . . came up to support the Prince's battle, and well there was need of it, for without this he would have been hard put to it. . . .[1]

You must know that the discomfiture of the French was very severe and the losses on their side very terrible; and all too many noble and valiant men were left on the field, dukes, counts, barons, and knights, whereby the realm of France was since much impoverished in honour, might, and good counsel. And you may be sure that if the English had pursued the enemy as they did at Poitiers

[1] Froissart here tells the story of the sending of a request for help to the King, and of his refusal, with the words, "Let the boy win his spurs".

still more would have lain dead there, even the King of France himself. . . . For he stayed on the field until it was very late, and when he departed he had with him not more than sixty men all told. Then my lord John of Hainault, who was guarding and advising him, and had already remounted him (for the King's charger had been killed by an arrow) took his bridle and led him away by force, saying, "Sire, come away, for it is time; do not so unwisely let yourself be undone here; you will recover another time what you have lost now ". . . .

I assure you that this day the archers of England gave great support to their side, for most men say that it was by their shooting that the affair was decided, although indeed there were valiant knights among the English who fought bravely, performing splendid feats of arms. But it should be clearly understood and admitted that the archers performed a great feat, for it was by their volleys when the battle began that the Genoese were defeated, the which gave great advantage. For all too many men-at-arms, richly armed and equipped, and well mounted, were thrown into confusion and undone through the Genoese, because they stumbled among them and fell one over another, so they could not rise or recover themselves.

And among the English there were plunderers and ruffians, Welshmen and Cornishmen, carrying great knives, and following up the men-at-arms and archers who opened the way for them; they found the French men in their perilous plight, and killed them all, great lords as they were. In this way there were many men killed that evening, which was great pity and harm; and the King of England was afterwards greatly angered, because they had not been held to ransom.

.   .   .   .

When Sunday morning came, there was so thick a mist that one could scarcely see the distance of half an acre.

There departed from the army, by order of the King and
the marshals, some five hundred men-at-arms and two
thousand archers, to make an excursion and see if they
could discover any bodies of French collected together.
This Sunday morning the levies of troops from Rouen and
Beauvais had set out from Abbéville in Ponthieu who
knew nothing of the previous evening's defeat, and they
came right upon this party of Englishmen, thinking at
first they were some of their own people. As soon as the
English saw who they were they fell upon them, and
there was a sharp fight; but the French were soon routed
and put to flight, in great disorder. There were slain in
the fields, by hedges and bushes as they fled, more than
7000, and had it been clear weather, not one would
have escaped. . . . I was told that of the levies of men
on foot sent from the cities and good towns there were
slain this Sunday morning four times as many as in
the great battle.

24.

[Letter said to have been sent by the French King, urging the Scots
to invade England. Inserted in Hemingburgh's "Chronicle".
(Latin—but possibly translated from a French original by the
Chronicler.)]

Right dear and well-beloved kinsman, true it is that
the King of England has already landed in the parts of
our realm towards Cotentin, and is tarrying there near
his ships; and the land of England is left void of defence
and unfortified, for the greater part of his army is with
him, and another part is in Gascony, and another divided
between the parts of Flanders and Brittany. Hence there
cannot be in England great store of armed and able men;
and it seems to all men that if you will put diligence and
care to the matter, you can inflict very great damage upon
him. Wherefore there are those who do not cease to

4 *

marvel greatly that as yet you have in no way done him
mischief, and do not yet do so, for you can never
have greater advantage than you have at present. And
so we ask and entreat you, by our mutual affection and
alliance, that you will not fail to take means of damaging
him and his whole country as well and stoutly as you can,
since the moment is now most favourable; so heartily
proving by your deeds the affection and promises that
you have pledged us. And we assure you that should he
hasten to return to England, we will at once, and without
delay send over our fleet with abundance of armed men,
for it is now fully prepared and ready. Make all speed,
therefore, to harm the said king, our enemy and your own,
for if you will take the business in hand well, you can
destroy and subdue the greater part of his land. And
cause us to be informed as to the news of your parts and
of your estate, the which may Our Lord prosper. May
the Holy Spirit vouchsafe to have you in his keeping.
Given at St. Denis in France, the 22nd day of July; to
our right dear and well-beloved kinsman the King of
Scots.

25.

[Enthusiasm in England at the Battle of Neville's Cross. Henry of
    Knighton's "Chronicle". (Latin.) The Scots crossed the border
    early in October, and marched south, destroying the border
    stronghold of Liddesdale, sacking Hexham Abbey, and burning
    Lanercrost. The battle was fought on 17 October, 1346.]

After David King of Scotland had carried out many
grievous raids in King Edward's absence upon the
northern parts of England, with much plunder and
slaughter of the inhabitants (to the grave scandal of the
Northern magnates, because they were thought by many
to have been complices in these wrongs, and consenting
to them) at last he invaded the East march of England,

in the year of Our Lord 1346, with a large army to the number of 36,000 men, well armed and arrayed after the manner of the French. They marched straight towards Durham, utterly refusing a truce, for they would not hear of it, or have any mercy until they should have tribute, head and foot, of all the inhabitants as far as the river Trent. For they had been led to suppose that there remained none in England who were not at the siege of Calais, save peasants and shepherds, and feeble and unwarlike priests. Wherefore the lord William de la Zouche, Archbishop of York, the lord Percy, and all the others of those parts, knights and squires, chaplains and clerks, with one accord ready to live and die for the salvation of the realm, all came together on one day, the Monday before the Feast of St. Luke, four miles beyond Durham. The Scots were a little distance beyond them, right valiant and full of confidence.

Lord William Douglas had gone on before the Scottish army, when the English suddenly fell upon him, and he was taken prisoner by a squire of the lord d'Eyncourt, a great many of his men being slain. When the King of Scots learned this, he prepared to fight with all speed, drawing up his army in lines of battle ; they filled the air with the sound of trumpets and bugles, and threw their battalions against the English. These however, putting their whole trust in God, holding the cause of right above death, and with full confidence in the sign of the Cross, which was borne before them among other banners, commended themselves to the divine mercy, by which no man is deceived, and flung themselves into the conflict with the greatest boldness. . . . At length by the divine mercy they were granted a joyful victory over their enemies. . . When the monks who were in the belfry of their Church saw the flight of the Scots, they lifted up their voices and filled the skies with loud shouts, calling

out and praising God, and singing the *Te Deum laudamus*
with tears of joy.   The English heard the sound as though
they had been close behind them, whence they derived
stronger faith and courage, and pursued their enemies the
more fiercely and drove them back.   For the monks of
Durham had made fine of £100 with the Scots, for themselves and their manors, and their tenants in the district,
to be paid on the following day without further delay,
and thus they were freed from the yoke.   The Scots had
purposed to march to Beverley and thence to York, for
they thought there were none in the land able to resist
them, but that they were all at the siege of Calais. . . .

The King of Scotland, who fled from the battle
wounded in the head with an arrow, was taken at
Merington by a yeoman of John Coupland and carried to
Bamburgh Castle, where, because he could not travel, he
stayed for a time in the keeping of Lord Percy, with
many other great men, until they were brought to London,
by the King's command.   In the meantime King Edward
sent orders to all the sheriffs and others, that no Scottish
prisoner should be set at liberty for any ransom whatsoever,
but that all should be kept in close custody; promising
that the King himself would make full satisfaction to all
the captors for the ransom of all and singular.   This
command was issued generally throughout all parts of
the realm, on pain of forfeit of life and limb.   Then,
immediately after the battle the English entered Scotland,
and took great booty of cattle and other goods, which
they carried off to England.

A certain man, who used to relate how he had seen it,
declared that when the priests of the Northern parts were
called out to battle against the Scots, he saw a great crowd
of them gathered together at Beverley; and when they
came to the end of the town, they took off their shoes,
and with bare heads, swords and arrows at their thighs,

and bows under their arms, ready for the expedition whereto they were summoned, advanced thus in procession. As they marched they called ceaselessly upon God and His saints, entreating His mercy and grace to prosper the business of their journey, to free the English people from their enemies who were seeking to destroy them. And truly, the country people, seeing their indescribable devotion, were stirred to wondrous contrition, and bowed their heads with tears and pious exclamations, imploring the Saviour's compassion to bring help in their great need. . . . The same thing is said to have been done by priests and people at York, and many other places.

26.

[Lines from a poem of Laurence Minot, describing the battle, probably written shortly afterwards, almost certainly not later than 1352. The spelling has been slightly altered.]

. . . Sir David the Bruse said he suld fonde [1]
To ride thurgh all Ingland wald he noght wonde ; [2]
At the Westminster hall suld his stedes stonde,
Whils our King Edward war out of the londe
  Bot now has sir David missed of his merkes [3]
  And Philip the Valays, with all thaire grete clerkes.

Sir Philip the Valais, suth for to say,
Sent unto sir David, and faire gan him pray
At [4] ride thurgh Ingland thaire fomen to flay [5]
And said none es at home to let [6] him the way
  None letes him the way to wende whore he will
  Bot with schipherd staves fand he his fill.

Fro Philip the Valais was sir David sent
All Ingland to win fro Twede unto Trent ;

[1] should try.   [2] turn back.   [3] object.
[4] To ride.   [5] terrify.   [6] hinder.

He broght mani berebag [1] with bow redy bent;
Thai robbed and they reved and held that thai hent; [2]
It was in the waniand [3] that thai furth went;
For couaitise of cataile tho schrewes war schent; [4]
 Schent war tho schrewes and ailed unsele [5]
 For at the Nevil cros nedes bud tham knele.

At the ersbisshop of York now will I begin,
For he may with his right hand assoyl us of syn;
Both Dorem and Carlele thai wald never blin [6]
The wirship of Ingland with wappen [7] to win;
 Mekill wirship thai wan, and wele have thai
  waken [8]
 For sir David the Bruse was in that tyme taken.

Whan Sir David the Bruse satt on his stede
He said of all Ingland haved he no drede;
But hinde [9] John of Coupland, a wight man in wede, [10]
Talked to David, and kend him his crede. [11]
 Thare was Sir David so dughty in his dede,
 The faire toure of London haved he to mede.

Sone than was Sir David broght unto the toure,
And William the Dowglas, with men of honowre;
Full swith redy servis fand thai there a schowre
For first thai drank of the swete, and sethin of the sowre.

Than sir David the Bruse makes his mone,
The faire coroun of Scotland haves he forgone;
He luked forth into France, help had he none
Of sir Philip the Valais, ne yit of sir John. . . . [12]

[1] "bag-carriers." [2] seized. [3] waning moon, "with bad luck".
[4] "Those rascals were disgraced." [5] "fared ill."
[6] cease. [7] weapons. [8] wakened. [9] dexterous.
[10] "active in armour." [11] "taught him a lesson."
[12] John, Duke of Normandy, Philip's eldest son.

27.

[A letter sent to England under his seal by the Earl of Lancaster,
describing his campaign in Gascony. (French.) Undated ; given
by Avesbury. The Earl had landed at Bayonne in the summer of
1345, and after a successful campaign, won the Battle of Auberoche
in October ; he continued his progress in 1346, capturing the
important town of Aiguillon, which was afterwards besieged by
the French.]

As for news of these parts, know that full three days
before the Feast of Our Lady's Assumption [1] we marched
from La Réole towards the parts of Bergerac, and brought
together there all the lords of Gascony and others who
were not then employed, with the intent of making a
raid, and we took counsel there with these lords. But
before our departing thence, some folk, knights and others,
came to us to ask for a truce on behalf of the French, who
were still laying siege to Aiguillon. But because we knew
that our lord the King was come into Normandy, we
would not agree to any truce ; whereupon the enemy
raised the siege, on the Sunday next before the Feast of
St. Bartholomew, and went off in a sorry fashion, for they
lost great part of their goods and men, and left behind
them their tents and most of their harness. So that as
soon as we knew of it, we held straight on our march into
Agenais, and came before Ville Réal, one of the King's
good towns, which surrendered to us, and other towns
and castles round about in great numbers. When we
had secured this town and the district round it, we
rode through the whole country, going straight towards
Tonneins and Aiguillon, which towns we also caused to
be made secure, and the surrounding districts. Then we
turned back again to La Réole, and stayed there full eight
days, holding all the country round it ; and there we took
counsel. We divided our army into three parts, and left

[1] 15 August.

the lord of la Brette, Sir Bernard de Brette, as Seneschal
of Gascony; Sir Alexander de Camont and others in the
parts of Bazadois; and the lord of Duras and other lords
of Agenais we left in that region.   Ourselves kept straight
on our march towards the parts of Saintonge with a
thousand men-at-arms.   We dislodged on the 12th day
of September, and lay that night in a good town that had
surrendered to us the same day, the town of Sauveterre.
On the morrow, when we had taken oaths of the men of
the town, we continued our march a good eight days, without attacking town or castle until we came to Chateauneuf,
which is on the river Charente; and there we caused the
bridge, that was broken, to be repaired, for the water was
so deep that one could not cross elsewhere, and crossed
over on the morrow.   The same day we had news that
Sir Walter Manny's men, who had safe-conduct from the
French to go to the King by land, were seized and imprisoned in the town of St. Jean d'Angely; and so it
proved; Sir Walter, with two others, had with much
difficulty made his escape.   So we kept on our road
towards the said town, and assaulted it, and took it by
storm, thank God, setting free the men from prison.   We
stayed there eight days, and secured the town; the townspeople made oath to us and became English, and they
have bound themselves to find 200 men-at-arms and
600 foot at their own cost as garrison of the town during
the war; in time of peace they will increase their payments each year to the King by 4,000 crowns more than
they were wont to pay to the King of France.   On the
morrow of Michaelmas we rode towards the city of
Poitiers, camping one night before the town of Lusignan,
which is a strong town, so that we attacked it and took
it by storm; the castle, one of the noblest and strongest
in France or Gascony, was surrendered to us.   We secured
the castle and the town, and left there a full hundred

men-at-arms, and others on foot. Then we rode before
the city of Poitiers, and summoned it, but they would do
nothing, for they thought their city was strong, and there
were men enough to hold it. So we assaulted the city on
the Wednesday after Michaelmas, and took it by storm,
and all those within were taken or slain. The lords that
were there, a bishop and some four barons, fled away on
the other side when they saw that the city was taken.
And we stayed there full eight days. At the writing of
these letters we were at the town of Saint-Jean, and we
are holding good towns and castles round about that have
been surrendered to us. So we have made a fair raid,
God be thanked, and are come back to Saint-Jean; we
think to continue our march from here to Bordeaux, but
this will be hard to do, for the enemy are mustered in the
district. But with God's help we hope to do well.

28.

[Letter describing the defeat of a French fleet coming to the relief
of Calais, off Crotoy, on June 25, 1347. (French. Inserted by
Avesbury in his "Chronicle" as describing the events of 25 June;
the letter itself bears no name or date. A translation is given
by Sir H. Nicolas in his "History of the Royal Navy".)
Towards the end of June the French had equipped a fleet, in
the hope of getting supplies through to Calais, but it was inter-
cepted by the English.[1] The letter said to have been found on
this occasion, addressed to the French King by John de Vienne,
Captain of Calais, was apparently forwarded by Edward to
Philip.]

Right dear Lord, please you to know that the next day
the wind, that was in the West, veered towards the East

---

[1] As early as March, 1346, Philip had arranged for the help of a large
Genoese fleet and 10,000 men. During the winter the French captains
Mistral and Marant had been revictualling the town, but this had
become more difficult in the spring. On 21 June, 1347, a large
convoy was given in charge of the Genoese captain d'Oria.

between 9 a.m. and noon, so that the Earls of Northampton
and Pembroke, the lords Morley, Talbot, Bradeston, and
the two admirals, with a great number of archers and
their retinues, and of the town levies, went on board our
ships and sailed towards Boulogne and Crotoy to look out
for the enemy, who had planned to victual Calais.   About
the hour of Vespers they fell in with them on this side of
Crotoy, numbering, as far as our people could see, 44
vessels, flunes,[1] galleys, and victuallers, loaded with various
provisions.   Some of the enemy who were in the rear
threw their victuals into the sea, and sailed away in the
direction of England, others to the port of Crotoy.   The
ten galleys abandoned their boats and cargoes, and made
for the open sea.   One flune and twelve victuallers with
their cargoes, that were in the van were so hotly pursued
that they ran as close to the land as they could, and all
on board leapt into the sea, and swam off so that there
remained not a single person alive in their ships.   But
the next night, just at daybreak, two boats came out from
the town into the open sea, the which were quickly
sighted by a mariner called William Roke, with one
Hickman Stephen ; whereupon one boat got back to the
town with much difficulty, and the other was chased
ashore.   In this there was taken a great master, the
captain of the Genoese galleys, and leader of the Genoese
who are in the town, and seventeen of these men with
him, as well as a good forty letters.   But before the said
captain was taken, he bound to an axe one letter containing
matter of great charge, and threw it into the sea ; but
this axe and letter were found when the tide ebbed—of
the which you will find a copy enclosed within this.   And
know that what I have told you before about this matter is
true, for I learned it from a knight who was on board with
the ships.

[1] A flune, or flouin—a light, swift ship.

[Copy of the letter enclosed, sent to the King of France by the
Captain of Calais.]

Right dear and most dread lord, I recommend me to you
as earnestly as I may, as one desiring greatly to hear good
news of your estate, the which may Our Lord by His grace
always maintain in prosperity. And if it please you to
hear the state of our town of Calais, be assured that at
the writing of these letters we were all well and of good
courage, greatly desiring to serve you, and to do whatever
may be to your honour and profit. But, most dear and
dread Lord, know that although our people are all well
and of good courage, yet the town is in sore need of corn,
wine, and meat. For know that there is nothing within
it that has not been eaten up, cats, dogs, and horses, so
that we can find nothing more in the town to live upon,
except we eat human flesh. For once before you wrote
that I should hold the town as long as there was food
left in it; and now we have come to that point that we
have no longer anything to live upon. And so we have
agreed among ourselves that unless we shall shortly
have succour, we will sally forth from the town into the
open, and fight for life or death. For it were better for us
to die honourably in the open than to eat one another.
Wherefore, most dread lord, apply what remedy you may
see fitting, for if remedy or counsel be not shortly had, you
will not have any letters more from me, and the town will
be lost, and we who are within it. Our Lord grant you
long and prosperous life, and make you of such mind, that
if we die for you, you will requite it to our heirs.

29.

[Letter from Edward III describing the arrival of the French army to
relieve Calais, and the failure of peace negotiations. The letter
is preserved in Avesbury's "Chronicle," and is printed from
Avesbury in "Foedera," III, i. (French. Undated, but written

before 3 August when the town surrendered.)   Philip of France
came to the heights of Sangatte on 27 July (S. Luce, "Froissart").]

Edward, by God's grace, King of England and France
and Lord of Ireland to the honourable Father in God, John
by the same grace Archbishop of Canterbury, Primate of
all England ; and to our Chancellor and Treasurer, greeting.—Because we believe that you will gladly hear news
as to the state of matters with us, we do you to wit that
this last Wednesday before the first of August our adversary of France with all his power came and camped near
us, on some high ground on the other side of the marsh.
And on his coming some of our host fell in with his men
and skirmished with them, taking prisoner a goodly
company of knights and squires.   On the same day the
cardinals [1] came to the end of the causeway, and sent their
letters to our cousin of Lancaster and other great men
of our host, praying that they would speak with them.
Wherefore, with our permission, our cousins of Lancaster
and Northampton went there, and the cardinals begged
them in very pressing manner that treaty might be had,
and said that they were assured that our adversary would
make us such offers of peace as would reasonably be acceptable.   And at the instance of the said cardinals, being
ready, as we are, and always have been to accept a reasonable peace whenever it may be offered us, we willingly
agreed to such discussion.   And therefore our cousin of
Lancaster had two pavilions set up on a spot within our
ground, between the two armies; where there came together, with the cardinals the Marquis of Juliers, our said
cousins of Lancaster and Northampton, our Chamberlain,
Sir Bartholomew Burghersh, Sir Reginald Cobham, and
Sir Walter Manny, on our part ; and the Dukes of Bourbon and Athens, the Chancellor of France, the Lord of

[1] Annibale Ceccano, Bishop of Frascati, and Etienne Aubert, Bishop
of Ostia.

Offémont, and Sir Geoffrey de Charny for our adversary. They held discussion together, and those treating for the other party began to speak of the town of Calais, and were all for surrendering the town in such manner that those within might go free with their goods and chattels; and then, when that was done, they would treat of peace. Our people replied that they were not charged to speak about the town, but to treat of peace, if a reasonable means might be shown. But those of the other side were obstinate about the matter of the town, so that they could only with much difficulty be brought to offer anything. But at last they offered the Duchy of Guienne, as the King's grandfather held it, and the county of Ponthieu. Our people answered that this offer was too small to requite so great damage. They treated so for three days without result, for those of the other side stood always upon parley about the town, to have saved the people within by some subtlety. And then upon the Tuesday, towards vespers, certain great men and knights came from our adversary to the place of treaty, and on his part offered our people battle so that we should be willing to come outside the marsh, and he would give us a fitting place for fighting whenever it pleased us, between then and the Friday evening next following. And they desired that four knights of our people, and four others of theirs should choose a fitting place for both sides. Upon this our people replied that they would cause this offer to be put before us, and would give them answer on the ensuing Wednesday. When this matter was shown to us, we took counsel with the great men, and other discreet persons of our council and our host, and trusting in God and our right, we caused answer to be made that we accepted their offer, and would willingly have battle. And we had our letters of conduct made out for four knights of the other side to come to our host, so that we might take four others of the same estate, and these eight knights should swear to go and view and seek out suitable places until they were agreed. But now, when those of the other side had heard this reply, they began to veer about in their offers, and to talk of the town all afresh as though putting aside the battle; in this way they would hold to nothing certain. And on the Thursday before daybreak our adversary departed with all his people, as though discomfited, making such haste that upon their going they burned their tents and great part of their harness. Our people pursued them close upon their heels, so that at the writing of this they were not yet come back. And for this cause we are not yet certainly resolved what we shall do further; but by all means we intend to go forward in the despatch of our war, with God's help, as speedily as we can.

30.

[Sir Thomas Dagworth's despatch to the Chancellor announcing the victory of La Roche Derien. (French.) Avesbury. During the night of 19-20 June, 1347, Dagworth, who had recently replaced the Earl of Northampton in Brittany, fell upon the army of Charles of Blois, who was besieging the English in La Roche Derien, and completely defeated him.]

Right dear and very honoured Lord—Please you to hear news from the parts of Brittany that my lord Charles of Blois had laid siege to the town and castle of La Roche Derien, and had in his company 1200 fresh men-at-arms, knights, and squires, and 600 others, and 600 archers of the district, 2000 cross-bowmen, and I know not how many of the common levies. And he had had great entrenchments of ditches made round him, and outside his fortified place he had caused all ditches to be filled, and the hedges to be cut down for the breadth of a good half-league round him, whereby my archers could not find vantage over him and his people, but were perforce obliged to fight in the open field. He and his people knew of my coming upon them by their scouts, and they were drawn up in arms all night. We came upon them, my comrades and I, on the 20th day of June, about the quarter before daybreak and by God's grace the business went in such manner that he lost the field, and was plainly discomfited, praised be God.

I had in my company about 300 men-at-arms and 4000 archers, besides Sir Richard de Totesham and Hankin de Isprede, and the garrison of La Roche Derien, who came out when it was daylight and they could make us out, and came to us right chivalrously against the enemy; for we came in conflict with the enemy before sunrise, in four battles, one after another. And there were slain in the fight the lord of Laval, the viscount of Rohan, the lord of Chateaubriand, the lord of Malestroit, the lord of Quintin, the lord of Rougé, the lord of Derval and his son and heir, Sir Ralph de Montfort, and many other knights and squires; between 600 and 700 men-at-arms, and I cannot tell you the number of common people. And there were taken that day my lord Charles of Blois, Sir Guy de Laval, son and heir of the lord of Laval who died in the battle, the lord of Rochefort, the lord of Beaumanoir, the lord of Lohéac, the lord of Tinteniac, and a great number of other knights and squires.

31.

[Parliament held on 14 January, 1348. "Rolls of Parliament," ii. 164. (French.) A truce had been made on 28 September, 1347.]

. . . The causes of the Parliament were set out by Sir William de Thorp, in presence of our lord the King, the prelates, earls, barons, and Commons of the realm there assembled. And there were two causes especially touching our lord the King and the whole realm of England, namely, the one cause as to the war that the King has undertaken against his adversary of France, by the common consent of all the great men and Commons of his land, in divers Parliaments held before this time, as has often been rehearsed—what shall be done about it when the present truce shall be at an end. And the other cause, as to the peace of England, how, and in what manner it can be better kept. And upon this the knights of the shires and the others of the Commons were commanded that they should treat together, and inform the King and the great men of his council what they thought about these matters.

The knights and others of the Commons having had deliberation thereupon for four days, at length made answer to the article touching the war in the following manner:—

Most dread lord, as to your war, and the disposing of it, we are so ignorant and simple that we know not, and are not able to give counsel thereon; and of this we pray your gracious lordship to hold us excused; and that it may please you to decide upon this point with the advice of the great men and discreet persons of your council, what shall seem best to you for the honour and profit of yourself and your realm. And we will willingly agree to what shall be thus ordained, and will hold it settled and established.

32.

[Proceedings in an irregular Parliament or Great Council,[1] 1353. "Rolls of Parliament," ii. 252. (French.) As early as 1351 formal peace negotiations were opened between representatives of the two kingdoms. In 1352 the new Pope Innocent VI (a cardinal of the Calais conferences) began to play an active part in promoting further discussions; in February, 1353, Edward appointed the Archbishop of Canterbury, the Duke of Lancaster, and others, to continue the negotiations.]

On the 7th day of October, our lord the King, the prelates, and great men being seated in the White Chamber,

---

[1] Cf. Stubbs, "Const. Hist.," ii. 429 (1896).

the Commons were summoned, and it was shown there by
Sir Bartholomew Burghersh, the King's Chamberlain . . .
how that our lord the King had considered how he could
best ease his people, who have so often been burdened with
impositions and heavy aids made to him before this time,
by reason of the war that he has maintained against his
adversary of France. . . . And how upon this matter he
lately sent persons of the most noble and excellent estate
of his realm, as the Archbishop of Canterbury, the Duke
of Lancaster, and other prelates and great men to Guînes,
to treat with the deputies of his adversary in the presence
of a cardinal whom our Holy Father sent there to act as
intermediary, and in no way as party, and to give him an
account of the discussion. And after this discussion the
King sent his confessor to the Papal court, to inform the
Holy Father in confession how far he would be willing to
go, in order that the war between himself and his foe
might cease (bearing in mind the mortality that there had
been from this cause, and the great mischiefs that he and
his people had suffered since the beginning of this same
war; and also being desirous of spending part of his time
in another war, more pleasing to God, and to His greater
honour)—namely, that if his adversary would restore to
him the Duchy of Guienne, as freely as any of his ancestors
held it, the Duchy of Normandy, and the County of Ponthieu, with the lands that he has conquered from his said
foe in France, Brittany, and elsewhere, and also the obedience of Flanders, whereof he is seized, all to be held freely,
without homage or other service; then he would willingly
resign the said crown, to bring the war to an end. Nor
even would he stay for Normandy, that he would not
willingly suffer that his foe should have it if it could be
shown that he had a right to it.

And as to this the Holy Father should, in a secret
manner, sound the wishes of his adversary, for otherwise

5 *

the King would assent to no other treaty of peace ; protesting always that in case his adversary would not accept this, his rights should be saved as fully as they had pertained to him before.

Since then the Holy Father has communicated nothing to our lord the King, although the King afterwards sent his clerk, Master William of Wittlesea, Archdeacon of Huntingdon, to him, to learn some result of the business ; but the Archdeacon has reported nothing to the purpose. Wherefore it seems to the King and to the great men and others of the Council that he must needs make ready for war against his foe as well for the defence of the realm, as to recover his rights ; for the which preparations he must needs have a great sum of money.[1]

33.

[Parliament of 28 April, 1354. "Rolls of Parliament," ii. 255. (French.)   On 30 March other deputies had been appointed, who arranged a truce until April, 1355.]

It was explained by Sir Bartholomew Burghersh the King's Chamberlain to the great men and Commons there present, how that there had been treaty between the ambassadors of our lord the King and of his adversary of France, and how there was good hope, with God's help, of a final and acceptable issue. But the King was unwilling to accept this without the assent of the great men and the Commons. Wherefore the Chamberlain asked them in the King's name if they would agree to peace, in case one might succeed in obtaining it by treaty and agreement of the parties. To which the Commons replied all with one accord, that whatever issue it should please the King and the great men to accept would be agreeable to them.

[1] The subsidy on wool and skins was continued for three years, the two last being conditional upon the renewal of war ; the whole to be spent only for purposes connected with the war.

Upon this reply the Chamberlain said to the Commons, "You are willing, then, to agree to a treaty of perpetual peace, if one may have it?" And the Commons replied unhesitatingly and with one voice, "Yea, Yea".

34.

[The breakdown of peace negotiations. "Chronicle" of Geoffrey le Baker. (Latin.) On 28 August, 1354, the Duke of Lancaster and others had been appointed to treat in the presence of the Pope ("Foedera," III, i. 283).]

. . . Then for the more securing of so great a relief, solemn messengers were sent from each kingdom to the Apostolic See, to wit, on behalf of the King of England, this embassy was discharged by the Bishop of Norwich, the Earl of Arundel and other knights; and they met at Avignon the Archbishop of Rouen, the Duke of Bourbon, Geoffrey de Charny, and others of the council of France. All the ambassadors were received with great honour, the Duke of Lancaster being met by many cardinals and bishops, who conducted him for two miles to the Pope's palace in the city. And at last, in the council of the Supreme Pontiff, in the presence of himself, the cardinals, and the ambassadors of both sides, the respective causes of each were put forward. The which having been heard, the English asked for the confirmation of the agreements lately made at Calais between themselves and the ambassadors of France there present. The Frenchmen replied that they would gladly have peace; but as for Aquitaine and the aforesaid counties, they said that the King of France could not permit, and they themselves would not consent, that these, with all the rights therein pertaining to the crown of France should be alienated from that Kingdom, whose integrity they had sworn to preserve. Nevertheless, they would agree that a meet lordship of the duchy and the counties, in the same manner as his ancestors had held Aquitaine, should come to the King of England ; so always that the sovereignty of the royal crown of France were reserved.

But the English, for the sake of having a lasting peace, asked that these lordships should be granted to their King absolutely and unconditionally ; for they considered how that same sovereignty had been wont to provoke former Kings of England and France to war, on account of homage and allegiance being delayed.   This request, however, was obstinately refused, although, as the Cardinal of Bologna bore witness, it had lately been admitted at Calais, and confirmed by persons having authority to do so.   And further, their argument touching their oath and the King's, by which, as they alleged, they were bound to maintain the honour of their Kingdom in its integrity, was met with the reply that, for the sake of a satisfactory peace, the Pope might be pleased to absolve them from their oath, and that, so far as the foregoing articles were concerned, it would be advisable for this to be done.   But in spite of that, the Pope did nothing fresh that was of any avail for the peace of the Church and the two King-doms.   Wherefore the ambassadors, who had been sent there at heavy expense, returned without achieving any result.

35.

[Letter from Sir John Wingfield to the Treasurer, describing the Black Prince's doings in Gascony, in the autumn of 1355. (French.) Avesbury. A joint invasion of Northern and Southern France was planned to take place in the summer of 1355, but the expeditions were delayed until the autumn. The Prince's army had been in Gascony since September.]

My Lord, as for news of our parts, please you to hear that at the writing of these letters my lord the Prince and all the earls, barons, bannerets, knights and squires were in good health. And in all this expedition my lord has lost no knight or squire except Sir John de Lisle, who was mortally hurt in most marvellous fashion by a crossbow-bolt on the third day after we came into the enemy's country, and died on the 15th day of October. And, my lord, please you to know that my lord has raided the county of Armagnac, and taken many walled towns there, and burnt and destroyed them, save certain towns that he has made secure. Then he went into the viscounty of Rivière, and took a good town called Plaisance, the chief town of the country, burning and destroying it, and all the country round about. Then he went into the county of Astarac, took many towns, and laid waste all the country; and next into the county of Comminge, where he took many towns and had them burnt, with the surrounding district. He took the chief town, that is called Samatan, a town as big as Norwich. Then he entered the county of Lisle, and took some of the walled towns, burning many other good towns as he passed through. Then he came into the lordship of Toulouse, where we crossed the river Gironde and another very wide one a league above Toulouse, for the enemy had broken all the bridges on both sides of the city saving those within it, for the river runs through Toulouse; at that time the Constable of France, the Marshal of Clermont, and the Count of Armagnac were therein, with great power. The city is very large, strong and fine, and well walled. There was no man in our host that knew a ford there, but by God's grace we found it. Then he went through the lordship of Tholosane, taking many good walled towns, the which he has burnt and laid waste, with all the surrounding country.

After that we came into the lordship of Carcassonne, taking many good towns before we came to Carcassonne; we took the town, which is larger, stronger and finer than York; and the whole of this town, and all the others in the district were burnt and destroyed. So we went on several days' march until we were passed through the country of Carcassonne and were come into the lordship of Narbonne, where we took and pillaged many towns until we came to Narbonne, the which held out against us, and was taken by storm.[1] This town is but little smaller than London, and lies on the Greek sea, only two short leagues distant from the open sea; there are a haven and landing-place, whose water comes right up to Narbonne. The town is only 15 leagues from Montpellier, 18 from Aigues-Mortes, and 30 from Avignon. And please you to know that the Holy Father sent his messengers to my lord, who were only seven leagues from him, when they sent a sergeant-at-arms, that was the Holy Father's sergeant-at-arms at the door of his chamber, with their letters to my lord, praying that they might have safe-conduct to come to him; and they showed him their errand from the Holy Father, that was to treat between my lord and his enemies of France. This messenger was two days in the host before my lord would see him or receive his letters; and it was on this occasion that my lord had news that the power of France was come forth from Toulouse, to the neighbourhood of Carcassonne, so that he wished to turn back upon them unexpectedly; and he did so. On the third day, when we were to have come upon them, they had tidings of us before daybreak and withdrew, disappearing into the mountains and strong places, and went by long marches back towards Toulouse. Some of the people of the district, who acted as their guides, to lead them by that road, were captured as they were returning; and because the Holy Father's sergeant-at-arms was under my guard, I made him question the

---

[1] Wingfield does not explain the fact, very clearly brought out by Froissart, that the English, here and at Carcassonne, failed to take the fortified "city" as distinguished from the open town.

guides who had been taken in this way; for the man
whom he questioned was the guide of the Constable of
France, and a native of that district, and he could easily
tell and know the bearing of the French from what he had
seen. I told the said sergeant that he might tell the
Holy Father and all the others at Avignon what he had
heard and seen. And as for the answer that my lord
made to the messengers, you would think yourself well
repaid if you knew all the manner of it. For he would in
no wise suffer them to approach nearer to him, but said
that if they wished to discuss anything, they should send
to the King, and that my lord himself would do nothing
except by the King's command. And as to his turning
back after his enemies, the crossing of the Gironde, the
taking of castles and towns on the march, and other things
that he did against them in the pursuit, they are right
noble and illustrious, in manner as my lord Richard
Stafford and Sir William Burton can tell you more fully
than I can send word by letter. My lord rode against his
enemies for eight whole weeks, and tarried not in all
these places save eleven days. You must know for certain
that since this war began against the King of France,
there has never yet been such loss or destruction as he has
suffered in this raid. For the districts and good towns
that have been laid waste in this expedition found the
King of France more every year to carry on his war than
did the half of his realm, not reckoning the changing of
his money each year, and the custom that he takes of
Poitou; as I shall be able to show you by good records
that were found in divers towns, in the houses of re-
ceivers. For Carcassonne and Limoux, that is as large
as Carcassonne, and two other towns near by found the
wages of 1000 men-at-arms each year for the King of
France, and beyond this, 100,000 old crowns, to maintain
his war. And you must know that, from the records

that we found, and as burgesses of the great towns, and other persons of the country have told us, the towns laid waste in Tholosane, and the towns of Carcassonne, and the city and country of Narbonne contributed every year, over and above the aforesaid sum, 400,000 old crowns. And with God's help, if my lord had wherewithal to carry on this war, and to secure the King's profit and honour, he could greatly extend our marches, and secure many places ; for our enemies are much confounded. And at the writing of these letters my lord had resolved to send all the earls and bannerets to stay in various places on the borders, to make raids and harass the enemy.

My lord, I cannot send you other news at present ; but what you shall desire of me please you at all times to command me by your letters, as one who is yours with all my might. My right honoured lord, may God grant you long life, joy, and health. Written at Bordeaux, the Wednesday [1] next before Christmas Day.

36.

[Another letter from Sir John Wingfield, to Lord Stafford. (French.) Avesbury, 2 January, 1356.]

Very dear lord, and right trusty friend, as for news since your departure, please you to wit that there are taken and surrendered five walled towns—namely, Porte Sainte-Marie, Clairac, Tonneins, Bourg Saint-Pierre, Castelsagrat, and Brassac, and seventeen castles. . . . And be pleased to know that Sir John Chandos, Sir James of Audley, and your people who are with them, with the other Gascons who are in their company, Sir Baldwin Botour and his company, and Sir Reginald Cobham took the town called Castelsagrat by storm. And the bastard of l'Isle, captain of the town, was slain as they made the assault, being pierced through the head by an arrow. Sir Reginald is

[1] 23 December (Kervyn de Lettenhove).

come back to Landak, and Sir Baldwin to Brassac, with
their company. Sir John and Sir James, with those of
their company remained at Castelsagrat, having enough
provisions of all kinds to last until Midsummer, except
fresh fish and greens, as they have sent us word by their
letters. So that you need not be concerned about your
good people. There are in the town more than 300 lances,
300 foot, and 150 archers; they have ridden up to Agen,
and burnt all their mills, and they have broken and burnt
all their bridges over the Gironde, taking a castle outside
the town, the which they secured. Sir John of Armagnac
and the seneschal of Agenois who were within the town of
Agen would not once put forth their heads, nor any of their
men, although our people have been twice before the town.
My lord Boucicaut had come up, as well as Sir Ernold of
Spain and Grismouton of Chambly with 300 lances and
300 Lombard foot; they are in the town of Moissac in
Quercy, but one league from Castelsagrat and one from
Brassac, so you may well imagine that there will be a
goodly company there to make trial of each other. Please
you to know that Sir Bartholomew is at Cognac, with six
score men-at-arms of my lord's household, and six score
archers; with the Captal de Buch, the lord Montferrand,
and the lord of Carton, who have in their company full 300
lances, six score archers, and 200 foot.

And there are men-at-arms in Taillebourg, Tonnay, and
Rochefort, so that when they are together, they may well
be 600 lances. At the making of these letters they were
out on an expedition to Anjou and Poitou; the Earls of
Suffolk, Oxford and Salisbury, the lord of Mucidan, Sir
Elie de Pomiers, with other Gascons, well over 500 lances,
200 foot, and 300 archers had been gone more than twelve
days towards the parts of Notre Dáme de Rochemade,
and were not yet returned. Sir John Chandos, Sir James,
and Sir Baldwin, and those of their company are also

departed on a raid, towards their own borders, and so likewise are Sir Reginald and those of the household, with the
Gascons in their company. The Earl of Warwick has
been at Tonneins and Clairac, to take these towns, and at
the writing of these he is gone towards Marmande to destroy their supplies, and whatever else he may. My lord
himself is at Libourne, and the lord of Pomiers at Fronsac,
but a quarter of a league away; my lord's people were lying
both at Saint-Emilion and at Libourne, and Sir Bernard
de Bret is with him. He is awaiting tidings of what shall
take place, and according to these he will go where it shall
seem best for his honour. At the making of these letters
the Count of Armagnac was at Avignon, and the King of
Aragon. And as to all other reports that there have been
in divers places, whereof you have heard, I can tell you no
more, save that you take care to send news to my lord as
soon as you can well do so. Right dear Sir, may Our Lord
grant you good life and long. Written at Libourne, the
2nd day of January.

37.

[Letter from the Black Prince to the Bishop of Hereford. (French.)
"Register" of Bishop Trillek of Hereford. The Prince's successes
were continued during the early months of 1356; towards the
middle of June the Duke of Lancaster landed with a large army
in Normandy, and important joint operations seem to have been
expected; but the Prince was detained in the South.]

Reverend father in God—as we have sure hope that it
is by the good and devout prayers of persons of Holy
Church and other Christians that the quarrel that we have
to pursue on behalf of our very honoured lord and father
the King, in these parts will reach the most favourable
issue, we earnestly entreat you, putting our trust in you,
that you will have the same especially in your devotion;
and will command all your subjects, as well the religious

as parsons, vicars, and others of your jurisdiction, to go twice each week in procession, praying for us; and to pray daily for us in good masses, by some special prayer to be appointed by you. So that by these devotions we may the better win the rights of our said dear lord, and our own. Reverend father in God, the Holy Ghost be guardian of you. Given under our secret seal at Bordeaux, on the 25th day of June.

38.

[" Letter of the Lord Prince of Wales, addressed to the Mayor, Alder-men, and community of the City of London, concerning news of the battle near Poitiers." (French.) Printed from the letter-books of the City of London by Sir H. Nicolas, in his edition of the " Chronicle of London ".[1] The Prince set out on his march early in August; the Battle of Poitiers was fought on 19 September.]

Right dear and well-beloved, concerning news from the parts wherein we are, be pleased to know that since the time when we informed our most dread lord and father the King that we were of purpose to make a raid against the enemy into the parts of France, we took the road towards the country of Perigord and Limousin, and straight on to-wards Bourges, in Vienne, where we thought to have found the King's son, the Count of Poitiers. And the principal cause of our going into these parts was that we expected to have news of our lord and father the King, as of his passage. And because we did not find the said Count, nor any other great force there, we drew towards the Loire, and sent our people to ride on and see if we could find a crossing anywhere; these encountered the enemy and they fought together, so that some of the enemy were slain, and taken. The prisoners said that the King of France had sent Grismouton, who was in this company, to give him certain tidings of us and of our power; and that for the

---

[1] A translation is given in Riley's " Memorials of London ".

same reason he had sent the lord of Creon, the lord Boucicaut, the Marshal of Clermont and others in another direction. The said prisoners also said that the King had made certain resolve to fight with us what time we were on the road towards Tours; and he was on the march in the neighbourhood of Orleans. The next day we had news there where we were lodged that the said lords of Clermont and Boucicaut were in a castle very near our camp; so we resolved to go there, and we came and camped round about them. We agreed to assault the place,[1] the which was taken by storm, wherein there were full many of their men taken and slain, and some of ours were slain there too. But the said lords of Clermont and Boucicaut withdrew into a strong tower that was there, the which held out for five days before it was won, whereupon they surrendered. There we were informed that all the bridges over the Loire were broken, and that we could nowhere have passage. Upon this we made our way straight to Tours, and stayed for four days before the town, wherein were the Count of Anjou and the Marshal of Clermont, with great force of men. And on our departing thence we took our road so as to escape any risks from the high floods, expecting to have fallen in with our dear cousin the Duke of Lancaster, from whom we had certain tidings that he would endeavour to come to us.

At this time the Cardinal of Perigord came to us at Montbezon three leagues from Tours, where he had much to say to us concerning a truce, and peace. Upon which parley we made answer that we had no power to make peace, nor would we intermeddle with it without the command and desire of our right honoured lord and father the King; nor, as to a truce, were we at that time of the opinion that it would be best for us to agree to one. For we were there more fully certified that the King had made

[1] Vierzon.

ready by all possible means to fight with us. So we drew on thence towards Châtelherault for the passage of the river Vienne, where we lay four days, waiting to know more certainly of him. The said King came with his power to Chauvigny, five leagues from us, to cross over the same river towards Poitiers, whereupon we resolved to hasten towards him, on the road that he must take, in order to have fought with him. But his battles were all passed before we could come to the place where we expected to encounter him, saving some part of their people, about 700 men-at-arms, who fought with ours. Here there were taken the Counts of Soussoire and Jounhy, the lord of Châtillon, and great plenty of others, were taken prisoner and slain, both of their men and ours. Our people pursued them as far as Chauvigny, full three leagues off; wherefore we were obliged to lodge that day as near that place as we could, to gather our men together. The next day we set out on our march straight towards the King. We sent on our scouts, who found him with his power ready for battle in the fields a league from Poitiers; so we went as near to him as we could, to take up our position. And we ourselves were on foot and in battle array, ready to fight with him, when the aforesaid Cardinal came up, begging right earnestly, for a little sufferance, so that parley might be arranged between certain persons from both sides, for the purpose of making accord, and having a good peace, which he undertook to bring about in good faith. Whereupon we took counsel and granted his request. Then certain persons from both sides were appointed to treat about this matter, the which treaty brought forth no result. Then the Cardinal wished to have procured a truce at his pleasure, in hindrance of the battle, but this we would not agree to accept. The French asked that certain knights of one side and the other might choose a fair place, so that the battle could in no wise fail; and in this wise it was delayed that day, and the battles of both sides stood all night in their places until the morrow about the hour of prime, and for any forces that were between them, one would not give the other vantage by undertaking the attack.   Then for lack of victuals as well as for other reasons it was agreed that we should set out on our march, keeping before them on their flank in such manner that if they desired battle, or to draw towards us in a spot that was not greatly to our disadvantage, we would accept it; and so it was done.   Whereupon the battle was joined two days before the Feast of St. Matthew; and, praised be God, the enemy was discomfited, and the King and his son taken prisoner, great plenty of other great men being captured and slain, as our dear batchelor Sir Nigel Loring our Chamberlain, the bearer of this who has full knowledge of it will be able more fully to explain to you, than we may write it.   To whom be pleased to give full faith and credence.   May Our Lord be pleased to keep you.   Given under our secret seal at Bordeaux, the 22nd day of October.

39.

[The capture of the French King, and the ransoming of prisoners after Poitiers.   Froissart.]

Truly this battle which was near Poitiers in the fields of Beaumanoir and Maupertuis was right great and perilous, and many deeds of arms were done there which all came not to knowledge, and the fighters on both sides endured much pain.   King John with his own hands did that day marvels in arms; he had an axe in his hands wherewith he defended himself.   In the breaking of the press there were taken near to him the Earl of Tankarville, Sir Jaques of Bourbon, count of Ponthieu, and the lord John of Artois, count of Eu; and a little above that, under the banner of the Captal de Buch was taken Sir Charles of

Artois and many other knights. The chase endured to
the gates of Poitiers; there were many slain and beaten
down horse and man for they of Poitiers closed their
gates and would suffer none to enter. Wherefore in
the street before the gate was horrible murder, men hurt
and beaten down. The Frenchmen yielded themselves
up as far off as they could see an Englishman; and there
were many English archers that had four, five, or six
prisoners. . . .

So many English and Gascons came up from all directions that perforce they broke up the ranks of the King's
battle, and the French were so mingled with their enemies
that at times there were five men upon one gentleman.
There were taken the lord of Pompadour, and the lord
Bartholomew de Brunes, and Sir Geoffrey de Charny was
slain with the banner of France in his hands; and the
lord Reynold Cobham took the Earl of Dammartyn. Then
there was great press upon the King, for eagerness to take
him, and such as were nearest cried, "Sir, yield you, yield,
or else you are but dead". There was a knight of St.
Omer, retained in wages with the King of England, called
Sir Denis de Morbecke, who had served the English for
about five years, because in his youth he had forfeited the
realm of France for a murder that he did at St. Omer. It
happened so well for him that he was quite near the King
when they were about to take him; he pushed through
the press by force of his body and arms, for he was tall
and strong, and said to the King in good French, "Sir,
yield you". The King, who was in sore straits, and too
hard pressed by his enemies, beheld the knight, and said,
"To whom shall I yield me? Where is my cousin the
Prince of Wales? If I might see him, I would speak with
him." Denis answered, "Sir, he is not here, but yield you
to me, and I will bring you to him". "Who be you?"
said the King. "Sir, I am Denis of Morbecke, a knight

of Artois, but I serve the King of England, because I am
banished the realm of France. . . . Then the King
answered, as I was afterwards informed, "I yield me to
you," giving him his right gauntlet, and the knight took
it, being greatly rejoiced. There was great press about
the King, for every man strove to say, "I have taken him,"
so that the King could not go forward with the lord Philip
his young son.

    .   .   .   .

Then the Prince had his banner set up high on a bush
and trumpets and clarions began to sound; the Prince
took off his basinet . . . and a little red pavilion was put
up wherein he entered, and drink was brought to the
Prince and to the lords who were about him, the which still
increased as they came from the chase, for they tarried
there and their prisoners with them. When the two
marshals were come to the Prince, he demanded of them
if they knew any tidings of the French King; they replied,
"No, Sir, not of a certainty, but we think he is either
dead or taken, for he has not gone out of the battle".
Then the Prince said to the Earl of Warwick and to Sir
Reynold Cobham, "I beg of you to go forth, and to ride
as far forth that at your return you may show me the
truth". These two lords took their horses and departed
from the place, and rode up a little hill to look about them.
Then they perceived a great flock of men-at-arms on foot
advancing very slowly. There was the King of France in
great peril, for Englishmen and Gascons had mastered
him; and had taken him from Sir Denis de Morbecke,
and separated him from him; and such as were of most
force were shouting, "I have taken him". The King,
who knew the rivalry there was among them to have him,
to escape the peril said, "Sirs, lead me courteously to my
cousin the Prince, and strive not together for my taking,
for I am so great a lord as to make you all rich". The

King's words somewhat appeased them, howbeit ever as they went they continued their brawling.

When the two aforesaid lords saw that strife among them they spurred their horses towards them, saying "Sirs, what is the matter?" They were answered "It is the King of France who is taken prisoner, and there be more than ten knights and squires that challenge the taking of him". Then the two lords broke up the press with their horses, causing every man to draw back, and ordered them in the Prince's name on pain of their heads to approach the King no nearer unless they were commanded. . . .

. . . .

When every man was come back from the chase, they found that they had twice as many prisoners as they were in number in all; then it was counselled among them, because of the great charge and doubt to keep so many, that they should put many of them to ransom incontinent in the field, and so they did. And the knights and squires who were prisoners found the Englishmen and Gascons right courteous; there were many that day let go only on their promise of faith and truth to return again between then and Christmas to Bordeaux with their ransoms. Then that night they lay in the field beside where as the battle had been. Some unarmed them, but not all, and they unarmed all their prisoners, and every man made good cheer to his prisoner; for whosoever took any prisoner in the battle, he was clear his, and he might quit or ransom him at his pleasure. . . . They let them ransom themselves and go quit more courteously than ever men did before; they constrained them no otherwise but that they asked them on their honour how much they could pay, without burdening them too much, and willingly believed what they told them. For they said that they would set no knight's or squire's ransom so

high but that he might pay at his ease and maintain his
degree according to his estate, and ride about to advance
his person and his honour.   The custom of the Germans
nor their courtesy is not such, for they have neither pity
nor mercy upon any gentlemen, but ransom them to the
full extent of their means, and beyond, and put them in
stocks and chains, and keep them in prison as straitly as
they can, to extort greater ransom from them.

All such as were in this battle with the Prince were all
made rich with honour and goods, as well by ransoming
of prisoners as by winning of gold, silver, plate, and jewels,
that were there found, and of chests filled with rich heavy
belts and fine cloaks.   There was no man that did set anything by rich harness, whereof there was great plenty,
for the French had come there richly arrayed, as weening
have had the day for themselves.

40.

[An echo of the Battle of Poitiers.   " Notification concerning the con-
    dition of Denis de Morbecke, in the matter of the cause between
    him and Bernard de Troye about the capture of King John of
    France in the Battle of Poitiers."   Entry on the Patent Roll,
    1360.   (French.)   " Foedera," III, ii. 467.]

The King to all those who shall see or hear these letters,
greeting.   It has been declared to us by our dear and
well-beloved Ralph Spigurnel, knight, John of Bucking-
ham, Dean of Lichfield, David de Wollore, and John de
Codington, clerks of the Chancery, sent by our Council in
England to view the condition of Denis de Morbecke,
knight, lying ill in the City of London, as it was said—
That they and others of our Council on the 10th day of
January last past, came to the house where the said
Denis is lodged, in a street near the Church called
Barking Chapel in the said City of London.   And they

found him in his chamber, lying in his bed, sorely ill, in
their opinion, and the said Ralph addressed him in the
following manner—"Sir Denis, you know how that lately
at Sandwich you were pursued by an appeal of one
Bernard de Troye, a squire of Gascony, by reason of the
taking of the King of France at the battle of Poitiers.
And because our lord the King was so busy about his
passage that he could not then give attention to the trying
of the said appeal, a day was then assigned you by his
Constable and Marshal to be before him wheresoever he
might be in the realm of France or England, at Candlemas next coming, to do and receive what should then
be adjudged by our lord the King upon the said appeal.
And this day and place you expressly accepted, wherefore
we are sent to you from the King's Council, to know
whether you are able and willing to perform what you
undertook in this manner."

Whereto Sir Denis at once answered openly before
the said Ralph, John, David, and John, and others
of our Council there, in the presence of notaries, that his
desire was always, and still is, to make his way to us to
perform his promise, and to do his duty in all things
touching the said appeal, if his body might suffice and
endure it, even though he were to die by the way; and as
to this he made a declaration at Sandwich before the
Constable and Marshal. But he thought that he could
not do so until God should have lent him better health,
and visited him with His grace.

And the better to know the truth, and that the said
Denis made no pretence in this matter, they made him
uncover his body, arms, hands, and feet; and when they
had seen these, it was the opinion of Ralph, John, David,
and John, and of the notaries, physicians, surgeons, and
all others who were come there for this cause, that the
said Denis was by reason of his sickness so prostrated,

wasted and reduced in all his members that he might
scarcely recover as long as he lived, unless a great miracle were performed for him.

And nevertheless Denis swore the same upon the
Holy Gospels ; and moreover, Master John Paladyn, phy-
sician, and John of Cornhill, surgeon, questioned about
this, swore on the Holy Gospels, and upon their honour, in
peril of their souls, that by reason of his sickness the said
Denis was so feeble that he had not strength to help
himself, nor to move feet, legs, arms or hands without
assistance.

The which matters aforesaid are all comprised in an
instrument drawn up hereupon ; and we, so that they
may come to the notice of all men, have caused these our
letters patent to be made, and sealed with our Great Seal,
in testimony of the truth.

41.

[As the result of renewed peace negotiations, the King of France
agreed in March, 1359, before the expiration of the Truce of
Bordeaux of 1357, to that Treaty of London whose provisions the
French Estates refused to ratify. Another invasion of France
followed in the autumn of 1359. The following account of the
King's train is given by Le Bel and is reproduced by Froissart.
It illustrates the impression made by his equipment.]

When King Edward was come to Calais, with the
Prince of Wales and his two brothers, he gave order to
unload the ships, for he did not wish to tarry there,
but to go and seek his dear cousin the Duke of Lancaster.
Thus he set out from Calais with the finest baggage-
train that was ever seen, for it was said that there were
full 6000 carts well furnished and drawn, that had all
come from England. Moreover he ordered his battles in
such striking fashion that it was most pleasing to see
them. He had appointed as his Constable my lord of

March, and made him ride half a league before him with
600 men-at-arms, of the best arrayed in the host, and
1000 archers.   Afterwards he ordered his own battle,
taking full 3000 men-at-arms and 5000 archers, and
rode always in close array after his marshal, so that he
might be able to fight at once, if need were.   After this
great battle came the waggons, that stretched full two
French leagues, and carried everything that one can
think of needed for his household and for fighting; as
hand-mills, and ovens for baking bread, for fear lest all the
ovens and mills on their march should be destroyed.
After this came the Prince of Wales and the Earl of
Richmond his brother, and they had in their battle 2500
mounted men-at-arms, nobly and richly equipped, 4000
archers and as many men on foot; and they did not leave
one groom by the way, but they could not march more
than three leagues a day.   You must know that it rained
constantly day and night, which was great hardship both
for the men and the horses.   They found all the country
laid waste, wherefore you may understand that all, high
and low, were in great straits, for bread, wine, meat, and
especially on account of the bad weather. . . .

And you must know that the noble King and his people
had full 10,000 to 12,000 waggons,[1] with three good horses
each, brought from England; and the lords brought on
their waggons tents and pavilions, forges and ovens, to do
what was necessary . . . ; and they had several skiffs and
small boats of leather, so subtly made that they could easily
hold three men for fishing on a lake or river, if it were
desired.   And so the lords and men of condition had fish'
during Lent, but the commons made shift with what
they might get.   And with all this, the noble King had
full 30 falconers, all with their hawks, and at least 60

[1] An increase upon his previous estimate.

couples of great hounds, and as many harriers, with
which he hunted every day.   The host was always
divided in three parts, and each division rode separately,
each with its van-guard and rear-guard, and they camped
a league apart.

42.

[The Treaty of Bretigny. Edward reached Paris in March, 1360, after
a long southward circuit. Yielding to the Papal Legate's frequent
requests for negotiation, he agreed to a conference on 3 April, but
the discussion was broken off, on the demand by the English
deputies for the terms of the London Treaty of March, 1359—
which amounted to a cession of the old Angevin Empire in full
sovereignty. Edward then attempted the siege of Paris, but was
obliged to abandon it. Negotiations were again suggested and
eventually agreed upon, the formal meetings opening on 27 April.
On 8 May a preliminary treaty was signed, being accepted by
both Kings shortly afterwards. In July King John of France
was brought to Calais, where the final treaty was signed on 24
October. From this definitive treaty certain stipulations (by
which the claims of Edward to the French crown and of John to
the sovereignty of the ceded territory were abandoned) were
omitted. These were to be replaced by mutual letters of renunciation, to be exchanged at Bruges in the following autumn ;
but the exchange was not actually made. (Cosneau, "Les Grands
Traités de la Guerre de Cent Ans" ; "Foedera," III, i. 514-18.)
(French.)]

Extract from the Articles as ratified at Calais.

1. First, that the King of England, in addition to what
he holds in Guienne and Gascony, shall have perpetually
and for ever for himself and his heirs, all the following, to be
held in the same manner as the King of France, and his
son, or any of his ancestors, Kings of France, held them ;
that is to say, what was held in demesne, in demesne, and
what in fee, in fee ; and according to the time and manner
specified below—

The city, castle, and town of Poitiers, and all the land

and country of Poitou, with the fief of Thouars and the lands of Belleville;

The city and castle of Saintes, and all the land and country of Saintonge, on both sides of the Charente;

The city and castle of Agen, and the land and country of Agenois;

The city and castle, and the whole country of Perigord, and the land and county of Pierregouis;

The city and castle of Limoges, with the land and country of Limousin;

The city and castle of Cahors, with the land and country of Caoursin;

The city, castle, and district of Tarbe, and the land, district, and county of Bigorre;

The county, land, and district of Gorre;

The city and castle of Angoulême, with the county, land, and country of Angoumois;

The city and castle of Rodez, and the land and country of Rouergue.

And if there be any lords, as the Count of Foix, the Count of Armagnac, the Count of l'Isle, the Count of Perigord, the Viscount of Limoges, or others, who hold any lands or places within the bounds of the said regions, they shall do homage to the King of England, and render all other services and payments due on account of their lands or places, in manner as they have done in times past.

2. Item, the King of England shall have all that he or any of the Kings of England in former times held in the town of Montreuil-sur-mer, and its appurtenances.

3. Item, the King of England shall have the whole county of Ponthieu; save that, if any alienations have been made by Kings of England at different times from the said county to persons other than the Kings of France, the King of France shall not be bound to restore them to

the King of England. And if such alienations have been made to former Kings of France, and the King of France holds them at the present time, he shall release them wholly to the King of England. Saving that, if the Kings of France have held them in exchange for other lands, the King of England shall either restore what was had in exchange, or leave in his hands the lands thus alienated. But if the Kings of England who were for the time being had alienated anything to persons other than the Kings of France, and these be since come into his possession, the King of France shall not be bound to restore them. Also, if such lands owe homage, the King shall deliver them to others, who shall do homage to the King of England; and if not, he shall give them to a tenant who shall render the services due; and this within a year from the time when he shall have left Calais.

4. Item, the King of England shall have the castle and town of Calais;

The castle, town, and lordship of Marck;

The towns, castles, and lordships of Sangatte, Coulogne, Ham, Le Wal, and Oye; with lands, woods, marshes, rivers, rents, lordships, advowsons of Churches, and all other appurtenances and places lying within the following limits and bounds. . . .[1]

5. Item, the King of England shall have the castle, town, and the whole county of Guînes, with all the lands, towns, castles, fortresses, places, tenants, homages and seignuries, woods and forests, and the rights in them, as fully as the late Count of Guînes held them at the time of his death. And the Churches and good people within the limits of Guînes, Calais, Marck, and other places aforesaid, shall be subject to the King of England as they were to the King of France and the Count of Guînes for the time being. And all the above, of Marck and Calais,

---

[1] These are carefully specified in detail.

contained in this present article and that immediately preceding, the King of England shall hold in demesne; saving the inheritance of the Churches, which shall remain wholly to them, wherever they be situated; saving also the inheritance of other persons of the districts of Marck and Calais, situated outside the town of Calais, to the annual value of £100 worth of land, and below, in current coin of the district, which shall remain to them. But habitations and inheritances situate in the town of Calais, with their appurtenances, shall remain to the King of England in demesne, to be disposed of at his pleasure. To the inhabitants of the town, county, and district of Guînes, all their demesnes shall be left, and they shall claim them fully, saving what is said of frontiers, limits, and bounds in the preceding article.

6. Item, it is agreed that the King of England and his heirs shall have and hold all the islands adjacent to the aforesaid lands, districts, and places, with all the other islands that he holds at present.

7. Item, it is agreed that the King of France, and the Regent, his eldest son, shall as soon as possible, and at latest before the Feast of Saint Michael within a year next coming, restore, deliver, and transfer to the King of England, his heirs and successors, all the honours, obediences, homages (etc.) . . ., and all rights that they have, belonging . . . by any cause, title, or colour of right, to the King or crown of France, on account of the aforesaid cities, counties, castles (etc.), and each one of them, wherever they may be. And they shall, by their letters patent, command all Archbishops, Bishops, and others of Holy Church; and all counts, viscounts, barons, and nobles; and all others whatsoever of the aforesaid places, that they shall obey the King of England and his heirs, as they have obeyed the Kings and crown of France. And by the same letters they shall acquit and absolve them from all homage,

oaths, obligations and subjection, made in any manner by any of them to the crown of France.

8. Item, it is agreed that the King of England shall have the aforesaid counties, cities, castles, etc., wheresoever they may be to hold heritably and perpetually for himself and heirs, that which the Kings of France held in demesne, in demesne, and that which they held in fee and service, in fee and service ; saving all that is said above in the article touching Calais and Marck.   And if, of any rights, jurisdictions, or profits, whatsoever pertaining to any of the aforesaid cities, counties, castles, and lands, which any Kings of England have held, alienations, donations, obligations, or charges have been made by Kings of France within the past 70 years, by any cause or manner whatsoever, all such donations . . . henceforth are and shall be utterly repealed and annulled.   And everything thus given, alienated or charged shall be restored and delivered to the King of England or his deputies as soon as possible . . ., saving all grants and alienations made to Churches, which shall remain peacefully to them in all the aforesaid districts and places ; so that the persons of the said Churches shall pray diligently for the said Kings, as for their founders.

9. Item . . ., that the King of England shall have and hold all the aforesaid cities, counties, castles, and districts, which have not formerly belonged to the Kings of England, as the King of France or his son hold them at present.

10. Item . . ., if within the limits of the said districts formerly belonging to the Kings of England, there were anything not so belonging, but being in the possession of the King of France on the day of the battle of Poitiers, which was the 19th day of September, in the year 1356, it shall remain to the King of England and his heirs.

.   .   .   .

13. Item, that the King of France shall pay to the King of England 3,000,000 gold crowns, of which two are worth a noble in English money. Whereof 600,000 crowns shall be paid to the King of England or his deputies at Calais within four months from the time of the King of France's arrival there. And within the year next following 400,000 crowns shall be paid in England, in the City of London; and thenceforth 400,000 crowns each year until the 3,000,000 be fully paid.

14. Also, that by the payment of the said 600,000 crowns at Calais, and by delivery of the hostages named below; and by the delivery to the King of England within the said four months of the town, castle, and fortresses of Rochelle, and the castles, towns and fortresses of Guînes, the King's person shall be released from prison, and he shall be permitted to leave Calais and return to his power without hindrance. But neither he nor his people shall bear arms against the King of England until he shall have performed what he is bound to do by the present treaty. . . .[1]

[John of Montfort to be restored to the County of Montfort and other lands not pertaining to the Duchy of Brittany. The claim to the Breton succession to be decided, if possible, by agreement before representatives of the two Kings, and of friends of the parties; any agreement so obtained to be enforced against the unwilling party; neither King under any circumstances to make war upon the other in support of either claimant. The King of France to retain the sovereignty of the Duchy. All districts, etc., transferred by the treaty to enjoy their liberties and franchises. The lands of Philip of Navarre and his adherents to be restored with full pardon. Persons banished or deprived during the war as adherents of either party to be reinstated.]

27. Item . . . the King of England shall, at his own expense, deliver all the fortresses taken and occupied by

[1] There follow the names of hostages and prisoners, and the arrangements to be made for them.

him and his subjects, adherents and allies, in France,
Touraine, Anjou, Maine, Berry, Auvergne, Burgundy,
Champagne, Picardy, and Normandy, and in all other parts
of the realm of France, save those of the Duchy of Brittany, and of the districts and lands which ought to belong
to him by the present treaty.

28. Item, the King of France shall deliver to the King
of England all towns, castles, fortresses and other aforesaid lands and places at his own cost.   And if there shall
be any persons rebellious, or refusing to restore to the King
of England any cities, towns, castles, etc., . . . which
ought to belong to him by the present treaty, the King of
France shall be bound to cause them to be delivered to the
King of England at his own cost; and in the same way
shall the King of England be bound to deliver the fortresses which ought by this present treaty to belong to the
King of France.   And the said Kings and their people shall
be bound to give mutual help to each other in this matter
when they shall be required, at the wages of the party who
shall make the request.

29. Item, that Archbishops, Bishops, and other prelates
and people of Holy Church, by reason of their temporalities, shall be subject to that one of the two Kings under
whom they hold their temporalities; and if they hold
under both Kings, they shall be subject to each of them
for the temporalities which they hold of each.

[Mutual alliance to be made between the two realms. The King of
France and his eldest son to abandon the Scottish alliance, and
to renounce such alliance directed against the King of England,
and his people or his heirs in future. Similarly, the King of England and his eldest son to abandon the Flemish alliance, and to
renounce such alliance directed against France in future.]

33. Item, the Kings shall obtain confirmation and support of all the above matters by the Pope.

34. Item, all subjects of the said realms who shall wish to study at schools and universities of the realms of France and England shall enjoy all privileges and liberties of such schools and universities, in the same manner as they could before the war, and as they do at present.

35. For the security and guarantee of all the above matters, the following securities shall be given— Letters shall be given under the seals of the Kings of France and of England, and their eldest sons. And they and their children and relatives, and the great men of their realms, 20 on each side, shall swear to keep the treaty.

And if there should be any person of the said realms rebellious, or refusing to agree to the above matters, the Kings shall do all in their power to reduce them to obedience, according to the tenor of the treaty. And with this, they shall submit themselves, their heirs and their realms, to the coercion of our Holy Father the Pope, so that against persons who shall be rebellious he may apply compulsion by sentence of excommunication, ecclesiastical censures, and other due means. And among the aforesaid securities and guarantees, the two Kings and their heirs shall renounce all wars, and all forcible measures, by their faith and oath. And if by the disobedience, or might of any subjects of the realm of France, or other just cause, the King of France or his heirs shall be unable to accomplish all the aforesaid matters, the King of England, or his heirs, or other for them, shall not, and ought not to make war against the King of France or his realm ; but together they shall strive to reduce the said rebels to obedience. . . . Similarly it shall be if any of the realm or the obedience of the King of England shall refuse to give up castles, towns, or fortresses in the realm of France, or to obey the treaty. . . .

36. [All previous agreements to be null and void.]

37. Item, that neither of the Kings shall procure or cause

to be procured, that any innovations or impediments be made by the Court of Rome or by others of Holy Church, contrary to the present treaty, against either of the said Kings, their adherents or allies . . . lands or subjects, by reason of the war or for other cause. . . .

And if our Holy Father or other shall wish to do so, the Kings shall hinder him, without pretence, to the best of their ability.

[*Stipulations omitted from the final treaty in October*, Cosneau, *ibid.* ; "Foedera," III, i. 487-94, Arts. 11 and 12.]

The French King and his son to release all claims upon the ceded districts and their inhabitants. . . . "Without retaining anything to themselves, their heirs and successors, or the Crown of France . . . whereby they, . . . or other Kings of France, might . . . challenge or demand in time to come anything of the King of England . . . or any of the aforesaid vassals and subjects, by reason of the aforesaid towns and places. So that all the aforesaid persons, their heirs and successors shall be in perpetuity liegemen and subjects of the King of England. . . .

And that the King of England and his successors shall have and hold all the aforesaid places, and they shall remain to them fully in their lordship, sovereignty and obeisance, allegiance and subjection, as the Kings of France held them at any time past; and the King of England . . . shall have all the aforesaid districts in full franchise and perpetual liberty as sovereign and liege lord, and as neighbour of the King and crown of France, without recognising any sovereignty in them, or doing any obedience, homage, resort, or subjection, and without in time to come doing any service or recognition to the King or the crown of France for any of the aforesaid places.

Also, that the King of France and his eldest son shall expressly renounce the said resort and sovereignty, and all rights . . . in all things which by the said treaty, ought to belong to the King of England. And similarly the King of England and his eldest son shall expressly renounce all those things which, by the present treaty, ought not to be delivered or remain to the King of England, and all the demands that he has made of the King of France, especially the claim and right to the crown and realm of France, and the homage, sovereignty and demesne of the Duchy of Normandy, Touraine, the counties of Anjou and Maine; the sovereignty and homage of the Duchy of Brittany, and of the county and districts of Flanders.

43.

["The Companies" (Froissart).[1]]

Soon after King John's return, the King of England sent trustworthy persons into the realm of France, to cause all manner of Englishmen to evacuate and depart from the garrisons that they held, and to command them in his name to restore the castles and strongholds to the King of France and his men, on pain of forfeiting the realm of England, and even their lives.

This ordinance was a great hardship to many, who had learnt to rob and pillage, and had advanced themselves and made their fortune by the war; and whereas before they had been poor grooms and servants, they thought that, if they returned, they could not live after the manner wherein they had been accustomed. So that many refused to obey, and did much evil in the land of France, as you shall hear. And those who obeyed, sold the strongholds that they held to the people of the surrounding country. True it is that the knights and squires, gentlemen of England obeyed the order, and departed from their towns and fortresses; but there were Germans, Flemings, men of

[1] MS. d'Amiens.

Brabant and Hainault, Bretons, Burgundians, rascally Frenchmen, Normans and Picards, and Englishmen of low condition, who had risen in the war, and had nothing to lose save what they held. These men continued in their mischief, for they declared that they must needs live. So they gathered together from divers places, and made war in the realm as fiercely as before. Wherefore the King of England was greatly displeased.

44.

[Parliament of 1369. Renewal of War. "Rolls of Parliament," ii. 300. (French.) The French King had accepted appeals made by the barons of Gascony against the hearth-tax imposed by the Prince in 1368. He was supported on the technical ground that the re-nunciations which should have been exchanged at Bruges, in completion of the Treaty of Calais, had not been carried out.]

The Bishop of Winchester, Chancellor, after describing what had taken place, continued :—

" . . . And by reason of the attempts thus made in the said Principality by our said adversary, contrary to the form of the Peace, the Prince sent his solemn messengers to show the same fully to our lord the King, explaining further, how that the Prince had called to him the wisest persons of the said Principality, and had discussed with them as to whether, by reason of these encroachments so openly made against the form of the Peace, the King might justly and reasonably resume and use the title of King of France. And they declared that the King might do so justly and in good faith."

And upon this point the Archbishop of Canterbury and the other prelates were charged by the King to hold discussion together, and to lay their advice before him.

On the following Wednesday, having had full deliberation upon the matter with which they were charged, they all made answer with one accord, that, by reason of the aforesaid causes, our lord the King might justly and with good conscience, resume and use the title of King of France. And the dukes, earls, barons, and other great men, and the Commons agreed to this in full Parliament. The which title the King resumed.

And on the 11th day of June, the King's Great Seal, that he had previously used, being put into custody, and another seal, stamped with the title of France, resumed, charters, letters patent, and writs were sealed. And all the seals in the King's other places were in the same manner changed on that day.. .

45.

[The Bishop of Norwich's Crusade, 1383. Walsingham. (Latin.) The English position was much weakened in 1369, the French having regained much of their lost ground. In 1370 expeditions were arranged in Gascony (resulting in the recapture of Limoges) and in Northern France. An expedition to Aquitaine under the Earl of Pembroke was frustrated by the defeat of his fleet off Rochelle. In 1373 John of Gaunt made his long and circuitous march from Calais ; but peace negotiations were resumed, and in June, 1375, a truce was completed, which was renewed until 1377. On the renewal of war at the beginning of Richard II's reign, the English were reduced to a defensive position, and interest centred mainly in naval matters ; the position was further complicated by John of Gaunt's claim to the throne of Castile. Various unsuccessful expeditions were planned in 1378, 1379, and 1380. In 1382 events in Flanders seemed to open the way for a renewal of efforts in that direction ; the Flemings had driven out their Count, who was now supported by France, and appealed to Richard's Government for help. In October, 1382, Parliament agreed to give support to Flanders, in preference to sending an expedition to Spain under the Duke of Lancaster. It was decided to take advantage of the Crusade recently proclaimed against the antipope, Clement VII, by Urban VI, in order to send an expedition to Flanders, against the "schismatic" French, supported by the resources of the Crusade. Bishop Despenser of Norwich had been commissioned by the Pope to

7 *

levy men and forces in England, to be employed against Clement VII's supporters.]

During Lent a Parliament was held [1] in London, wherein for many days there was discussion about the commission granted by the Supreme Pontiff to the Bishop of Norwich, and as to his setting out against the schismatics; and there was much violent contention. For one party, whose hearts God had touched, desired that he should set out, as the Champion of the Church, against the enemies of Christ, while the others opposed it, for they declared that it was not safe to entrust the King's people of the realm to an inexperienced priest. And there was open breach between them. And for this cause the business of the Pope and the whole Church was delayed until that Sunday whereon there is special mention throughout the whole Church of Our Lord's Cross and Passion.[2] At length,—after many evasions by the leaders of the realm, and after many debates had been interposed, but utterly crushed by God's grace, and by the praiseworthy firmness of the knights of Parliament—on that same Sunday, whereon Holy Church sings of the going forward of the royal banners, suddenly the whole faction present in that Parliament, that had held out so strongly against Christ's business, and the advancement of the faith of the Cross, gave way, as though struck by the thunder of that solemn antiphon, "Behold the Cross of the Lord, let his enemies be scattered," and gave decision after the wishes of the crusading Bishop ".

[1] 23 February.

[2] The 5th Sunday in Lent. The decision of the previous Parliament had met with opposition in some quarters, especially among the Duke of Lancaster's friends.

46.

["Rolls of Parliament," iii. 149. (French.)]

Also be it known, that after the said Bishop of Norwich had taken consideration for a little time, he came before the King and the lords of the realm in Parliament and made another offer, in the following form; namely, that if it pleased the King to allow him the "fifteenth" last granted by the laity of the realm, he would then serve the King for a whole year in his wars, within the realm of France, with 2500 men-at-arms, and 2500 archers, all well arrayed and mounted. And of this number, 1000 men-at-arms and 1000 archers, should if it pleased God, be on the sea, equipped and ready to cross over to the relief and succour of the town of Ghent and the country of Flanders, within 20 days next after the first payment to him of the said "fifteenth". And he would take upon himself the expenses of their transport and other charges, and would undertake to carry this out in aid of the King.

But although it appeared to the King and his Council, and to the lords of the realm that this offer was most loyal and generous, if it might be performed; nevertheless, it was very necessary that the King should have the assistance of persons who should be captains, and governors of the host. For it is well known to everyone that so great a force could scarcely remain long in a prosperous condition without the management of great and noble persons, lords and others. Therefore the Bishop was asked, from the King, to assist the King and Council by giving the names of the captains whom he thought of having with him in the said expedition. To this the Bishop replied, that if it might please the King to accept his offer, and to hand over the expedition to him in manner as he requested, he would undertake to have with him the best captains of the realm, after the King

and the other royal persons.   But he said that he would
not make known their names in particular until he was
sure that the expedition would be given to him.   Upon
this, the Bishop was asked, what lord of the realm he
wished to have with him, to be the King's Lieutenant
in the host ? since a King's Lieutenant was very necessary
in such an important and difficult business, who should
have authority to take cognizance of crime, and of doing
other necessary things ; and this office had never hitherto
been discharged by a prelate, or other person of Holy
Church.

The Bishop answered that he would set down in writing, and deliver to the King, the names of certain lords ;
begging the King to choose from these the person most
pleasing to him for this business, and to appoint him his
Lieutenant ; who should be charged to be obedient to the
Bishop in all matters touching the Crusade.   And the
Bishop agreed, on his part, to defer to the Lieutenant in
all things touching the Lieutenancy.   He promised, moreover, that if within the said year it should happen that the
kingdom of France should be converted to the support of
the true Pope Urban, he would from that time be bound
at once to lay aside the banner of the Crusade, and serve
the King in the war under his own banner, with the
number of men defined above, until the end of the year.

When this offer had been rehearsed in full Parliament,
before the King and all the Commons, it seemed to all to
be good, and highly profitable for the whole realm, if it
were well carried out; and therefore it was accepted by
our lord the King.   And then afterwards, when the Bishop
had delivered the names of four persons from whom the
King should choose his Lieutenant, the King, desiring the
common profit of the realm, wished that none should have
ground for accusing the lords of the realm, for that this
expedition that appeared so profitable, was without good

cause hindered or set aside by them; he agreed therefore
that since the Commons of the realm had given their
counsel upon it, it should be granted and rehearsed in full
Parliament that if the Bishop could not come to an agreement with any of the lords named by him, or with other
sufficient person worthy of bearing the dignity of Lieutenant;—in that case the King would be willing that the
Bishop should have the Lieutenancy, and the government
and control of the host, in all matters, after the manner of
his proffer.

47.

[Walsingham. "Historia Anglicana," 1383. (Latin.)]

In these circumstances the Bishop sent letters sealed
with his seal throughout the whole Kingdom, giving to
rectors, vicars and curates power of hearing the confessions of their parishioners, and of granting the boon of
plenary absolution and remission, according to the form of
the Papal Bull, to those who should make any contribution whereby the business of the Crusaders might be advanced. Therefore, when it was known that so great a
blessing had come to the English people, the inhabitants
of the whole realm, being desirous of not receiving so
great a boon in vain, were inflamed with faith and devotion, so that those who felt themselves fit to set out
made ready with all speed, while those who seemed un-
suitable, bestowed liberally of their goods, with the advice
of their confessors. . . .

And thus there was scarcely anyone to be found in the
whole breadth of the realm who did not offer himself for
the business, or contribute somewhat of his goods. . . .
So that that which had before seemed impossible to the
King's Councillors and to the enemies of the expedition,
now began to seem possible, whence the Bishop, poorest

among the Bishops of the realm, was furnished with the
resources for so great an expedition.

[KNIGHTON].—For the Bishop gathered together an incredible sum of money, gold and silver, jewels, necklaces,
rings, and other ornaments, especially from ladies and other
women ; for it was said that one lady gave him £100. And
so other women contributed, some more, some less, and
many, it was believed, beyond their means, that they might
obtain the benefit of absolution for themselves and their
friends. And in this way the hidden treasure of the realm,
that was in the hands of women, was put in jeopardy.
Men as well as women did thus, rich and poor, according
to their means and beyond . . . for otherwise they did not
receive absolution. . . . Many provided armed men, others
found archers, while many others set out at their own
expense. For the Bishop had wonderful pardons, with
plenary absolution, from Pope Urban VI, by whose authority both the living and the dead, on whose behalf sufficient
contribution was made, were absolved from all offences by
himself and his commissaries. For it was said that some
of his commissaries declared that at their command angels
would come down from above, snatch souls from their
pains in purgatory, and carry them off at once to heaven.

48.

[Walsingham. *Ibid.*, 1383. News of the Bishop's first successes.]

When therefore these good tidings were made known in
England, by some who had been present at the taking of
Gravelines and Dunkirk, and who, as witness of the truth
of their accounts, had brought home with them horses,
oxen, and household goods, at once the whole country,
allured by hope of booty became eager to set out. And
without further deliberation many London apprentices and
servants, assuming the white hoods, with red crosses on

their right side, and red scabbards at the left, set out, against the will of their masters and lords. This example was followed by others from almost the whole of England, who, leaving their friends, their kin and families, set out, unarmed save with swords, bows, and arrows. And not only did laymen do this, but the professed of all orders, having asked permission, but not obtained it, presumed to undertake the expedition, to their great hurt and discredit. For they did not decide upon this journey only for Christ's sake, but in order to see their country, and the world. These inexperienced men and rustics hurried up from all directions, until they came to the sea, where Sir John Philpot, who was looking after the Bishop's affairs, provided shipping. There were many who had nothing for their expenses, beyond their passage, for they thought that if they had once crossed the sea, they would want for nothing, but everything would come to them at will. So a great many were carried abroad, and they hastened to the Bishop, who had then advanced further, and come to the town of Ypres, that was full of riches, renowned for its buildings, and well fortified with fighting men. . . .

And now the number of those who had crossed over was so great, that 60,000 were estimated to have come from England.

The Bishop, therefore, when he considered the arrival of so great a multitude, who were not practised in arms, nor even possessed them, was very vexed, and sent to Sir John Philpot, asking him to allow none to cross in future, save those who were practised and able.

49.

["Rolls of Parliament," iii. 151. (French.) The Bishop's successes were brought to an end by his unsuccessful siege of Ypres ; his forces were dispersed by the arrival of a strong French army, and took refuge in their garrisons, which, however, were rapidly sur-

rendered to the French.   In September, Bishop Despenser returned to England with the rest of his army, under the strong
suspicion of having made a bargain with the French to surrender
Gravelines.   In November, 1383, Parliament met, and he was
impeached for his conduct of the expedition.   Some points of the
Bishop's defence.]

First, as to the charge brought against him, that he had
not served the King for the term which he had promised,
nor for the half of it,—the Bishop said that by the aforesaid covenant he was bound, and moreover he was charged
by his liege lord, especially and before all else, to go with
his force to the relief of the town of Ghent.   And by
reason of this charge, as soon as he had landed abroad,
he made his way towards that town; and on the march,
as it pleased God, he came in conflict with the enemy,
both at Gravelines and Dunkirk and elsewhere.   And at
last, when the men of Ghent had met him, and they had
talked and taken counsel together as to what was best to
be done, both for their succour, and for the success of his
expedition, the final intention of the men of Ghent was
this, namely, that they should lay siege to the town of
Ypres.   For they asserted that Ypres was not well enough
stocked with men and supplies to hold out against the
forces of England and Ghent.   And they said further, that
if the town of Ypres were won, that held the keys of all
Flanders, the rest would very soon be conquered.   And
so by the instigation and comfort of the men of Ghent,
and with the consent of all the English captains who were
with the expedition, siege was laid to the town.   But
during the siege, many of his men perished of divers grave
sicknesses, and many were killed and wounded; and a
great number of the good-for-nothing rascals who were
mutinous and disobedient to him returned to England
with their pillage.   And therefore, and owing to the departing of the men of Ghent from the siege, the English

captains saw that after their departure the host was very
greatly diminished, and so shrunken by the aforesaid
causes, that the English would not and could not hold the
field against such a force as the French had assembled.

And thus, giving due consideration to these excuses
alleged by him, and to the labours of the Bishop himself
and his people in this expedition, and to the honour and
profit of the King and the realm; and especially considering
that, by reason of the said expedition, a truce, and offer
of peace discussions had been made by our adversary of
France—which, if it pleased God, would open the way to
a final peace ;—and also that what had occurred ought not
in reason to be charged to his default, especially since it
had come about rather by the fortune of Providence than
in other manner ; it seemed to him that as to this article,
he should be held excused.

Also, as to the charge that he did not make his due
muster at Calais—he said that to hasten the coming of
his people in the expedition for the relief of Ghent in
manner as he had promised, he crossed to Calais before
his other captains, with such persons, in small number,
as he could get together.   And he did not tarry more than
two or three days after his landing at Calais, but forthwith
made his way towards Gravelines, and with the Lord's
help, took it.   And then, when he was come before Ypres,
although for the aforesaid cause he did not make his full
muster at Calais, nevertheless he had before Ypres his full
number of men in each degree, and more.   And this he
was ready to prove by good and sufficient witness, or in
other reasonable manner that the King should assign.
And thus, as to that point, it seemed to him that he was
not blameworthy.

And as to that it was said that he had not with him
the best captains of the Kingdom after the royal persons—
it appeared to him that he had good and sufficient captains.

But he would have had better, if they had been given license and permission; as the Lord Neville, who offered in the King's presence to go with the expedition, if it should please the King to give him leave—the which leave was denied him. And thus, as to that, it seemed to him that he was in no way to blame.

And touching the charge, that he was said to have refused to have a Lieutenant—he said that it was true that the King sent letters and messengers to him in Flanders, where he then was with his army, touching this matter; whereto he replied by his own letters, returning thanks to his liege lord to the utmost of his power, for that it pleased him to think of him, and to be tender of him and his estate. And these same letters made express mention that whenever the King and his council wished to appoint such a Lieutenant it would be well pleasing to him. Thus he did not refuse to have the said Lieutenant, but held himself well satisfied with whatever the King might ordain. And thus it seemed to him that as to that also he was in no way to be blamed; but rather, as for other causes alleged on his part, and for other services that he had before rendered to the King and the realm, he should have deserved reward and thanks, and not displeasure. Entreating our lord the King that it might please him to accept his excuses truly put forward, and to be gracious lord to him, if it seemed to his Highness that he had nothing offended in this part.

Whereto the Chancellor replied. "It is true that when you were in Flanders, after that you had stayed there a little time, certain news came to our lord the King and his council in England, many times, by letters and by other manner, sent to him from Flanders by the captains of your host, that the host was daily in worse condition for want of a Lieutenant, and of good governance. Then the King caused the matter to be discussed with the Earl of Arundel, and finally an agreement was come to with the Earl that he should be the King's Lieutenant in the host, and should come to you in haste, with a sufficient number of good men-at-arms and archers, in succour of you and the host, if you would agree to this. For without your consent the King would have nothing done in the matter, and therefore he sent you his letters and messenger, to have your opinion. And you answered by your letters, which are yet ready at hand to be shown, in such manner that by the form of the said letters,—which are made with double meaning—and by other words of yours reported elsewhere, it may evidently appear that you did not wish to have a Lieutenant.

"And although you have now alleged this last matter contained in your letters as an excuse (as is not sufficient, your said letters being well understood) nevertheless, this is in no way to the purpose as to what is charged against you before—namely, that you utterly refused to have a Lieutenant before your departure from the realm, according to the first offer made to you as well as since. Whereby, and also from want of good captains and governors, all the mischief has happened to your host."

[The Bishop was informed that his other excuses were insufficient, that he would be held guilty, and would be expected to pay fine and ransom at the King's pleasure—for which purpose the temporalities of his bishopric would be seized. He was also asked to give particulars as to the persons retained with him, and the amount of their service, so that they might be called upon to complete it.]

Also, on another occasion the Bishop, declaring that, inasmuch as he had been in many ways disturbed and interrupted in giving his answers to the articles wherewith he was impeached, by captious words and otherwise, he had left out and forgotten great part of what

he had to say in his excuse, begged the King that for
God's sake he would appoint him another day in this
Parliament, and a seemly hearing without interruption ;
and then, he said, with the Lord's help, he would excuse
himself so clearly as should reasonably suffice.   This
request was granted, and another day appointed, namely
the 24th day of November.

On that day the Bishop, rehearsing the four articles
previously charged against him in Parliament, in presence
of the King himself, made answers very nearly as he had
done before, upon all the aforesaid matters ; Adding—that
at the time when he had news that the van of the
French army had entered Flanders, and when upon this
the siege of Ypres was abandoned, he had resolved to
encounter the said vanguard, and to have fought with
them.   But this intention he was not able to carry out
for as much as the captains of his host would not agree
to it ; but they and others of his army opposed him so
strongly that of necessity, and for fear of the enemy, they
were obliged to depart and take refuge in their fortresses.
Therefore the Bishop returned to the town of Gravelines,
and would have held it well enough against all men, and
did hold it, until the other captains had surrendered their
fortresses to the French.   And then there came to him
some Englishmen, telling how that there were some 6000
or 7000 of the English on the sands near Calais, who had
been turned out of the surrendered fortresses, to their
great mischief and hardship ; because they had nothing
to live upon, and could not have admission to the town of
Calais.   And inasmuch as the truce lately made was to
expire within the next two or three days, the French were
purposing to attack them, and kill them all as soon as it
was at an end ; And this slaughter, if it should take place,
would reflect principally upon the Bishop himself, and
then upon the other captains, to greater mischief and

villainy than anything else could be. Therefore they charged him in the King's name to surrender the town to the enemy, or at once destroy it, and make his way to the succour of these people, and thence to England. For they said that if anything but good happened to these people on the sands, they would charge the Bishop for it before the King himself. Wherefore, said the Bishop, he was obliged of necessity to dismantle and quit the town of Gravelines although it grieved him to do it, as his own conquest from the enemy . . . and also because before this, a letter had come from the King, commanding him, if there were great want of victuals in the town (as in truth, there was) to evacuate it, and save himself and his people. . . .

[These excuses were not accepted, and judgment was given against him as before, after another long speech by the Chancellor, in which his arguments were demolished. The trial of several of his captains followed.]

B. Naval Affairs and Home Defence.

50.

[Measures for defence : (a) Notice to all sheriffs, 15 August, 1338. "Foedera," II, ii. 1055. (Latin.)]

[With reference to a previous order that beacons should be prepared—] . . . We have now understood that a great many galleys and ships of war are newly gathered on the sea, to invade our realm in hostile manner, and to inflict what other evils and injuries they can as well upon merchants and other our faithful lieges as upon other our adherents, or persons coming to our realm. And being desirous of preventing this wickedness, and of providing, as we are bound, for the defence and salvation of our realm and of our faithful lieges, we do command you that immediately upon receipt of these letters you shall cause beacons to be made, as well upon hills distant from the sea as in other

places near the sea-coast, in such places, and as often, and
in such manner as shall seem to you expedient, and as was
formerly wont to be done; and to be sufficiently guarded
by men of the district, and lighted as often as danger shall
threaten.

[(b) Order for the defence of London, 23 October, 1338.
"Foedera," II, ii. 1062.]

To the mayor, aldermen, and sheriffs of London.

Because our enemies gathered together in galleys, in
no small numbers, have entered our realm in divers parts
in hostile manner, and do propose shortly to attack our
said city, to perpetrate therein what evils and wickedness
they can; we, being desirous of providing for the salvation
and defence of the city, do strictly enjoin you to cause the
city with all possible speed to be enclosed and fortified towards the water with stone or boards, against such hostile
attacks; and to cause piles to be fixed across the Thames,
in defence of the city as shall best seem expedient. And
you shall cause all persons having rents in the city, as well
religious as others, of whatever estate, to aid in the said
defence, sparing none in this matter, so that it may be
hastened in the speediest possible manner.

[(c) Order to all sheriffs of counties lying on the sea coast, 20
November, 1338. "Foedera," II, ii. 1066.]

Because we have understood for certain that our enemies
from abroad are daily preparing to invade our realm, in
order to commit therein what evil and wickedness they
can—for this reason we have ordained by the advice of our
council, for the more speedy warning of our people of the
approaching attacks of the enemy, and for the better avoid-
ing of their malice, that one bell only shall be rung in all
churches within a distance of seven leagues from the sea;
and that if peril shall threaten from such hostile attacks,
all the bells shall be rung in each of these churches, for

the defence of our people, and to give warning for the repulse of our enemies.

[(d) Notice to the mayor and sheriffs of London. 22 March, 1342. *Ibid.* II, ii. 1190.]

Because we understand that there are within our realm of England many persons spying upon our secret business, and others who send letters into France and elsewhere, for the purpose of giving information to our enemies, to their great comfort, and to our own manifest prejudice, we, wishing to avoid the perils which hereby may befall, do command you to cause all persons approaching the port in order to have passage, or entering our realm there, of whom suspicion may be had, to be searched; to seize all letters of credence and others which you may find to be suspicious, as a result of this search, and to cause these to be sent into the Chancery with all speed, and the persons who brought them to be kept in safe custody.

51.

[Early attacks on the English Coast.]

(a) MURIMUTH. A.D. 1338.—In the fourth year of Pope Benedict XII, the twelfth year of the reign of King Edward III, and the sixty-fourth year of the present writer's age, the galleys of the King of France seized five large ships of the King of England lying in the harbour of Sluys (which were, however, almost empty), while the sailors were in the town, and carried them off to the parts of Normandy. And on the Monday after Michaelmas, fifty galleys full of armed men came suddenly to Southampton about the ninth hour, and all that day they pillaged the town, carrying off whatever they could to their ships. They stayed in the town all night, all the inhabitants being driven away or slain. And on the morrow, perceiving that

8

the men of the country were gathering together, they fired the town in five places, and went back to their ships.

1339.—In this year, on the Eve of the Annunciation,[1] there came eleven galleys to Harwich, and they attacked the town, and fired it in three places; but the fire did little damage, on account of the wind, that was unfavourable. And the levy of the district quickly came out against them, resisting them valiantly, and so they withdrew, but small destruction having been done. . . .

Also in this year just before Pentecost the King of France's pirates came in galleys and pinnaces, to the neighbourhood of Southampton, and because they saw that the country was well prepared to resist them, they immediately withdrew. And because they dared not land there, nor in the Isle of Wight, which was well fortified, they betook themselves to other open places, and thieves as they were, did a great deal of damage. Afterwards, on the feast of Corpus Christi, they burned some fishermen's cottages at Hastings, and killed several men. They made their appearance many times off the Isle of Thanet, Dover, and Folkestone, but did little damage in those places, unless it were to poor fisher folk, because the country was always ready to resist them.

(b) KNIGHTON.   1339.—About the feast of St. James the French came with a very great force to the port of Sandwich, namely, with 32 galleys, 20 great ships and 15 small ones; but they dared not land, because the English were prepared for them, but turned off to the port of Rye, where they did much mischief. Then the English came up from the sea, and they sought refuge in flight. The English pursued them to Boulogne, setting fire to a great part of that town, and hanged twelve of the ships' captains, returning to England with the ships they had captured at Boulogne.

[1] 24 March.

(Later.) Robert de Morley, admiral, went to Normandy with his fleet and the fleet of the Cinque Ports, and they burnt five towns . . . and they burnt there 80 ships belonging to the fleet of the Normans.

(c) MURIMUTH. 1339. — In the ports of Devon and Cornwall, and towards Bristol, the French seized several ships which they found alone, burning them and killing the sailors and others whom they found on board. And on Tuesday, Wednesday, and Thursday in Whitsun week these same pirates or others landed at Plymouth in Devon, and burnt the greater part of the town. They were turned back by Hugh de Courtenay, Earl of Devon, a man almost eighty years of age; and other knights of the country, with the men of the country, fought with them, at first losing some of their own men. But at last, having rallied their forces, they slew all the pirates whom they found on land, driving them into the sea so that 500 were drowned, as it was estimated by persons who were present.

(d) FROISSART. 1338.—[Philip of France] caused his great fleet that he kept at sea to be much strengthened, whereof Sir Hugh Quiéret, Behucet, and Barbevaire[1] were captains and leaders. These three master rovers kept great store of hired fighters, Genoese, Normans, Picards, and Bretons, and that winter they did much mischief to the English. . . . They pillaged them sorely, capturing the beautiful large ship called the "Christopher," laden with goods and wools that the English were taking to Flanders, which ship had cost the King of England a great sum of money to build. But these people lost it to the Normans, and were all thrown overboard.

[1] Egidio Bocanegra.

8*

52.

[The Duties of an Admiral. (French.) From the "Black Book of the Admiralty," vol. i. Rolls Series. The translation is the one there printed, as done by Thomas Bedford, Registrar of the Admiralty under James II, but one or two slight alterations have been made, mainly as suggested in notes made by the Editor of the "Black Book". These rules were drawn up almost certainly between 1338 and 1351 ; there are some grounds for assigning them to the period 1338-1340. They are printed also in Nicolas' "History of the Royal Navy".]

I. When one is made admiral, he must first ordain and substitute for his lieutenants deputies, and other officers under him some of the most loyal, wise and discreet persons in the maritime law and ancient customs of the seas which he can anywhere find, to the end that, by the help of God and their good and just government, the office may be executed to the honour and good of the realm.

II. Item, the admiral ought afterwards, with all the haste that he can conveniently, to write to all his lieutenants, deputies and other officers whatsoever throughout all the sea-coasts through the whole realm, to know how many ships, barges, balingers, and other vessels of war the King may have in his realm, when he pleaseth or need shall require, and of what burthen they are, and also the names of the owners and possessors thereof.

III. Item, to know likewise by good and lawful inquests, taken before the same lieutenants, deputies, or other officers of the admiral, how many fighting mariners there are in the realm ; And the reason is because that in case the King or his Council ask his admiral concerning the same, he may then truly and justly represent to them the number, as well of the ships, barges, balingers, and other vessels of war, and the names of the owners and possessors thereof, as the number of all fighting mariners throughout the Kingdom; and so the King and his Council shall always certainly know his strength by sea.

IV. Item, it is to be taken notice that when the admiral rides on horseback to get any men of war together, or about any other business of the King or the realm, if he be a knight batchelor he shall have 4s. sterling a day for his wages, and if he be an earl or a baron, he shall have for wages according to his estate and degree. . . .

VII. And besides (if the admiral be a knight batchelor) he shall have every day at sea 4s. for himself; and for each knight going in his company, 2s., and for every squire armed 12d. a day; and shall have in consideration of 30 men-at-arms at the end of each quarter of a year, 100 marks, and so he shall have for every one; and shall also have for each archer 6d. a day, and so every one of his captains shall have their wages of him. And if the admiral is a baron, he shall have 6s. 8d. a day, and if he is an earl, he shall have 13s. 4d. a day.

VIII. After that a ship or fleet is come and arrived in one or several ports of the Kingdom, to go and stay at sea by command of the King and order of the realm for the defence thereof, with a certain number of soldiers or archers in the company of the King or his Lieutenant, the admiral ought by his office to elect and order for the King's person, if he is present, otherwise for his Lieutenant, the best and most able ship of the Kingdom, which shall be called the chamber of the King or his Lieutenant; and if the King be present, then the controller of his household is to make choice of some of the best ships of the whole fleet, that is to say one ship for the Hall, another for the Wardrobe, a third for the Larder, and the fourth for the Kitchen, and more if it be necessary. And if the King hath son or sons, brother or brothers, uncle or uncles with him, then good, able and sufficient ships shall be ordered, assigned and delivered for their persons before the admiral elect, take, or make choice of any ship for himself. The admiral ought to assign and deliver to each of the lords and captains, according to their quality, sufficient shipping as well for their persons as for their victuals, if he have shipping to do it. . . .

XII. And the admiral is governor of the mariners, and ought to govern and maintain them in their laws; and the admiral is bound by his office, if the King be present in his own person, every day before nightfall to sail after the King, and to know his pleasure, what course they shall steer that night and the day following, and in that manner in the King's absence he ought to do to his Lieutenant. And afterwards all the ships and other vessels are to come together about the admiral, and to know what course he will steer, and he shall acquaint them therewith as well as he can; and afterwards those that know it shall communicate it to the others. And because that every one shall follow the admiral, the admiral ought always to carry a light, unless it be for certain necessary causes otherwise ordained by the King, his Lieutenant, or by the admiral.

XIII. Item, if the King is in his own person in the fleet, then there ought to be in his ship three great lanthorns, one whereof ought to be higher than the other two, and these two others shall be hanged even. And the King may have more lanthorns if he pleaseth, if the master of the ship thinks it fit, to the end that all those in the fleet may know the ship wherein the King is; the King's Lieutenant shall carry three lanthorns as is above said, but no more.

XIV. Item, the admiral ought every night that the fleet is at sea to carry two great lanthorns at the two parts of the masthead of the ship wherein he is, to the end that he may be known to be admiral. And if he

hath under admirals, he may let each of them carry one
lanthorn and no more at the top of his mast, for seeing
and knowing the fleet, and to the end that the ships of the
fleet may not be separated for want of light. . . .

XVIII. Item, it is to be noted that at what convenient
time the admiral pleaseth to call the captains and the
masters of the fleet together, he shall hang up in the
middle of the mast of the ship a flag of counsel, so that
it may be known and perceived in all parts of the fleet,
either in port or at sea; and then immediately the captains and masters of ships are bound without delay to
come with their boats well manned on board the admiral's
ship, there to hear and do what the King's counsel shall
have ordained. And if the King or his Lieutenant is
there, they ought to do to them as it is ordained they
are to do to the admiral; and if any one of the fleet doth
refuse so to do, he shall be punished as a rebel, and according to the maritime law.

53.

[The Battle of Sluys.   (Froissart, Lord Berners' translation.)]

This was on Midsummer eve, 1340, all the English fleet
was departed out of the river of Thames and took the way
to Sluys.   And the same time between Blankenberghe
and Sluys, on the sea was Sir Hugh Quiéret, Sir Peter
Bahuchet, and Barbenoire, and more than seven score
great vessels, besides others.   And there were of Normans,
Genoese and Pickards about the number of 40,000.   There
they were laid by the French King to defend the King
of England's passage.   The King of England and his
came sailing till he came before Sluys; and when he saw
so great a number of ships that their masts seemed to be
like a great wood, he demanded of the master of the ship
what people he thought they were.   He answered and

said "Sir, I think they be Normans laid here by the French King, and hath done great displeasure in England, burnt your town of Hampton, and taken your great ship the 'Christopher'." "Ah," quoth the King, "I have long desired to fight with the Frenchmen, and now shall I fight with some of them, by the Grace of God and St. George, for truly they have done me so many displeasures, that I shall be revenged, and I may." Then the King set all his ships in order, the greatest before, well furnished with archers; and ever between two ships of archers he had one ship with men-at-arms; and then he made another battle to lie aloof with archers, to comfort ever them that were most weary, if need were. And there were a great number of countesses, ladies, knight's wives,[1] and other damosels that were going to see the Queen at Ghent. These ladies the King caused to be well kept with 300 men-at-arms and 500 archers.

When the King and his marshals had ordered his battles, he drew up the sails, and came with a quarter wind, to have the vantage of the sun (which as they came up had been in their faces). And when the Normans saw them turn back, they marvelled why they did so, and some said "They think themselves not meet to meddle with us, wherefore they will go back". They saw well how the King of England was there personally, by reason of his banners. Then they did apparel their fleet in order, for they were sage and good men of war on the sea, and did set the "Christopher," the which they had won the year before, to be foremost, with great plenty of Genoese crossbowmen on board; and with many trumpets and instruments, so set on their enemies. There began a sore battle on both sides; archers and crossbowmen began to shoot, and men-at-arms approached and fought hand-to-hand; and the better to come together, they had great

---

[1] "And merchants' wives of London" (Froissart).

hooks and grapers of iron, to cast out of one ship into another, and so tied them fast together. There were many deeds of arms done, taking and rescuing again; and the great ship "Christopher" was at the first won back by the Englishmen, and all that were within it taken or slain. Then there was great noise and cry, and the Englishmen approached and fortified the "Christopher" with archers, and made him to pass on before to fight with the Genoese. This battle was right fierce and terrible [1]; for battles on the sea are more dangerous and fiercer than the battles by land; for on the sea there is no reculying nor fleeing; there is no remedy but to fight and to abide fortune and every man to show his prowess.

Of a truth, Sir Hugh Quiêret and Sir Peter Béhuchet and Barbenoir were right good and expert men of war. This battle endured from the morning till it was noon, and the Englishmen endured much pain, for their enemies were four against one, and all good men on the sea. There the King of England was a noble knight of his own hand for he was in the flower of his youth; in likewise so was the Earl of Derby, Pembroke, Hereford, Huntingdon, Northampton and Gloucester, Sir Reynold Cobham, Sir Richard Stafford, the Lord Percy, Sir Walter Manny . . . and divers other lords and knights, who bore themselves so valiantly, with some socours that they had of Bruges, and of the country thereabout, that they obtained the victory. So that the Frenchmen, Normans, and others were discomfited, slain, and drowned.

[1] For these Normans and Genoese were all sea-rovers . . . and had spent their whole lives in seeking adventures of arms on the sea. Also, to say truth, the English are good seafaring people, for they are bred to it (MS. de Rome).

54.

[Edward III's letter to the Duke of Cornwall, announcing the Battle of Sluys. (French.) Printed by Nicolas in his "Royal Navy," vol. ii., Appendix—where the translation is given on p. 61. From the Archives of the City of London, Register F.]

Right dear son, We well believe that you are desirous of having good news of us, and how it has fared with us since our leaving England, and so we have you to know that on the Thursday after we left the port of Orwell we sailed all that day and the night following; and on the Friday about the hour of "noune" we came off the coast of Flanders, off Blankenberghe, where we had sight of the fleet of our enemies, which were all gathered together in the port of Zwyn; and because the tide did not then suit to meet them, we remained there all that night. And on the Saturday, St. John's day, soon after the hour of 'noune,' with the tide, in the name of God, and in the confidence of our just quarrel, we entered into the said port against our enemies, who had placed their ships in very strong array, and made a right noble defence all that day, and the night after. But God, by his power and miracle granted us the victory over our enemies, for which we thank him as devoutly as we can. And we have you to know that the number of our enemies' ships, galleys, and great barges, amounted to nine score, which were all taken, save 24 in all, which made their escape; and of these some are since taken at sea. And the number of men-at-arms and other armed people amounted to 35,000, of which number it is estimated some 5000 escaped; and the rest, as we are given to understand by some persons who are taken alive, lie dead in many places on the coast of Flanders.[1] On the other hand, all our own

[1] "In this battle there were dead . . . full 30,000 men slain and drowned, as it was said; great part of whom the tide washed up on the shores of Sluys and Cadsand, and some were found fully armed just as they had fought." (Le Bel.)

ships, that is to say, the "Christopher" and the others which were lost at Middleburgh, are now retaken, and there are captured in this fleet 3 or 4 ships as large as the "Christopher". The Flemings were of good will to come to us at the battle, from the beginning to the end. So that God our Lord has shown abundant grace, for which we and all our friends are ever bound to render grace and thanks to him. Our intent is to remain quiet in the river, until we have made certain agreement with our allies and our other friends of Flanders as to what is to be done. Right dear son, may God keep you. Given under our secret seal in our ship, the "Cog Thomas," on Wednesday [1] the eve of St. Peter and St. Paul.

55.

[The fight with the Spaniards on the sea. (On Sunday, 29 August, 1350, off Winchelsea.)

(a) From a letter of the King to the Archbishop of Canterbury. "Foedera," III, i. 201, 10 August, 1350, at Rotherhithe. Entered on the Close Roll. (Latin.)]

We think it is not unknown to you how that the Spaniards, with whom we had purposed to renew the alliance made in former times between their Kings and our ancestors, by the marriage of our offspring, have now . . . with their confederates many times attacked our people, merchants and others, travelling by sea with wines, wool, and other goods, murdering and putting them to death most cruelly ; and they have destroyed no small part of our shipping, and perpetrated other innumerable mischiefs, and do not cease daily to do so. And now they are so puffed up with arrogance that, having gathered together an immense fleet, fortified with armed men, in the parts of Flanders, not only are they presuming to boast that they will completely destroy our shipping and dominate the English sea, but

[1] 28 June.

they expressly threaten to invade our realm, and utterly
to subdue the people subject to us; [the accustomed prayers
and processions are to be ordered throughout the diocese]
. . . since we, trusting in the Divine mercy, upon whose
bidding, and not on human might, victory depends, do
purpose to set out against these our enemies, for the defence of Holy Church and the succour of our realm.

[(b) FROISSART.   Ed. Luce, vol. iv.   The account is not included
in Lord Berners' translation.   It is given by Johnes, whose
translation is here mainly followed.][1]

At this time there was much ill-will between the King of
England and the Spaniards, on account of some mischiefs
and pillages that the Spaniards had committed at sea
against the English.   Whereby it happened that in this
year the Spaniards who had been in Flanders for their
merchandise were informed that they would not be able
to return home without meeting the English fleet: They
took counsel upon this, but did not take much account of
it; and they amply provided their ships at Sluys with arms
and good artillery, and hired all manner of men, soldiers,
archers, and crossbowmen, who would take their pay.
They waited for each other, and did their business.

When the King of England, who hated the Spaniards
greatly, heard that they were making great preparations,
he said openly " We have for a long time spared these
people, for which they have done us much harm, without
amending their conduct; on the contrary, they grow more
arrogant, for which reason they must be chastised as they
pass our coasts ".   His people readily agreed to this pro-
posal, and were eager to engage the Spaniards.   The King
therefore issued a special summons to all gentlemen who
were then in England, and went to the county of Sussex,
which lies on the sea between Southampton and Dover,

[1] A translation is also given in " A Mediæval Garner," G. G. Coulton.

opposite to Ponthieu and Dieppe; and kept his court in a monastery on the coast, whither the Queen also came. . . .

When the Spaniards had completed their cargoes, and laden their vessels with cloth, linen, and whatever they thought would be profitable to take back to their own country, they went on board their ships at Sluys. They knew that they should meet the English, but took little account of it, for they had marvellously provided themselves with all sorts of artillery, and with great bars of forged iron, made to throw on ships and sink them, together with great stones. When they saw that the wind was favourable to them, they weighed anchor; there were 40 great ships, of such a size and so beautiful that it was a fine sight to see them. High upon their masts they had battled platforms, full of flints and stones, with soldiers to guard them; and from the masts their streamers, emblazoned with their arms, fluttered in the wind so that they were beautiful to look upon. And it seems that if the English had a great desire to meet them, the Spaniards were still more eager for it, as I will tell you afterwards. The Spaniards were full 10,000 men, altogether, with the soldiers whom they had hired in Flanders; so they felt confident and strong enough to meet the King of England and all his power at sea. And with this intent they came sailing on before a fresh and favourable wind, past Calais.

The King of England, who was at sea with his fleet had already made his plans, and given orders as to how they were to fight, and what was to be done. He had appointed the Lord Robert of Namur master of a ship called the "King's Hall," on board of which was all his household. The King took his stand in the prow of his ship, dressed in a black velvet jacket, and on his head he wore a black beaver hat, which became him well. And he was that day, as I was told by those who were with him then, as joyous as ever he was in his life. And he made his minstrels play on their horns a German dance, that Sir John Chandos, who was there, had lately brought back; and for entertainment he made the same knight sing with his minstrels, taking great delight in it.   And from time to time he looked up to the turret at his masthead, for he had set a watch there, to tell him when the Spaniards were in sight. Whilst the King was thus amusing himself with the knights, who were all glad to see him so gay, the watchman, who had caught sight of the Spanish ships, said, "Ho I see a ship coming, and it seems to me a Spaniard".   The minstrels were silent, and he was asked if he saw more than one; a little after he said "Yes, I see two, now three and four;" and then, when he saw the whole fleet, "I see so many that, God help me, I cannot count them".   Then when the King and his knights knew that they were the Spaniards, he caused the trumpets to sound, and all the ships came together, and ranged themselves in good order for the fight, for they knew that they would have battle, since the Spaniards had such a great fleet. It was then late, about the hour of vespers. The King had wine brought, and he and all his knights drank, and then put their basinets on their heads. The Spaniards soon drew near, and they might easily have passed without fighting, if they wished, for they were in large ships, and had the wind in their favour; . . . but through pride and presumption they disdained to sail by, but bore down upon them and began the battle.

When the King of England saw from his ships their order of battle, he said to the helmsman of his vessel, "Lay me alongside that Spaniard who is coming towards us, for I will have a tilt with him". The mariner dared not disobey the King's order, but laid the ship as he was ordered against the Spaniard, who was coming swiftly before the wind at full sail; and if the King's ship had not been large and stout, she would have been sunk, for

she met the great Spanish ship with such force that it was
like the crash of a tempest. And with the shock, the
turret on the mast of the King's ship caught that of
the Spaniard, so that it broke his mast, and all in his
turret fell into the sea and were drowned. The King's
ship received such a shock that she let in water; the
knights saw this, and bestirred themselves to bale it out,
saying nothing to the King of the matter. Then said the
King, looking at the ship that he had attacked, "Grapple
my ship to that one, for I will take her"; but his knights
replied, "Sire, let this one go, you will have a better".
So that ship sailed on, and another great ship came up,
whereto the King's knights grappled theirs with chains and
iron hooks. Then began a fierce and cruel battle, the
archers shooting, and the Spaniards fighting and defend-
ing themselves valiantly.

The fight was not in one place, but in ten or twelve at
a time; whenever they found themselves equal to the
enemy or superior, they grappled them and performed
wonderful feats of arms. But the English had no advantage, for the Spanish ships were much higher and larger, so
that they had great advantage in shooting, and casting
down bars of iron, which caused the English to suffer
greatly.

The knights on board the King's ship, which let in
water, and was in danger of sinking, strove hard to overcome the Spanish ship to which they were grappled, and
did many great deeds of arms; until at last it was won, and
all on board put to death. Then the King was told of the
peril they were in, and how his ship was fast letting in
water, and he was advised to go on board the ship they
had just taken. He took this advice, and went on board the
Spanish ship, and the knights and all who were with him,
and left their own empty; and then they meant to sail on
and attack the enemy, who was still fighting gallantly, his

crossbowmen shooting iron bolts from great bows, which harassed the English greatly.

This battle on the sea between the Spanish and English was well and fiercely fought; but it began late, so that the English made great efforts to finish the business well, and discomfit their enemies. Also the Spaniards, who are used to the sea, and were in great and strong ships, acquitted themselves to the utmost of their power. On the other part there fought the young Prince of Wales, and those of his charge, their ship being grappled to a great Spanish vessel, and he and his people suffered much, for their ship was pierced in many places, and the water rushed in so that for all their efforts to bale it out, she filled up more and more. The people with the Prince were in sore fear of this, so they fought fiercely to win the Spanish ship, but they could not have her, for she was strongly held and defended.

Upon this peril wherein the Prince and his people stood, there came the Duke of Lancaster sailing by the Prince's ship; he saw at once that they had the worst of the engagement, and that their ship was in sore straits, for they were throwing out the water on all sides. So he fell upon the other side of the Spanish vessel, crying " Derby to the rescue," and attacking the Spaniards fiercely, so that they did not endure for long; but their ship was won, and they were all thrown overboard, not one being spared. Then the Prince and his people at once went on board her, and scarcely had they done so before their own ship sank, so that they knew the great peril they had been in.

The English knights and barons fought well in other directions, each according as had been agreed upon, and there was full need of their valour, for they found a tough adversary; so that late in the evening, the ship the " King's Hall," whereof Sir Robert of Namur was captain, was grappled by a great Spaniard, and there was a sharp fight. And because the Spaniards wanted to master this ship at their ease, and to secure her with all who were within, they strove to carry her off with them; and setting all their sails, and taking advantage of the wind, they went off with her, in spite of all that Sir Robert and his men could do. For the Spanish ship was much larger and heavier than theirs, so that she had great advantage. Thus they passed by the King's ship, crying "Rescue the 'King's Hall'"; but they were not heard, for it was already late, and if they had been seen, they could not have been succoured. And I believe that the Spaniards would have carried them off easily, but for the right valiant feat of one of Sir Robert's servants, called Hankin. For with his drawn sword in his hand, he leapt on to the Spanish ship, ran to the mast, and cut the rope which bore the sail, so that it became useless; and then with great agility he cut the four main ropes that directed the mast and the sails, so that the sails fell to the deck, and the ship stayed, and could not go forward. Then Sir Robert of Namur and his people came up with drawn swords, attacking those within so vigorously that they were all slain and thrown overboard, and the ship was won.

I cannot tell of all these men, nor say "This one did well," or "This one did better"; but while it lasted the battle was sharp and bitter, and the Spaniards gave the King of England and his men enough to do. Nevertheless, at last the victory remained for the English. The Spaniards lost 14 ships,[1] and the rest saved themselves by flight. When they had all disappeared, and the King saw he had none left to fight with, he caused his trumpets to sound the retreat, and set out for England, where he landed at Rye and Winchelsea soon after nightfall.

[1] English chroniclers increase the number to 24 or 26.

· 56.

[(a) An order for the arrest of ships. (Latin.)   "Foedera," III, i. 476. The King, to Robert de Causton and John de Wesenham.   15 March, 1360.   Such orders for the seizure of shipping for the Government's use were constantly issued, according to circumstances, when any expedition was prepared.]

Because it is ordained by the magnates and others of our Council that there shall put to sea with all speed one fleet of ships with the Admiral of the West, and one from the Admiralty of the North, well supplied with men-at-arms, armed men, and archers, and with victuals, to resist the malice of our enemies of France, who have recently invaded our realm, and seized the town of Winchelsea, slaying persons therein, and doing much damage. . . .

We, fully trusting in your loyalty and discretion, have assigned you, separately and together, to arrest all large ships and barges suitable for war, in all ports and other places northward from the mouth of the river Thames; and to cause them without delay to be provided with men-at-arms, archers, armed men, and victuals for one month, and to come together at a certain place appointed according to your judgment; so that in each large ship there shall be placed 40 mariners, 40 armed men, and 60 archers, and in each barge, as many as is suitable and expedient—to be chosen by the makers of the array as well from the men of the good towns near the coast, as from the men of those parts to be arrayed by them; taking so much money as shall suffice for one month for the wages of these same men each day, namely, for each knight, 2s., for each squire, 12d., for an armed man, 6d., an archer, 4d., and a mariner, 3d.

—And to cause victuals and other things necessary for the supply of the ships to be taken and borrowed from the merchants and other good men of these parts, for which prompt payment shall be made from the first payments of the "15th" and "10th" lately granted by the community of the counties of our realm, for the wages and expenses of men-at-arms, and for the setting out for the defence of the realm.

—And to put out to sea with all speed, with the ships thus arrayed, against our enemies, by reason of the present necessity, together with other ships that are now on the sea, and ready to come from the Western parts.

And you shall have power of arresting all persons whom you shall find rebellious or resisting in the execution of the foregoing, and of detaining them in prison until we shall otherwise have ordained concerning them. . . .

[(b) **Writ authorising the impressment of mariners.** (Latin.) "Foedera," III, i. 428. 7 June, 1359. Similar writs were issued on behalf of a number of other shipmasters at the same time.]

The King to all and sundry sheriffs, mayors, bailiffs, officers, and other faithful lieges, etc., greeting. Know that we have assigned our beloved Thomas Clark, master of a ship called the "Edward," to choose and take 60 mariners, wheresoever they can be found, within liberties or without, as well within the liberty of the Cinque Ports as elsewhere, and to put them into his said ship, for the management of it, to stay there at our wages; and to seize and imprison all whom he shall find rebellious or contrary. . . .

Therefore we order you to be intendant to the said Thomas, and to give him advice and assistance whensoever he shall give you notice in our name. . . .

[(c) **Writ summoning certain persons to give advice to the Council.** (Latin.) "Foedera," III, ii. 880. 26 October, 1369.]

To the Warden of the Cinque Ports, and the Mayors and bailiffs of other important ports.

Because we have learned for certain that our adversary of France and other our enemies his adherents, are preparing, with great multitude of ships and men-at-arms, to destroy the shipping of our realm of England, and to hinder the passage of merchants and merchandise of our said realm, and to injure merchants and other our lieges in all ways that they possibly can, unless forcible resistance be made to them with all speed—we, being desirous of resisting the malice of our said enemies, as is fitting, and of providing for the safety of the ships, merchants, and merchandise of our realm, so far as we can, do command you, that immediately upon receipt of these letters, you shall choose in each town of these ports,[1] two of the more sufficient and discreet men, who are best acquainted with foreign parts, and have most knowledge and experience in the management of ships, merchants, and merchandise, and other matters; and you shall cause them to come before us and our Council at Westminster on the Octaves of St. Mark next, at latest, to give advice and information to us and our Council, with the advice and assent thereof, as to what shall be done for the safety of ships, merchants, and merchandise, and their passage to and fro, and for the greatest advantage and security of our realm and people, against the said enemies, and for their destruction.

57.

[(a) Statement by the Commons as to the causes of the decay of shipping. (French.) "Rolls of Parliament," ii. 307. 1371.]

Item, the Commons put forward, that it may please our lord the King to know the principal causes whereby our shipping[2] is so nearly destroyed.

In the first place, the arrests of ships that have often been made a long time before our lord the King had occasion to make use of them; during which time those who owned them have always borne all the expenses connected

[1] The Cinque Ports—this writ was addressed to the Warden.
[2] La navie.

with them at their own cost, as well of the mariners
as of all other appurtenances, without making any profit
in the meantime. Whereby many of them have been
so impoverished that by insufficiency they have abandoned this calling, and allowed their ships to rot and be
ruined.

On the other hand, the merchants of the land, from
whom the support of shipping must come, have been
restrained from their voyages and other business by
various ordinances, so that they have had no need of
shipping. And for this reason, the mariners have in great
part left that labour, and sought their living in other
ways, and the ships have been laid up to rot.

And also, the masters of our lord the King's ships,
whenever they have been given notice to prepare for any
voyage, have, by colour of their office, taken the masters
of other ships to serve them, and the other ablest men in
them; so that the ships of other owners have been left
without direction, and for this reason many of them have
been ruined, and those who owned them undone.

[(b) Complaint of weakness on the sea. (French.) "Rolls of Parliament," ii. 311. 1372.]

Item, the Commons pray, as also the merchants and
mariners of England, that whereas 20 years back, and
always before that time, the shipping of the realm was
so noble and plentiful in all ports and good towns on
the sea and on rivers, that all countries used to consider
and to call our said lord the King of the sea, and
feared him the more, both by sea and land, by reason of
the said navy—it is now so diminished and ruined by
various causes, that there remains barely sufficient to
defend the country against royal power, if great need
arose. . . .

58.

[(a) Richard II's Navigation Act. "Statutes of the Realm," ii. 18.
St. 5 Ric. II, i. c. 3. 1381.]

To increase the shipping of England, which is now
greatly diminished, it is assented and accorded that none
of the King's lieges shall from henceforth ship any
manner of merchandise, going out or coming into the
realm of England, except in ships of the King's ligeance;
and every person of the said ligeance who after the Feast
of Easter next ensuing, at which Feast this ordinance
shall first begin to be of force, shall ship merchandise in
other ships or vessels upon the sea than those of the said
ligeance, shall forfeit to the King all his merchandise
shipped in other vessels, wherever they may afterwards
be found, or the value of them. Of which forfeiture the
King wills and grants that he who shall discover, and
duly prove that any person has forfeited anything against
this ordinance, shall have the third part for his labour, of
the King's gift.

[(b) "Statutes," *ibid.* ii. 128. St. 6 Ric. II, i. c. 8. 1382.]

Although lately . . . it was ordained that no liege
subject of the King . . . should in anywise ship merchandise or goods . . . in any ships . . . except in ships of
the King's ligeance; yet . . . it is ordained and granted,
that the said ordinance shall hold good so long as able
and sufficient ships of the King's ligeance shall be found
in the ports where the said merchants shall happen to
resort; so that thus they shall be bound to freight these
ships with their merchandise before all other ships, under
the aforesaid penalty; but otherwise it shall be lawful for
them to hire other suitable ships, and freight them with
their goods and merchandise, notwithstanding the former
statute.

59.

[How the Earl of Pembroke departed out of England to go into Poitou (1372), and how the Spaniards fought with him in the haven of Rochelle. Froissart, Lord Berners' translation.]

So the season came that the Earl of Pembroke should depart, and so took his leave of the King and all his company. And Sir Otho of Grandson was ordained to go with him; he had no great company with him but certain knights by the information of Guichard d'Angle; but he had with him such certain sum of money to pay the wages of three thousand men of war. And so they made speed till they came to Hampton and there tarried 15 days abiding wind, and then they had wind at will, and so entered into their ships and departed from the haven in the name of God and St. George, and took their course towards Poitou. King Charles of France who knew the most part of all the counsell in England, I cannot tell how or by whom, but he knew well how Sir Guichard d'Angle was gone into England, to the intent to get out of the King a good Captain for the county of Poitou; and also he knew how the Earl of Pembroke should go thither, and all his charge. The French King was well advised thereof, and secretly sent an army of men of war by the sea, of Spaniards at his desire, because his own men were gone to King Henry of Castile, because of the confederation and alliance that was between them. The Spaniards were 40 great ships and 13 barques, well purveyed and decked, as these Spanish ships be. And sovereigns and patrons of that fleet were 4 valiant captains, Ambrose de Boccanegra, Cabeça de Vaca, Don Fernando de Peon, and Ruy Diaz de Rojas.

These Spaniards had been at sea, awaiting the return of the Poitevins and the coming of the Earl of Pembroke, for they well knew it was their intent to come to Poitou, wherefore they lay at anchor off the town of Rochelle. And so it happened that the day before the vigil of St. John the Baptist in the year 1372 the Earl of Pembroke and his company were to arrive in the haven of Rochelle; but they found the aforesaid Spaniards before them, who intended to prevent their landing, and were right glad of their coming.

When the Englishmen and Poitevins saw the Spaniards and perceived how they must needs fight with them, they comforted themselves howbeit they were not equally matched, neither of men nor of ships; but they armed themselves and put themselves in good order, their archers before them, all ready to fight.

And then the Spanish ships which were well purveyed with a great number of men of war and brigands, with crossbows and cannon, with great bars of iron and plummets of lead to cast down, began to approach, making great noise; these great ships of Spain took the wind to fetch their turn, against the English ships whom they had but little feared and so came upon them with full sail spread. So thus at the beginning there was great cry and noise of the one and the other, and the Englishmen bore themselves right well, and there the Earl of Pembroke knighted certain of the squires for honour. There was a great battle and hard, the Englishmen had enough to do, for the Spaniards who were in ships so great that they towered above the English vessels, had great bars of iron and stones, and cast them down to sink the English ships, and hurt many a man right sorely. And among the knights of England and Poitou great nobleness of knighthood and prowess was shown. The Earl of Pembroke fought and met his enemies right fiercely, and did that day many a noble feat of arms, and in like manner so did Sir Otho de Grandson, Sir Guichard d'Angle, the lord of Puyane, and all the other knights.

From what I have heard recorded by those who were there in the battle before Rochelle, the English and Poitevins who were there showed clearly how they desired to win praise in arms, for never did they bear themselves more valiantly; for they were but few in regard to the Spaniards, and with much smaller ships, that it might well be marvelled how they endured so long. But the noble knighthood that was in them supported them and held them in strength, for if they had been like in ships, the Spaniards had taken but little ado of them, for they held their lances so close together that none durst abide their strokes without they were well armed and pavessed. But the casting down of plummets of lead, and great stones and bars of iron hurt and troubled them marvellously sore and hurt and wounded divers knights and squires. The people of the town of Rochelle easily saw this battle, but they made no advance to come to help the Earl of Pembroke and his company, who so valiantly there fought with their enemies, but did let them alone. Thus in this battle and strife they endured till it was night and then they departed from each other and they cast their anchors. But this first day the Englishmen lost 2 barges laden with their provisions and all that were in them were put to death. The same night Sir John of Harpenden who was then Seneschal of Rochelle made great entreaty to them of the town, to the Mayor Sir John Caudrier [1] and others that they should arm them, and cause to be armed all the commonalty of the town, and to enter into barges and ships and go to aide and comfort their people, who all the day had so well fought with their enemies. But they of the town, who had no will to the matter excused themselves, and said they had enough to do to keep the town, and how they were no sea men nor wist not' how to fight the

---

[1] M. Luce points out that he was not in office at this time—the Mayor was Piere Boudré.

Spaniards on the sea, but if the latter were on land they
said they would then gladly go forth. So the Seneschal
could not get them forth for all that he could do.

The same time within the town there was the lord of
Tonnay-Bouton, Sir Jaques of Burgeres and Sir Mauburni
de Lignières, who also desired them to go forth. But
when they saw that their request could not avail, these 4
knights went and armed them and all their company, such
as would go forth with them, the which was but a small
number. So they entered into 4 barges and at the breaking of the day when the flood came they went to their
company who gave them great thanks for their coming.
And there they showed unto the Earl of Pembroke and Sir
Guichard d'Angle how that they would not be succoured or
supported by those of the town of Rochelle. And then
since they could not amend it they answered that they
must abide the grace of God and the adventure of fortune
and that the time would come when they of Rochelle would
repent of it. When the day was come and the flood came
up and it was high tide, the Spaniards weighed up their
anchor, making great noise with trumpets, and put them
in good order as they did the day before, and got under way
their great ships strongly armed and purveyed, and took
the advantage of the wind to close in the English ships
who were nothing to the number of the Spaniards. And
so the aforesaid 4 captains of the Spaniards came forward
in good order. The English and Poitevins saw well their
order and so drew all together and set their archers before
them. Therewith came on the Spaniards at full sail and
so began a fierce and cruel battle ; then the Spaniards cast
great hooks of iron with chains and grappled their ships to
the English ships so they could not depart. With the
Earl of Pembroke and Sir Guichard d'Angle there were
22 knights who right valiantly fought with lances and
swords and such weapons as they had. Thus fighting

they continued a long space, but the Spaniards had too great advantage of the English men, for they were in great ships and cast down great bars of iron and stones the which sore travailed the English men. Thus shouting, struggling and fighting with each other they endured till 3 of the clock;[1] there were never men that endured more travail on the sea than the English did that day, for the most part of their men were sore hurt with the casting down of bars of iron and stones, so that Sir Aymerie of Tharse that valiant knight of Gascony was there slain and Sir John Langton that was knight of the body to the Earl of Pembroke.

To the Earl's ship there were grappled 4 great ships whereof Cabeça de Vaca and Don Fernando de Peon were captains, and in them were many good fighting men, and they did so much that they entered into the Earl's ship, where was done many a valiant feat of arms, and thus the Earl was taken, and all that were in his ship taken or slain. . . . And on the other hand the Poitevins, Sir Guichard d'Angle, the lord of Puyane, the lord of Tonnay-Bouton, and in another ship Sir Otho de Grandson were fighting with Ambrose Boccanegra, Ruy Diaz de Rojas, until all the knights were taken by the Spaniards so that none escaped being captured or slain, and all these people were in danger of like fate. But when they had taken the chief masters they left slaying of servants for their masters desired that they would forbear, saying how they would pay for all. . . .

And you must know that besides the loss of so many good knights and squires as were taken and slain, the King of England that day had the greatest loss, for by this discomfiture he lost afterwards the whole country. . . . And as I was told, the English ship wherein was all the treasure and riches wherewith Sir Guichard d'Angle should have paid all the wages of the soldiers in Guienne,

[1] Nine o'clock (Nicolas).

perished, and all that was therein, so that nothing thereof came to any profit.   All that day, the which was the vigil of St. John the Baptist, and that night, and the next day till it was noon, the Spaniards lay still at anchor before Rochelle, making great joy.   And it fortuned so well to a knight of Poitou, called Sir Jaques of Surgeres, for he spoke so fairly and gently to his master that he was quit with the paying of 300 francs.   He came on St. John's day to dinner in the town of Rochelle.   By him there it was known how the day had sped, and who were slain and who were taken; and divers burgesses of the town showed by semblance how they were sorry and displeased, howbeit they were indeed right joyous, for they never naturally loved the Englishmen.

60.

[Walsingham, "Historia Anglicana".   Notices of 1385.   (Latin.)]

Concerning the folly of our people on the sea :—
    . . . Meanwhile a fleet was being prepared in all the English ports; fighting men were gathered together in great numbers, and the Master of the Hospital of St. John, and Lord Percy, brother of the Earl of Northumberland were placed in command as admirals.   But for the whole summer they were destined to keep an idle lookout on the sea, frequently seeing the French fleet, at one time sailing by them, at another openly making mock of them; yet they did not think fit to do anything against those on board, being prevented either by private disagreement or by mere folly.   But not thus the men of Portsmouth and Dartmouth! not thus did they decree to remain idle; no man had hired them to inflict damage upon the enemy, but they were spurred on by their own inborn valour. For, having no fear in the face of a great multitude of

ships, dreading no attacks of the enemy, they crossed the sea with a small company, and sailed over to the Seine, where without difficulty they sank four of the enemy's ships, and carried off four more, with a barge belonging to the lord of Clisson whose equal was not to be found in the kingdoms of England or France—wherein they won such booty as was enough to satisfy the most covetous, and to relieve their want.

[The French King's invasion schemes were delayed by events in Flanders, and by tempests]. . . . To say nothing of the damage inflicted upon him on land, he suffered great mischiefs on the deep, by the loss of his men and goods; for there came a dreadful tempest, while his fleet was returning from Sluys, that scattered his ships and dashed them to pieces, casting many of the sailors on the shores of the King of England, to wit, at Calais, and the neighbouring places. For on Holy Cross day, two great galleys, and a ship of another kind, called a "lyne," with a barge and two balingers, were wrecked off the town of Calais, and the townspeople took captive 500 Frenchmen and Normans who came to the harbour when their fleet was sunk; among whom was Robert Bremville, a very wealthy man and most influential among all the merchants of France. On the third day following, 72 French ships returning from Sluys, were trying to make their way past Calais, but the Calais men put out, and fought against them, winning 18 ships and a great barge, wherein were slain or taken 60 armed men. Three days later, after this fight, 45 great ships returning from Sluys, and endeavouring to round Calais, were hindered by our people, for the men of Calais, when their coming was known, took arms against them, and fought for more than six hours; at last the victory fell to our men, who put to flight all these ships but two, and a cog, wherein two French admirals were taken, with much plunder. But two of these ships were so large that they could not be brought into Calais harbour, wherefore they were sent to Sandwich. The larger of the two had been hired at Sluys by the lord of Clisson for 3000 francs, and it was a new ship only built that same year. The Normans had hired the cog from Estland for 5000 francs, so that it might be a protection and defence for them as they went back to their own country; but none the less, when the English attacked them, it could not avail to defend itself from being taken, and it fell a prey to them. There were captured and slain in these ships 256 men, both sailors and hired troops.

61.

[Renewed fear of invasion, 1386. (*Ibid.*)]

When it was understood for certain that the King of France had collected his ships and made ready his army, and was of purpose to invade England, the Londoners, timid as hares and nervous as mice, sought conflicting counsel on all sides, peered into dark places, and began to mistrust their own strength, and despair of resistance as though the city were on the point of being taken. Those who in peace had arrogantly boasted that they would drive all the Frenchmen out of England, now when they heard the rumour, albeit unfounded, of the enemy's approach, thought that all England could scarcely protect them. And so, as though drunken with wine, they rushed to the city walls, breaking and tearing down all the adjacent houses, and timorously doing everything that they were wont to do in the greatest extremity. Not one Frenchman had yet set foot on a ship, no enemy had put to sea, yet the Londoners were as fearful as though all the surrounding country had been conquered, and they saw the enemy before their gates.

BOOK II. SOCIAL HISTORY.

1.

[Stanzas from a poem written early in Edward III's reign. "Political Poems," Wright, Camden Society, p. 338. The poem, which is of considerable length, professes to describe "the evil times of Edward II"; but it illustrates the feeling prevalent among the poorer classes throughout the century. The spelling has been slightly altered.]

But were the King well advised, and wolde work by skill
Little need sholde he have such poor to pile
Thurfte him not seek tresot so far, he might finde near
At justices, at sheriffs, cheitors,[1] and chanceller, and at
    les,
Such might finde him enough, and let poor men have
    peace.

For whoso is in such office, come he never so poor
He fareth in a while as though he had silver ore
They buy londs and ledes,[2] ne may them none astonde,
What should poor men be i-piled, when such men beth in
    lond. . . .

But schrewedliche, for sooth, they don the Kinges heste
When every man hath his part, the King hath the leste
Every man is about to fill his owen purse;

[1] Escheators.   [2] Possessions.

143

And the King hath the least part, and he hath all the
curse, with wrong
God send truth into this lond, for tricherie dureth too
long. . . .

2.

[The following details of travelling expenses are taken from a long
and interesting account kindly supplied by Mr. Stamp, of H.M.
Record Office, to whom the Editor is also indebted for the translation. The extract illustrates merely a small part of the travelling
and labour involved in connection with the matter in question—
the Bishop proved most elusive, and had to be "followed at a
distance" through various parts of his diocese. P.R.O. Exch.
Accts., 348/10.]

Expenses incurred in the appropriation of the churches
of Filmersham and Grendon. (1365-6.)

In primis, for the expenses of Richard de Barowe and a
servant with two hired horses going from Cambridge to
London to obtain the King's letters of Privy Seal to the
Bishop of Lincoln for the forwarding of the appropriation
of the aforesaid churches, and returning thence—7 days
15s. 4d.

Item, for the expenses of the aforesaid Richard and a
servant with two hired horses going from Cambridge to
Lincoln, to present such letters to the Bishop and to get
an answer thereupon, and returning thence to Cambridge
—8 days   17s.

Item, for the expenses of the aforesaid Richard and a
servant with two hired horses from Cambridge to Chartsey
to take the answer of the King's letters, staying there
and returning to Cambridge—7 days   14s. 4d.

Item, for the expenses of the aforesaid Richard from
Cambridge, with two hired horses, to Windsor, to obtain
new royal letters again to the Bishop, staying there and
returning to Cambridge—6 days   13s. 5d.

Item, for the expenses of the aforesaid Richard and
servant with two hired horses from Cambridge to the
Bishop's manor called Stoweparc, to present the King's
letters to him, who promised that on his next coming to
Lincoln he would forward everything that lay in his
power to forward, staying there and returning thence to
Cambridge—7 days   14s. 2d.

Item, for the expenses of the aforesaid Richard and
servant with two hired horses from Cambridge to the
Bishop's manor of Lidington, staying there and inquiring
as to the Bishop's passage towards Lincoln, beseeching
also his good will for the forwarding of the aforesaid and
returning thence to Cambridge—5 days   9s. 3d.

3.

[The Black Death.   Chroniclers' notices (Latin), 1348-9.]

(a) KNIGHTON.—In this year there was a general mortality among men throughout the whole world.   It broke
out first in India, and spread thence in Tharsis, thence to
the Saracens, and at last to the Christians and Jews; so
that in the space of a single year, namely, from Easter to
Easter, as it was rumoured at the court of Rome, 8000
legions of men perished in those distant regions, besides
Christians. . . .

Then the dreadful pestilence made its way through the
coast land by Southampton, and reached Bristol, and
there perished almost the whole strength of the town,
as it were surprised by sudden death; for few kept their
beds more than two or three days, or even half a day.
Then this cruel death spread on all sides, following the
course of the sun.   And there died at Leicester, in the
small parish of St. Leonard more than 380 persons, in the
parish of Holy Cross, 400, in the parish of St. Margaret's,
Leicester, 700; and so in every parih, in a great multitude.

Then the Bishop of Lincoln sent notice throughout his whole diocese giving general power to all priests, as well regulars as seculars, of hearing confessions and giving absolution to all persons with full episcopal authority, except only in case of debt. And in this case, the debtor was to pay the debt, if he were able, while he lived, or others were to be appointed to do so from his property after his death. In the same way the Pope gave plenary remission of all offences to all receiving absolution at the point of death, and granted that this power should endure until Easter next following, and that every one might choose his own confessor at will.

In the same year there was a great murrain of sheep everywhere in the kingdom, so that in one place more than 5000 sheep died in a single pasture; and they rotted so that neither bird nor beast would approach them. There was great cheapness of all things, owing to the general fear of death, since very few people took any account of riches or property of any kind. A horse that was formerly worth 40s. could be had for half a mark, a fat ox for 4s., a cow for 12d., a heifer for 6d., a fat wether for 4d., a sheep for 3d., a lamb for 2d., a large pig for 5d.; a stone of wool was worth 9d. Sheep and oxen strayed at large through the fields and among the crops, and there were none to drive them off or herd them, but they perished in remote by-ways and hedges in inestimable numbers throughout all districts, because that there was such great scarcity of servants that none knew what to do. For there was no recollection of such great and terrible mortality since the time of Vortigern, King of the Britons, in whose day, as Bede testifies, the living did not suffice to bury the dead.

In the following autumn a reaper was not to be had for less than 8d., with his food, a mower for less than 10d., with food. Wherefore many crops rotted in the fields for want of men to gather them. But in the year of the pestilence,

as has been said above, of other things, there was so great
an abundance of all kinds of corn that they were scarcely
regarded.

The Scots, hearing of the dreadful pestilence in England,
surmised that it had come about at the hand of an aveng-
ing God, and it became an oath among them, so that, according to the common report, they were accustomed to
swear " be the foul deth of Engelond ". Thus, believing
that a terrible vengeance of God had overtaken the English,
they came together in Selkirk forest with the intention of
invading the realm of England, when the fierce mortality
overtook them and their ranks were thinned by sudden and
terrible death, so that in a short time some 5000 perished.
And as the rest, the strong and the feeble, were making
ready to return to their own country, they were pursued
and surprised by the English, who killed a very great
number of them.

Master Thomas Bradwardine was consecrated by the
Pope as Archbishop of Canterbury, and when he returned
to England, he came to London, and was dead within two
days. He was renowned above all other clerks in Christendom, especially in theology and other liberal sciences. At
this time there was everywhere so great a scarcity of priests
that many churches were left destitute, without divine
service, masses, matins, vespers or sacraments. A chaplain
was scarcely to be had to serve any church for less than
£10 or 10 marks, and whereas when there was an abundance of priests before the pestilence a chaplain could be
had for 4, 5 or 11 marks, with his board, at this time there
was scarcely one willing to accept any vicarage at £20 or
20 marks. Within a little time, however, vast numbers
of men whose wives had died in the pestilence flocked to
take orders, many of whom were illiterate, and as it were
mere laymen, save so far as they could read a little,
although without understanding.

10 *

In the meantime the King sent notice into all counties of the realm that reapers and other labourers should not receive more than they had been wont, under a penalty defined by statute; and he introduced a statute for this cause.   But the labourers were so arrogant and hostile that they paid no heed to the King's mandate, but if anyone wanted to have them he was obliged to give them whatever they asked, and either to lose his fruits and crops, or satisfy their greed and arrogance.   But the King levied heavy fines upon abbots, priors, knights of great and less degree, and others great and small throughout the countryside when it became known to him that they did not observe his ordinance, and gave higher wages to their labourers; taking 100s. from some, 40s. or 20s. from others, according as they were able to pay.   Moreover he took 20s. from each plough-land throughout the kingdom, and notwithstanding this, he also took a " fifteenth ".

Then the King caused many labourers to be arrested, and sent them to prison, many of whom escaped and went away to the forests and woods for a time, and those who were taken were heavily fined.   Others swore that they would not take wages higher than had formerly been the custom, and so were set free from prison.   The same thing was done in the case of other labourers in the towns. . . . After the pestilence many buildings both great and small in all cities, towns, and boroughs fell into ruins for want of inhabitants, and in the same way many 'villages and hamlets were depopulated, and there were no houses left in them, all who had lived therein being dead; and it seemed likely that many such hamlets would never again be inhabited.   In the following winter there was such dearth of servants for all sorts of labour as it was believed had never been before.   For the sheep and cattle strayed in all directions without herdsmen, and all things were left with none to care for them.   Thus necessaries became so dear that what had previously been worth 1d. was now worth 4d. or 5d. Moreover the great men of the land and other lesser lords who had tenants, remitted the payment of their rents, lest the tenants should go away, on account of the scarcity of servants and the high price of all things—some half their rents, some more, some less, some for one, two, or three years according as they could come to an agreement with them. Similarly, those who had let lands on labour-rents to tenants as is the custom in the case of villeins, were obliged to relieve and remit these services, either excusing them entirely, or taking them on easier terms, in the form of a small rent, lest their houses should be irreparably ruined and the land should remain uncultivated. And all sorts of food became excessively dear.

(b) GEOFFREY LE BAKER.—[The pestilence] deprived first the sea-ports in Dorset, and then the whole district of almost all their inhabitants, and spreading thence it raged so violently throughout Devon and Somerset as far as Bristol that the people of Gloucester would not let those of Bristol come into their parts, for they all thought that the breath of persons who lived among those who were thus dying was infected. But at length it invaded Gloucester, yea Oxford, London and at last the whole of England, with such violence that scarcely one person in ten of either sex survived. Since the cemeteries did not suffice, fields were chosen for burying the dead ; the Bishop of London bought that croft in London called " Nomannes lond," and the lord Walter Manny the one called " the newe chierche hawe," where he founded a religious house for the burial of the dead.[1] Suits in the King's Bench and Common pleas came

---

[1] Sir Walter purchased 100 acres of land outside " the bar of West Smithfield " from St. Bartholomew's Hospital, in 1349, for a cemetery ; according to his own statement 5000 persons were buried here in that year. His new Chapel of the Annunciation built there gave its name to the ground (" Dict. of Nat. Biography ").

of necessity to a standstill.   A few noblemen died, among
whom were the lord John of Montgomery, Captain of Calais
and the lord Clisteles, who both died in Calais and were
buried in London, at the house of the brothers of St.
Mary of Carmel.   But innumerable common people and
a multitude of monks and other clerks known to God alone
passed away.   The pestilence seized especially the young
and strong, commonly sparing the elderly and feeble.
Scarcely any one ventured to touch the sick, and healthy
persons shunned the once, and still, precious possessions of
the dead, as infectious.   People perfectly well on one day
were found dead on the next.   Some were tormented with
abscesses in various parts of their body, and from these
many, by means of lancing, or with long suffering, recovered.
Others had small black pustules scattered over the whole
surface of their body, from which very few, nay, scarcely
a single person, returned to life and health.   This great
pestilence, which began at Bristol about the Feast of the
Assumption, and at London about Michaelmas, raged in
England for a whole year and more, so that many villages
were utterly emptied of every human being.

(c) AVESBURY.—It began in England, in the neighbourhood of Dorchester, about the Feast of St. Peter ad
Vinculas, A.D. 1348, immediately spreading rapidly from
place to place, and many persons who were healthy in the
early morning, before midday were snatched from human
affairs; it permitted none whom it marked down to live
more than three or four days, without choice of persons,
save only in the case of a few rich people.   On the same
day of their death, the bodies of 20, 40, 60, and many
times more persons were delivered to the Church's burial
in the same pit.   Reaching London about the feast of
All Saints, it slew many persons daily, and increased so
greatly that from the feast of the Purification until just
after Easter, in a newly-made cemetery in Smithfield the

bodies of more than 200 persons, besides those that were buried in other cemeteries of the same city, were buried every day. But by the intervention of the Grace of the Holy Spirit, it ceased in London on Whitsunday, continuing to spread towards the north, in which parts it also ceased about Michaelmas 1349.

(d) *Chronicon Angliae.*—A great mortality spread throughout the world, starting from the northern and western regions, and raging with such great slaughter that scarcely the half of mankind survived. And towns that were formerly very thickly populated were left destitute of inhabitants, the plague being so violent that the living were scarce able to bury the dead. For in some religious houses, of 20 monks, scarce two survived. For, to say nothing of other monasteries, in the monastery of St. Albans more than 40 monks died in a short space of time. And it was estimated that scarcely a tenth part of the people had been left alive. The pestilence was immediately followed by a murrain among beasts. At that time revenues wasted away, and for want of husbandmen, who were nowhere to be found, lands remained uncultivated. And such misery followed these misfortunes that the world never afterwards had the opportunity of returning to its former condition.

4.

[Concerning the further prorogation of Parliament, owing to the increase of the pestilence. (Latin.) "Foedera," III, i. 182. Entry on Close Roll. Writ issued to all sheriffs, and to persons individually summoned to attend, 10 March, 1349.]

Whereas lately, by reason of the deadly pestilence then prevailing, we caused the Parliament that was summoned to meet at Westminster on the Monday after the Feast of St. Hilary to be prorogued until the quinzaine of Easter next—and because the aforesaid pestilence is increasing

with more than its usual severity, in Westminster and in
the City of London and the surrounding districts, whereby the coming of the magnates and other our faithful
lieges to that place at this time, would probably be too
dangerous—for this, and for certain other obvious reasons
we have thought fit to postpone the said Parliament until
we shall issue further summons.

5.

[The Ordinance of Labourers, 18 June, 1349. "Statutes," i. 307.
"Foedera," III, i. 198. (Latin.) "Calendar of Close Rolls,'
1349-54, p. 87 (summary).]

Because lately a great part of the people, and especially
of labourers and servants has died during the pestilence,
and some, perceiving the pressing need of the lords, and
the great scarcity of servants, refuse to serve unless they
receive excessive wages, while others prefer to beg in idleness than to get their livelihood by labour. We . . . have
had treaty and deliberation upon this matter with the prelates, nobles, and òther experienced persons assisting us, by
whose unanimous counsel we have ordained :—that every
man or woman in our realm of whatever condition, free
or bond, being able in body, and below the age of 60 years,
not living in merchandise, nor exercising any craft, nor
having wherewith to live of his own resources, nor land
of his own in whose tillage he may employ himself, and
not serving another,—if he shall be required to serve in
any suitable service, considering his condition, shall be
bound to serve him who required him, and shall receive
only such wages, allowances, hire or salary, as were accustomed to be offered in the place where he is to serve,
in the 20th year of our reign, or in the average five or six
years preceding.

Provided that lords shall have preference before others
in retaining in their service their villeins, or the tenants

of their villein land; so, however, that they retain in this
way only as many as shall be necessary for them, and not
more.

And if any . . . shall be required to serve, and will not
do so, if it be proved before the sheriff, bailiff, lord, or the
constable of the town where this occurred, he shall at
once be arrested . . . and sent to the nearest gaol, to remain there . . . until he shall find security for serving in
the aforesaid manner. And if any reaper, mower, or
other labourer . . . retained in any service, shall withdraw
without reasonable cause before the term of his agreement,
he shall suffer penalty of imprisonment; and none shall
receive or retain him in his service, upon the same penalty.

And that none shall pay . . . higher wages . . . than
were wont to be paid . . ., nor shall any otherwise exact
or receive them, on pain of doubling that which was thus
promised . . . to him who shall feel himself aggrieved. . . .
And if any lords of towns or manors shall presume to infringe this ordinance, suit shall be made against them in
the county courts . . . or other our courts, for the treble
thus paid by them or their servants.

[The ordinance is to apply to all artificers and workmen.]

Also, that butchers, fishmongers, hostelers, brewers,
bakers, pulters, and all other sellers of victuals, shall be
bound . . . to sell them for a reasonable price, having regard to the price whereat such victuals are sold in the
neighbouring districts; so that they shall have a moderate,
not excessive profit, reasonably to be required according
to the distance of the places whence such victuals are
carried. . . .

[Mayors and bailiffs of cities, boroughs, market-towns
and sea-ports, are to inquire as to offenders, and to levy the
penalties; they are to be severely fined if convicted of
negligence.]

And because many able-bodied beggars refuse to labour so long as they can live by asking alms, giving themselves to idleness and ill-doing, and sometimes to theft and other crimes, no person shall, on pain of the aforesaid imprisonment, give anything under colour of pity or alms to such as are able to labour, or encourage them in idleness ; so that they may be compelled to labour for their living.

6.

[Parliament of February, 1351. "Rolls of Parliament," ii. 225. (French).]

(a) From the statement as to the causes of summons :—

. . . Because the King is informed that the peace of the land is not well kept, and that there are many other misprisions and defaults which need to be redressed and amended, as by maintenance of parties and quarrels in the country, and also by reason of the servants and labourers, who will not labour and work as they were wont. And also because the treasure of the realm is carried out of the country in many ways, so that it is much impoverished and in point of being destitute of money, and put to mischief; and for other defaults that there are, our lord the King has caused his Parliament to be summoned at this time.

(b) Petition to the King:—that it may please him to have regard . . . how since this pestilence his Commons are greatly undone and ruined, and by it cities, boroughs, and other towns and hamlets throughout the land are decayed and daily falling into decay, and many are clean depopulated, that were wont to contribute to the tax of the "15th" and "10th," and other charges. . . . And now by . . . this last tax, which is charged at the same amount upon those who are left, they are ruined and undone, to their great mischief, so that they can scarcely live.

(c) Also, his Commons pray, that because since the pestilence the labourers will not work, taking for their labour as it was agreed by the King and his Council, nor do they pay any heed to fines and redemptions, but do worse and worse from day to day—it may please the King that corporal penalty shall be imposed on them, with fines, when they shall be duly convicted.

"The answer to this petition appears in the statute made now in this Parliament."

7.

[The Statute of Artificers and Servants. "Statutes of the Realm," i. 311. 25 Ed. III, Stat. 2, cc. 1-7. (French.) Also "Rolls of Parliament," ii. 233.]

Whereas late, against the malice of servants, which were idle . . . our lord the King ordained . . . that such manner of servants . . . should be bound to serve, receiving such salaries and wages as were accustomed . . . and that the same servants, refusing to serve, should be punished by imprisonment . . .; whereupon commissions were made to divers people in each county to inquire and punish all those who offended against it—And now, because he is given to understand by the petition of the Commons in this present Parliament, that the said servants, having no regard to this ordinance . . . withdraw from serving the great men and others, unless they have allowance and wages to the double or treble of what they used to take. . . .

In the same Parliament, with the assent of the Prelates, Earls, Barons, and other great men, and of the said Commons . . . the under-written matters are ordained and established :—

First, that all carters, ploughmen, shepherds, swineherds, dairywomen and all other servants shall take allowance and wages as were wont to be paid in the 20th year of our reign, and for three or four years before; in such wise that in the districts where wheat was wont to be given they shall take for the bushel 10d., or wheat at the will of the giver, unless it be otherwise ordained.

And that they be allowed to serve by the whole year or other usual term, and not by the day. And that none take in the time of haymaking . . . except at 1d. the day, and mowers of meadows 5d. for the acre, or 5d. for the day; and reapers of corn in the first week of August, 2d., and in the second 3d., and so until the end of August, and less in districts where less was wont to be given, without food or other courtesy being asked, given, or taken.

And that such workmen shall carry their instruments openly in their hands to market towns, and shall be hired there in a common and not a secret place.

Also that none take for threshing a quarter of wheat or rye more than 2½d.; and for the quarter of barley, oats, peas, and beans, 1½d., if so much was wont to be given. And in districts where it used to be the custom to reap by certain sheaves, and to thresh by so many bushels, they shall take no more, nor in other manner, than they were wont in the said 20th year and before.

And that the said servants be sworn twice a year before the lords, seneschals, bailiffs, and constables of each township to keep and perform these things.

And that none of them shall leave the town where he dwells in the winter for service in the summer, if he can have employment in the same town. . . . Saving that the people of the counties of Stafford, Lancaster, and Derby, and those of Craven and of the Marches of Wales and Scotland and other places, may come in August to labour in other counties, and safely return as they have been accustomed to do before this time.

And that those who refuse to make such an oath, or to fulfil what they have already sworn or undertaken, shall be put in the stocks by the said lords, bailiffs, and constables of towns for two or three days, or sent to the nearest gaol, to stay there until they are willing to submit. And that between now and Whitsun stocks shall be made in every town for this purpose.

Also that carpenters, masons, tilers and other roofers of houses shall not take more for the day for their work than they were accustomed ; to wit, a master carpenter 3d., and others 2d. ; a master mason on free stone 4d., and another mason 3d. ; and their servants 1½d. A tiler 3d. ; and his boy 1½d. ; and other thatcher with ferns and straw 3d., and his boy 1½d. Also a plasterer and other worker of mud walls and their boys in the same manner, without meat or drink ; that is from Easter to Michaelmas, and from then less, according to the rate and discretion of the justices who shall be assigned for this purpose. And that those who make carriage by land or water shall take no more for such carriage than they did in the said 20th year, or three years before.

Also that cordwainers and shoemakers shall not sell boots, shoes, or other things touching their mystery otherwise than they did in the said 20th year. And that goldsmiths, saddlers, furriers, sporriers, tanners, corriers, tailors, and all other workmen, artificers, and labourers, and all other servants not specified, be sworn before the said justices to do and employ their crafts and offices as they were wont to do in the said 20th year, and before, without refusing because of this ordinance.

And if any such servants, labourers, workmen or artificers, after such oath, infringe this ordinance, they shall be punished by fine, ransom, or imprisonment, according to the discretion of the justices.

And that seneschals, bailiffs, and constables of towns be sworn before the justices to inquire diligently by all the good ways they can, of all those infringing this ordinance,

and to certify the justices of their names, whenever they
shall come into a district to hold their session; so that the
justices . . . shall cause them to be arrested, to come before the same justices to answer for such contempts, so
that they may make fine and ransom to the King, if they
be convicted, and beyond this, to be committed to prison,
until they shall have found surety to serve and do their
crafts, and sell vendible goods, in the aforesaid manner.

And in case any of them break his oath, and be convicted
of it, he shall have 40 days' imprisonment; and if he be
convicted another time, a quarter's imprisonment; so that
each time they offend and be convicted they shall have a
double penalty.

And that the same justices, each time they come into the
country, shall inquire if the seneschals, bailiffs, and constables have made good and loyal certification, or have
concealed anything for gifts, procurement, or affinity, and
punish them by fine and ransom, if they be found guilty.

And that the same justices shall have power to inquire
and make due punishment of such ministers, labourers,
workmen, and all other servants whatsoever, and also of
hostelers, and those who sell victuals in retail, and other
things not specified . . . and to hear and determine. . . .

And that the justices inquire in their sessions if the said
ministers have taken anything from the said servants, and
shall cause to be levied upon each of the ministers what
they shall find them to have taken, with the fines and ransoms made, and delivered to the collectors of the "15th"
and "10th," in alleviation of the townships . . . and also
the amercements of those who shall be amerced before
them. And in case the excess found in a township shall
exceed the quantity of the "15th" of that township, the
remainder shall be levied and paid by the collectors to the
nearest poor towns, in aid of their "15th," by the advice
of the justices. And when the "15th" ceases, it shall be

raised to the King's use, and answered for to him by the sheriff of the county.

And that the said justices make their sessions in all the counties of England at least four times a year, namely, at the Feasts of the Annunciation of Our Lady, of St. Margaret, of St. Michael, and St. Nicholas; and also at all times when it shall be necessary according to their discretion.

And that those who in the presence of the justices say or do anything in encouragement or maintenance of the said servants and labourers against this ordinance, shall be severely punished according to the discretion of the justices. And if any such labourers, artificers, or servants flee from one county to another because of this ordinance, the sheriffs of the county where they be found shall, at the order of the justices in the counties whence they have fled, cause them to be arrested and carried to the nearest gaol of the same county to remain there until the next session of the justices.

[Knighton.]

In the same year the statute of servants was declared, and from that time they served their masters worse from day to day than they had done before.

8.

[From a mandate of the Archbishop of Canterbury to compel chaplains to serve churches; and to receive moderate wages; 3 August, 1350. (Latin.) Wilkins, "Concilia," iii. 1.]

. . . The general complaint reaches us, and that effective teacher, experience, shows us, that the priests now surviving, not considering that they have been preserved from the perils of the late pestilence to perform their ministry for the sake of God's people . . . and not on account of their own merits; and not blushing, in that their insatiable avarice is mischievously drawn into an example by other workers, disregard the cure of souls . . . not caring to undertake such cure, or bear the burdens pertaining to it, and betake themselves to the celebration of annuals and other private masses.   And, not contented with the accustomed stipends, they exact excessive payment for their services, so that under an unpretentious name, and with but light labour, they may claim more profit than if they had cure of souls.   Whence it will come to pass, unless their unreasonable appetite be restrained, that many churches, prebends, and chapels will remain utterly destitute of the services of priests.

9.

[Petition of the Commons, 1354. (French.) "Rolls of Parliament," ii. 261.]

The Commons also ask that since, by reason of the great cheapness and abundance of corn in the realm, labourers and artificers are not willing to serve a whole half year, or a quarter, nor take allowance of corn as they were wont to do formerly, but will only serve by the day, taking all their hire in money; and also they take bovates [1] and half bovates from the lords, the which is not sufficient to maintain them or keep them occupied, to excuse themselves from serving by terms, and the remainder of the time they serve by the day, taking their hire in money . . . that it may please our lord the King and his Council that the Statute of Labourers be expressly declared on this point, and fitting remedy be ordained in other ways against these mischiefs.

Answer.—As for this article, the Statute is sufficient upon the point, if it be used and well executed.

[1] The eighth part of a plough-land.

10.

["Statutes of the Realm," i. 366. (French.) St. 34 E. III, c. 11.
(1360).]

It is assented in this present Parliament that the Statute
of Labourers formerly made shall stand in all points, except the pecuniary penalty, as to which it is accorded that
from henceforth the labourers shall not be punished by
fines and ransoms; and it is agreed that the Statute shall
be enforced by punishment . . . in the following manner;—
that the lords of townships may arrest and imprison them
for 15 days, if they will not submit, and then send them
to the nearest gaol, to remain until they are willing to do
so. . . .

And that in this ordinance shall be comprised carpenters
and masons, as well as all other labourers . . . and that
they henceforth take payment by the day, and not by the
week, or in other manner. . . .

And that all alliances and conspiracies of masons and
carpenters made . . . between them shall be henceforth
undone and annulled; so that each mason or carpenter . . .
be compelled by his master whom he serves to do all work
that pertains to him, of freestone or rough stone; and also
every carpenter, according to his degree.

11.

[Knighton, 1362. (Latin.)]

In this . . . year, on January 13th . . . there arose an
excessively violent and horrible storm of wind, greater, as
men believed, than had ever before been known, for woods,
orchards, and trees of all kinds were prostrated, more than
can well be told, many being torn up by the roots in
incredible fashion. . . . It destroyed churches, mills, bel-
fries, walls and houses, and did inestimable damage to
buildings in London. . . .

11

In the same year the people were overwhelmed by a general mortality, which was called the second pestilence. Both great and small folk died, especially infants and the young.

12.

[Extract from a petition, 1363.   "Rolls of Parliament," ii. 279. (French.)]

"Since by the pestilences and the great winds divers extraordinary mischiefs have occurred, so that various manors, lands and tenements, held of our lord the King in chief, as well as others, are all desolate, wasted and ruined, as well the tenant and villein holdings as the chief manors, and such tenants in villeinage as were before cannot now be found . . . and to escape these mischiefs, and to have some profit from their lands, and wastes, the lords of such decayed places lease them, in whole or in part, for a life tenancy."

13.

[Petition in Parliament, 1376.   "Rolls of Parliament," ii. 340. (French.)]

To our lord the king and his sage Parliament, the commons show and entreat that, whereas various ordinances and statutes have been made in divers Parliaments for the punishment of labourers and artificers and other servants, the which have continued subtly, by great malice aforethought, to escape the penalty of the said Ordinances and Statutes; so that as soon as their masters accuse them of mal-service, or wish to pay them for their services according to the form of the Statutes, they take flight and depart suddenly out of their employment, and out of their own district, from county to county, hundred to hundred and town to town, in strange places unknown to their masters; so that they know not where to find them to have remedy or suit against them by virtue of the afore-

said Statutes. And if such vagrant servants be outlawed
at the suit of party, there is no profit to the suitor, or
harm or chastisement for such fugitive servant, because
they cannot be found, and never think of returning to the
district where they have served in this way. And that
above all greater mischief is the receiving of these vagrant
labourers and servants when they have thus fled their
masters' service, for they are taken into service immediately in fresh places, at such high wages that example
and encouragement is given to all servants to go off into
fresh districts, and from master to master, as soon as they
are displeased about anything. And for fear of such flight,
the commons dare not now challenge or offend their servants, but give them whatever they like to ask, in spite
of the Statutes and Ordinances made to the contrary, and
this principally for fear of their being received elsewhere
as is said. But if such fugitive servants were universally
seized throughout the realm, at their coming to offer their
services, and put into the stocks, or sent to the nearest
gaol, to stay there until they had confessed whence they
had come, and from whose service; and if it were known
in all districts that such vagrants were to be arrested in
this way and imprisoned, and not received into the service of others, as they are, they would have no desire to
flee out of their district as they do, to the great impoverishment, ruin, and destruction of the commons, if remedy
be not applied as speedily as possible. And be it known
to the King and his Parliament that many of the aforesaid
wandering labourers have become mendicant beggars, to
lead an idle life, and they generally go out of their own
district into cities, boroughs, and other good towns to beg,
when they are able-bodied, and might well ease the community by living by their labour and service, if they were
willing to serve. Many of them become " staff strykers,"
and lead an idle life, and commonly they rob poor people

11 *

in simple villages, by two, three, or four together, and are
evilly suffered in their malice.   The greater part generally
become strong thieves, increasing their robberies and
felonies every day on all sides, in destruction of the realm.

14.

[The effect of the war on social customs and habits.   Walsingham,
"Historia Anglicana," i. p. 272.]

In the year of grace 1348, which is the 22nd year of
the reign of King Edward, third from the Conquest, when
peace had been secured throughout the whole of England, it seemed to the English that as it were a new
sun was rising over the land, on account of the abundance
of peace, the plenty of all goods, and the glorious victories.
For there was no woman of account who did not possess
somewhat of the spoils of Calais, Caen, and of other cities
across the sea; garments, furs, pillows and household uten-
sils, tablecloths and necklaces, gold and silver cups, linen
cloths and sheets, were to be seen scattered throughout
England in different houses.   Then the ladies of England
began to pride themselves upon the apparel of the ladies
of France, and while the latter lamented the loss of their
things, so the former were rejoicing at having obtained
them.

15.

["Eulogium Historiarum," c. 1362.   From Camden's "Remains".]

The Commons were besotted in excess of apparel, in
wide surcoats reaching to their loins, some in garments
reaching to their heels, close before and flowing out on the
side, so that on the back they make men seem women,
and this they call by a ridiculous name, "Gown".   Their
hoods are little, tied under the chin, and buttoned like
the women's, but set with gold, silver, and precious stones.
Their liripipes reach to their heels, all jagged.   They have

another weed of silk which they call a paltok. Their
hose are of two colours, or pied with more, which with
latchets which they call herlots they tie to their paltoks.
Their girdles are of gold and silver, rich people's worth
20 marks, and those of the middling sort, as squires and
other freemen, worth 100 shillings or five marks, or 20
shillings, when all the time they have not 20 pence in
their coffers. Their shoes and pattens are snowted and
piked more than a finger long, cocking upwards, which they
call "crakows," more like the Devil's claws than men's
trappings, which are fastened to the knees with chains of
gold and silver. And thus they are garmented which are
lions in the hall and hares in the field. They are slow to
bestow gifts, but eager to receive them, forward in jesting,
but wearied by serious discourse. Whence it appears that
this people, on account of the too lavish gifts of God,
grows wanton in pride, luxury, gluttony and the other
deadly sins, whence it is to be feared that a divine scourge
will come upon them.

16.

["Statutes," i. 378; 37 E. III, cc. 8-15 (1363); also "Rolls of Parliament," ii. 278. (French.) A sumptuary ordinance, issued at the
request of the Commons, but withdrawn upon petition in 1365.
Minute regulations are drawn up for the apparel of all ranks;
the following rules were considered suitable for the poorer classes.]

It is ordained . . . first, as to grooms, as well the servants
of great men as of traders and craftsmen, that they shall
be served once a day with meat or fish, the rest with other
food, as milk, cheese, butter, and other such victuals according to their estate. And they shall have cloth for
their apparel whereof the whole cloth does not exceed two
marks. . . . And that they shall not use any article of gold
or silver, or embroidered or enamelled, or of silk. . . .

And their wives, daughters and children shall be of the

same condition in their apparel; they shall wear no veils
exceeding 12d. each. . . .

And that carters, ploughmen, drivers, oxherds, cowherds,
shepherds, swineherds, dairywomen, and other keepers of
beasts, threshers of corn, and all manner of men engaged
in husbandry, and other people who have not goods and
chattels worth 40s., shall wear no cloth save blanket and
russet, 12d. the yard. They shall wear no girdles, and
shall have linen according to their condition. They shall
live upon such food and drink as is suitable, and then not
in excess.

17.

[The use of the English tongue. "Statutes," i. 375; 36 E. III (1362),
I, c. 15. (French.)]

Because it is often shown to the King by the prelates,
dukes, earls, barons, and all the commons, what great
mischiefs have happened to many persons, because the
laws, customs, and statutes of the realm are not commonly
known, by reason that they are pleaded, set forth and
judged in the French tongue, which is too unknown in
the said realm. So that people who plead or are impleaded
in the King's courts and others, have no knowledge or
understanding of what is said for or against them by their
sergeants or pleaders— Also that according to reason
the said laws and customs would the sooner be learned
and known, and better understood in the tongue used in
this realm, and so everyone could better conduct himself
without breaking the law, and better safeguard his inheritance and possessions. And in various other regions and
countries where the King and the nobles and others of
this kingdom have been, there is good governance and full
right is done to all men, because their laws and customs
are learnt and used in the tongue of the land.— For the
above causes the King has ordained and established that

all pleas which shall be pleaded in any of his courts
before any of his justices, . . . or before any other of his
ministers, or in the courts and places of other lords of the
realm, shall be shown, pleaded, defended, answered and
debated in the English tongue. . . . And they shall be
entered and enrolled in Latin.

18.

[Arguments for the translation of the Bible into English.   Wyclif.
   English version of " De officio pastoralis " (Early English Text
   Society); about 1378.]

. . . And here the friars with their fautours sayn that it
is heresy to write thus Goddis lawe in English, and make
it knowen to lewid[1] men. . . . It semeth first that the
wit of Goddis lawe shulde be taught in that tunge that is
more knowen. . . .

Also the worthy realm of France, notwithstanding all
lettings,[2] hath translated the Bible and the Gospels, with
other true sentences of doctors out of Latin into Frenche,.
why shoulden not Englische men do so?   As lords of
England have the Bible in Frenche, so it were not against
reason that they should have the same sentence in English. . . .

. . . And herfore friars have taught in England the
Paternoster in Englische tongue, as men see in the play
of York, and in many other countries.[3]   Sithen the Paternoster is part of Matthew's gospel, as clerks know, why
should not all be turned into English? specially sithen all
Christian men, learned and lewid, that shall be saved,
must algates sue[4] Christ, and know his lore and his life.
But the Commons of Englishmen know it best in their
mother tongue.

[1] Lay, unlearned.   [2] Hindrance.
[3] Districts.   [4] Follow.

19.

[Higden, "Polychronicon". Before 1363. (Trevisa's translation.)]

... Children in scole, ayeinst the usage and manner of all other naciouns beeth compelled for to leve hire own langage, and for to construe hir lessouns and hire thynges in Frensche, and so they haveth seth the Normans came first into Engelond. Also gentil men children beeth i-taught to speke Frensche from the tyme that they beeth i-rokked in hire cradel, and kunneth[1] speke and play with a childes broche. And uplondisshe men wil likne hym self to gentil men, and fondeth[2] with greet busynesse for to speke Frensche, for to be i-tolde of.

[Trevisa's own note, 1385.]

This manere was moche i-used to for firste deth, and is sithe sumdel i-chaunged. For John Cornwaille, a maister of grammer, chaunged the lore in grammer scole, and construccioun of Frensche into Englische; and Richard Pencriche learned the maner techynge of hym and of other men of Pencrich; so that now, the yere of oure Lord a thousand thre hundred and four score and fyve ... in alle the gramere scoles of England, children leveth Frenche and construeth and lerneth in Englische. And heveth therby avauntage in oon side and disavauntage in another side; hire avauntage is, that they lerneth hir grammer in lesse tyme than children were i-woned to do; disavauntage is that now children of grammer scole conneth no more Frenche than can hir left heele, and that is harme for them and they schulle passe the see and travaille in straunge londes, and in many other places. Also gentil men haveth now moche i-left for to teche hire children Frensche.

[Higden]. ... All the longage of the Northumbres, and speciallich at York, is so scharp, slitting, and frotynge and

---

[1] Can, know how to.   [2] Try, seek.

unschape, that we southerne men may that longage
unnethe understonde. I trowe that that is bycause that
they beeth nigh to straunge men and naciouns that
speketh strongliche, and also bycause that the kynges of
Englond woneth alwey fer from that countrey. For they
beeth more i-turned to the south contrey, and if they
gooth to the north contrey they gooth with greet help and
strengthe. The cause why they beeth more in the south
contrey is for hit may be better corne londe, more people,
more noble citees, and more profitable havenes.

20.

[The character of the English. Higden, "Polychronicon" (Trevisa's translation).]

Notheles men of the south beeth esier and more mylde;
and men of the north be more unstable, more cruel, and
more unesy; the myddel men beeth somdele partyners
with bothe. Also they woneth hem to glotonye more than
other men, and beeth more costlewe in mete and in drynke
and in clothyng. . . . These men been speedful bothe on
hors and on foote, able and redy to alle manere dedes of
armes, and beeth i-woned to have the victorie and the
maistrie in everich fight wher no treson is walkynge; and
beeth curious, and kunneth wel i-now telle dedes and
wondres that thei haveth i-seie. Also they gooth in dyvers
londes, unnethe beeth eny men richere in her owne lond
othere more gracious[1] in fer and in straunge londe. They
konneth betre wynne and gete newe than kepe her owne
heritage; therfor it is that they beeth i-spred so wyde and
weneth that everich londe is hir owne heritage.[2] The
men beeth able to al manere sleithe and witte, but to fore

[1] "More fortunate in far coasts"—a fifteenth century translation;
this gives the sense of the original.

[2] Similarly, "trowing all the world to be a country to them".

the dede blondrynge and hasty, and more wys after the dede; and leveth ofte lightliche what they haveth bygonne. Therfore Eugenius the pope seide that Englisshe men were able to do what ever they wolde, and to be sette and putte to-fore alle othere, nere that light wytte letteth.[1]   And as Hannibal saide that the Romayns myghte nought be overcome but in hir owne cuntray; so Englische men mowe not be overcome in straunge londes, but in hir own cuntray they beeth lightliche overcome.   These men despiseth hir owne and preiseth other menis, and unnethe beeth apaide with hir owne estate;[2] what byfalleth and semeth other men, they wolleth gladlyche take to hem self.   Therfor hit is that a yeman arraieth hym as a squyer, a squyer as a knight, a knight as a duke, and a duke as a king.

21.

[Life in London.   From a petition in Parliament, 1354.   "Rolls of Parliament," ii. 258.   (French.)]

Whereas the city of London is the dwelling-place of our lord the King and of all the great men and great part of the commons, and foreign merchants and others, more than anywhere else in the realm, . . . in the said city there is such great dearness of victuals, as of wines, meat, fish, hay, oats, poultry, and all other things, that for the most part they are sold three times as dearly as they were bought, to the great damage of the King, the great men, and the commons, especially giving occasion to foreign merchants, who come to England for the staple or other advantage of the realm, to refrain from coming, owing to this, and for default of justice in the city—to the bad example of all the cities, boroughs, and market towns in England.

[1] "If inconstancy did not prevent them."
[2] "Never content of the state of their degree" (15th cent. translation).

22.

[Notice to the Mayor and Sheriffs, 1355. (Latin.) " Foedera," III, i. 303.]

Because armourers and others who have armour for sale,. anticipating the need of the great men and other our faithful lieges, who are shortly to set out with us for the defence of the realm, for such armour, are now attempting to sell all kinds of armour . . . at too excessive price, and otherwise than it used commonly to be sold before the announcement of the expedition; to the no small loss of ourselves and our lieges, and the evident hindrance of our setting out—We command you . . . to cause speedy search to be made in all houses of armourers and others who have arms for sale, and to cause these to be appraised, taking into consideration the value of the metal and the making and preparing of them, and sold at a moderate profit . . . so that by your negligence, and the cunning malice of these armourers, the said expedition be not delayed.

23.

[Ordinance for the keeping of the peace within the city and its suburbs, 1363. (French.) " Foedera," III, ii. 705.]

For the keeping of our lord the King's peace in the city of London and its suburbs, it is ordained by the King and his Council, with the assent of the mayor, aldermen, and community of the city, as follows :—

That none shall be so bold to go wandering in the city or its suburbs after the hour of curfew, rung at the Church of Our Lady at Bow, unless it be one known to be of good report, or his servant, for good cause, and then with a light; the which curfew shall be sounded at dusk.

And if any be found wandering contrary to this ordinance, he shall at once be arrested and sent to Newgate prison, to stay there until he has paid a fine to the City for his contempt, and given surety for his good behaviour.

Also that none . . . come armed into the City or its suburbs, nor bear arms by day or night, except the servants of the great lords of the land, bearing their masters' swords in their presence ; the sergeants-at-arms of our lord the King, Madame the Queen, the Prince, and the King's other children ; and the officers of the city, with those who shall accompany them, to help them in keeping the peace. . . . Upon the same penalty, and with forfeit of their arms and armour.

Also, that every hosteler and innkeeper shall warn his guests to leave their arms at their inns, when they are lodged there ; if they do not do so, for lack of warning by the host, and if they shall be found bearing arms, contrary to this ordinance, the host shall be punished by fine or imprisonment. . . .

Also . . . if any person draw a sword or knife, even though he do not strike, he shall pay half a mark to the city, or stay in prison for 40 days ; if he strike another with his fist, though he have not drawn blood, he shall pay 2s. or eight days' imprisonment ; if he draw blood with his fist, he shall pay 40d. or have twelve days' imprisonment. And before they are set free, such persons shall give surety for their good behaviour. . . .

Also that no trader or other, having a dwelling in the city, shall keep in his employment or service, or in any other manner, men other than those for whose good behaviour he is willing to answer to the King and the people. . . .

Also, that each alderman shall cause good watches to be made in his ward, for the better keeping of the peace, so that, if ill come from default of the watches, the alderman shall answer for it at his peril. . . . And he shall keep the names of all persons living or staying with the dwellers in his ward, as well those who are put into private places for work, as others.

24.

[The abuse of Purveyance. From the letters addressed to Edward III, probably by Archbishop Simon Meopham, before 1333, "De Speculo Regis Edwardi," ed. Moisant. (Latin.)]

"My lord King, behold what deceits are practised by your court in these days. Proclamation is made in the markets that none shall take oats or other things from any persons unless he pay for them as he is bound, under heavy penalty—And none the less, the harbingers of your court, and various grooms and servants, take many goods by violence from their owners, bread, beer, eggs, poultry, beans, peas, oats, and other things, for which scarcely any payment is made. . . .

And they take men and horses during agricultural labour, and plough beasts and beasts of burden, to labour for two or three days in your service, receiving nothing for their labour."

25.

["Statutes," i. 371. (French.) 1363. According to the law, the position had changed very greatly since 1333, several important statutes further restraining it having been passed before 1340. During the century the custom was followed by other great persons.]

For the grievous complaint which has been made of purveyors of victuals for the households of the King and queen, and their eldest son, and of other lords and ladies of the realm, the King of his own will, without motion of the great men or commons has granted and ordained, in ease of his people, that from henceforth no man of the said realm shall have right of taking, but only himself and the queen his companion. And moreover . . . it is ordained and established that upon such purveyances henceforth to be made for the households of the King and queen, ready payment shall be made in hand, namely, the price for which such victuals are sold commonly in the neighbouring markets.

And that the hateful name of purveyor be changed, and named buyer; and if the buyer cannot well agree with the seller of that which he requires, then the takings which shall be made for the said two households shall be made by view, testimony, or appraisement of the lords, or their bailiffs, constables, and four good men of every town, and that by indenture to be made between the buyers and the said lords or bailiffs. . . .

And the takings shall be made in fitting and easy manner, without duresse, compulsion, menace, or other villainy, and in such places where there is greatest plenty, and at a meet time. And that no more be taken than be required for the same two households; and that the number of the buyers be diminished as much as well may be; and such persons shall be buyers as be sufficient to answer to the King and his people. . . .

And that none be bound to obey the buyers of other lords against his will, nor those of the said two households, unless they make ready payment in hand. . . .

And for the carriage . . . for all manner of takings and buyings to be made . . . ready payment shall be given, in the same manner as for the takings. . . .[1]

And if any buyer, after the new commissions be made, make any takings or buyings, or any taking of carriage in other manner than is specified . . . he shall have punishment of life and limb, as in other statutes is ordained of purveyors.

---

[1] It was customary for payment to be made by means of receipts, or tallies, payable often at some place a considerable distance away.

26.

[Petition in Parliament, 1376. " Rolls of Parliament." (French.)]

The commons pray that whereas in times past our lord
the King and his progenitors used to have their own
carriage, namely, horses and carts for the service of their
household—now the purveyors of his household, in default
of his own carriage, and of good management, take horses,
carriages and carts of the poor commons, for ten leagues
around where the King is keeping his household, as well
those of persons belonging to districts three or four score
leagues away, passing along the road, as of persons dwelling in the same district. . . . Wherefore they entreat, as a
work of charity, that it may be ordained that our lord the
King be served for himself and his household with carriage
. . . at his own cost, without burdening or damaging the
poor commons.

27.

[Livery and Maintenance. "Statutes," ii. 74 (1390) ; 13 Rich. II,
c. 3. (French.)]

Because by the laws and customs of our realm, which by
the oath made at our coronation, we are bound to preserve,
all our lieges within the said realm, as well poor as rich,
ought freely to sue, defend, and have justice and right,
and the accomplishment and execution thereof, in any of
our courts and elsewhere, without being disturbed or oppressed by maintenance, threat, or in any other manner ;—
and now so it is, that in many of our Parliaments hereto-
fore held, especially in the Parliaments held last at Cambridge and Westminster, grievous plaint and great clamour
hath been made to us, as well by the lords spiritual and
temporal as by the commons of the said realm, of the great
and outrageous oppressions and maintenance made to the

damage of us and our people, in divers parts of the realm, by divers maintainors, instigators, barettors, procurours, and embracers of quarrels and inquests in the country, many of whom are all the more encouraged and bold in their maintenance and evil deeds aforesaid, because they are of the retinue of lords and others of our realm, with fees, robes and other liveries called liveries of company—

We have ordained and straitly forbidden, by the advice of our great council, that any prelate or other man of Holy Church, or batchelor, squire, or other of less estate, give any manner of such livery called livery of company.

And that no duke, earl, baron, or banneret give such livery of company to a knight or squire, if he be not retained with him by indenture for the term of his life, for peace or war, without fraud or evil device, or unless he be a domestic and familiar dwelling in his household; nor to any valet called yeoman archer, nor other of less estate than squire, if he be not in like manner a familiar abiding in his household.

And that all lords spiritual and temporal, and all others of what condition or estate they be, shall utterly oust all such maintainors . . . from their fees, robes, and all manner of liveries, and from their service, company and retinue, without receiving any such in their retinue in time to come; and that no lord spiritual or any other who hath or shall have people of his retinue, shall suffer any that belong to him to be a maintainor . . . in any manner, but shall put them away from his service, as soon as it can be discovered. . . .

And that none of our lieges, great or small, of whatever condition or estate, whether he be of the retinue of any lord or other person whatever not being of a retinue, shall undertake any quarrel other than his own, nor maintain it by himself or by other, secretly or openly; and that all those who use and wear such livery called livery of company, contrary to this our ordinance, shall leave them off altogether within ten days after the proclamation of this ordinance, without using or wearing them any more afterwards.

BOOK III. ECCLESIASTICAL AFFAIRS.

1.

[Petition to the King in Parliament against the provision of aliens to English benefices, 1343. "Rolls of Parliament," ii. 144. "Petition of the Community." (French.)]

Whereas aliens hold so many benefices in this land, and the alms that were wont to be distributed from them are withdrawn, much of the treasure of the land is carried beyond the sea, in maintenance of your enemies, the secrets of the realm are revealed, and your liege clerks in this country have the less advancement;—and now lately several cardinals have been made, to two of whom the Pope has granted benefices in this land amounting to 6000 marks a year. . . . And the commons have heard that one of these two cardinals, to wit, the cardinal of Périgord, is the King's fiercest enemy at the papal court, and the most hostile to his interests. And from year to year the country will be so filled with aliens that it may be a great peril, and scarcely any clerk over here, the son of a great lord or other, will find a benefice wherewith he may be advanced—Wherefore the commons beg a remedy, for they cannot, and will not, endure it longer; and that it may please the King to write to the Apostolic See . . . requesting the Pope to suspend these charges and recall what has been done. . . .

Answer.—The King is advised of this mischief, and he is willing that remedy and amendment may be ordained,

178

between the great men and commons, if it can be agreed upon; and also he wills and agrees that good letters shall be made to the Pope touching this matter, as well in the name of the King and the great men as of the commons.

2.

[The letter, 8 May, 1343, inserted by Murimuth in his "Chronicle". (Latin.)]

To the most holy father in God, our lord Clement, by divine providence sovereign bishop of the holy church of Rome and of the Church universal, his humble and devoted sons the princes, dukes, earls, barons, knights, citizens, burgesses and all the commons of the Kingdom of England, assembled in th-   rliament holden at Westminster in the quinzaine o_ ᴜaster last past, devoutly kissing his feet with all reverence and humility. Most holy father, the holy discernment, government, and equity which are manifest in you and ought to reign in so holy and high a prelate, head of holy Church, by whom all holy Church and the people of God ought, as by the sun, to be enlightened, give us sure hope that the just prayers, to the honour of Jesus Christ and of his holy Church, offered by us to your Holiness, will be graciously hearkened to by you, and all faults and wrongs be done away and removed, in fruitful accomplishment and remedy, by the grace of the Holy Ghost, who hath chosen and accepted you for such high state, and by you applied and graciously ordained. Wherefore, most holy father, we all in full consultation, by common assent do in lively manner set forth to your Holiness that the noble Kings of England, and our forefathers and predecessors and we, according to the grace of the Holy Ghost, to them and to us devised and giving each one in his devotion, have ordained and established, founded and endowed within the kingdom of England cathedrals and collegiate churches, abbeys and

12 *

priories, and other divers religious houses, and in them
have ordained, and to the prelates and governors of the
said places have given, lands, possessions, patrimonies,
franchises, advowsons, and patronages of dignities, prebends, offices, churches, and other many benefices: to this
end and intent, that the cure and government of such
benefices might be given to such persons, as that by them
the service of God and the Christian faith might be
honoured, increased, and embellished, hospitalities and
alms given and maintained, Churches and buildings
honourably preserved and kept, devout prayers offered up
therein for founders, poor parishioners aided and comforted; and that by them those whose cure they should
have might in their own tongue, in confession and otherwise, be fully taught and instructed. And inasmuch,
most holy father, as you cannot have notice of the faults
and shortcomings of the persons and places so far removed, if you be not informed thereof, we, having full
knowledge of the faults and shortcomings and of the
state of the persons and places aforesaid within the said
kingdom, do make known to your Holiness that, by means
of divers reservations, provisions, and collations granted
by your predecessors, apostles of Rome, and by you, most
holy father, in your time more largely than they were
wont to be, as well to foreign and divers nations and to
some our enemies not having knowledge of the tongue nor
the condition of those whose government and cure should
belong to them, as to others who are not fit, there come
to pass dangers and mischiefs which are these—the souls
of parishioners are imperilled, the service of God is destroyed, alms are withdrawn, hospitalities impoverished,
churches and buildings thereto belonging fallen into decay, charity stinted, cure of souls and the government
which belongeth thereto brought to naught, devotion of
the people checked, honest persons of the realm unad-

vanced, as well as many scholars, the treasure of the realm carried away, contrary to the intent and pious will of the founders. Which faults, shortcomings, dangers, and scandals, most holy father, we cannot nor ought not to suffer or endure. Therefore we humbly beg that the faults, shortcomings and divers perils which may thence come to pass being discreetly considered, it may please you both to recall such reservations, provisions, and collations, and to ordain that they be not henceforth made, and to apply fitting remedy for the evils which may thence arise, follow and ensue ; and that the benefices, buildings, and rights thereto belonging may to the honour of God be had in charge, defended and governed by persons of the said realm. And may it please your Holiness to signify unto us by your holy letters your intention upon this our petition without captious delay, understanding for certain that we shall on no account fail to apply our care and travail to get remedy and fitting correction in the matters aforesaid.

In witness whereof to these our letters patent we have set our seals. Given in full Parliament at Westminster, on the 8th day of May, the year of grace 1343.

3.

[Presentation of letters from England to the Pope, 1343. Cotton MS. Nero D. 10, *apud* Murimuth. Rolls Series. Appendix. (Latin.) The King had also addressed private letters to the Pope, which were now presented.]

Sir John de Shoreditch, a knight of much wisdom, and professor of law, was appointed to bear these letters to the Pope. And on the same day of his arrival at Avignon, after dinner, he went to the Pope's chamber and presented the letters to him in the name of the King and the magnates of England. The Pope, being aware of the reason of his coming, had summoned all the cardinals to the court, and shut them within his private chamber, himself remaining in the great chamber. And when Sir John had made his reverence, he was taken into the private chamber, where the Pope placed himself in his chair of state, in the presence of all the cardinals, before whom Sir John presented his letters. Whereupon he was removed from the private chamber, and the Pope had the letters read; after which he was again led into the chamber.

Then he had to listen to many harsh words, and among other things the Pope said that he had not made provision to vacant benefices for any aliens, save only two. Whereto Sir John replied, in presence of all the cardinals, "Holy Father, you have appointed to the Deanery of York the lord of Périgord, whom the King and all the nobles of England hold for a mortal enemy of the King and the realm". Finally the Pope said, "We know who drew up and dictated those letters, and we know that you did not do it; but one there is who is stinging us, and we will punish him. We know everything!" He added that a certain knight was repeating infamous things about his person and about the Roman Church; whereat the Pope showed himself much offended. And he said that he would write an answer as to the matters contained in the aforesaid letters to the King and the community.

Having heard this the Cardinals withdrew from the palace, as it were somewhat gloomy and perturbed. And Sir John made haste to get away from Avignon, lest perchance he should meet with some hindrance. . . .

4.

[Murimuth.]

From all this it may be gathered how the Apostolic See strives to apply the wealth of the realm of England to itself, both directly and by means of the cardinals and others about the papal court, in whose hands are the best benefices of the kingdom. . . . To such an extent that the riches carried abroad to the Roman court and to foreigners exceed the King's accustomed annual revenue; and from this same treasure, as it is believed, the King's enemies are in great part comforted. . . . Whence, it is become a proverb at the papal court that the English are good asses, bearing all the intolerable burdens laid upon them.

But no remedy can be applied against these by the bishops and prelates, because, since they are themselves almost all promoted by the Holy See, they dare not utter a word whereby they may offend it. While the King and the nobles, though they have ordained a remedy, yet by lavishing letters and prayers in favour of unworthy dependants, they impudently procure the contrary, and they are lukewarm in every good purpose.

5.

[A demand for English Cardinals. Geoffrey le Baker, 1350. (Latin.)]

The King wrote to the Supreme Pontiff entreating that he would advance some clerk of his realm to a cardinal's rank, declaring that he wondered greatly, in that the Roman court had not vouchsafed to receive any Englishman into that sacred order for a long time. . . . The Pope wrote in reply, that the King should make choice among the clerks of his realm of those most fit for this honour, and the Holy Father would willingly consent to his desire touching those chosen, provided that they were approved by the verdict of the cardinals, as is meet for the sought-for dignity, to the honour of God and the Universal Church.

The King chose Master John Bàteman, Bishop of Norwich, and Ralph de Stratford, Bishop of London, and presented them by his letters, to the Papal court; and

they awaited the completion of the business at the said
court for a long time, but in vain. In the meantime,
however, John of Valois . . . presented many of his clerks
for promotion by the grace of the Apostolic See, from
whom the Pope created twelve cardinals.

6.

[The first Statute of Provisors. "Statutes of the Realm," i. 316.
Also "Rolls of Parliament," ii. 232. (French.) The Statute
opens with a long preamble, referring to the Statute of Carlisle
of 1307, and rehearsing the circumstances leading to it.]

. . . It is shown to our lord the King, by the grievous
complaint of all the community of his realm . . . that now
of late our holy father the Pope, by the procurement of
clerks and otherwise, hath reserved, and doth daily reserve
to his collation generally and especially, as well archbishoprics, bishoprics, abbeys, and priories as all other
dignities and other benefices of England which . . . be of
the advowry of people of Holy Church, and give the same
as well to aliens as to denizens, taking of such benefices
the first-fruits and many other profits. . . . Our lord the
King, seeing the mischief and damages before mentioned,
and having regard to the statute made in the time of his
grandfather (which statute holdeth always its force, and
was never undone nor annulled in any point, and therefore
is he bound by his oath to cause it to be kept as the law of
his realm, though that by sufferance and negligence attempt
hath since been made to the contrary) . . . hath ordained
and established—

That the free election of archbishoprics, bishoprics, and
all other elective benefices and dignities in England, shall
be held henceforth in the manner as they were granted by
the King's progenitors, and founded by the ancestors of
other lords.

And that all prelates and other people of Holy Church

who have advowsons of any benefices, of the gift of our
lord the King and his progenitors, or of other lords and
donors . . . shall have their collations and other presentments freely in manner as they were enfeoffed by their
donors.

And in case that any reservation, collation, or provision
be made by the Court of Rome of any archbishopric,
bishopric, dignity, or other benefice, in disturbance of the
aforesaid elections . . ., so that such reservations, collations or provisions should take effect at the time of the
voidance, at the same voidance our lord the King and his
heirs shall have and enjoy for that time the collation to
archbishoprics . . . and other elective dignities which are
of his advowry, such as his progenitors had before free
election was granted. . . .

And that if such reservation . . . be made of any house
of religion of the King's advowry, in disturbance of free
election, our lord the King . . . shall have the collation
for that time, to give the dignity to a suitable person.

And in case that any reservation . . . be made by the
Court of Rome of any church, prebend, or other benefice
which be of the advowry of people of Holy Church, of
which the King is the advowee paramount immediate; at
the time of voidance, when such reservation . . . should
take effect, the King and his heirs shall have the presentation . . . for that time; and so from time to time when
such people of Holy Church shall be disturbed in their
presentments. . . . Saving to them the right of their
advowson and presentation when no collation or provision
thereof is made by the Court of Rome; or when they
shall dare and be willing to make presentation, . . . and
their presentees are able to enjoy the effect of their
presentments.

And in the same manner every other lord . . . shall
have the collations or presentments to the houses of

religion which be of his advowry, and to benefices of Holy
Church which belong to the same houses.

[If they do not present within a half-year, and the
Bishop take no action, the King shall present.]

And in case that the presentees of the King or of other
patrons of Holy Church, or of their avowees . . . be
disturbed by such provisions, so that they may not have
provision of such benefices . . . or they which be in
possession of such benefices be impeached upon their
possession by such provisors, then the said provisors, their
procurators, executors, and notaries, shall be attached by
their body and brought to answer; and if they be convicted they shall remain in prison without being let to
mainprise or bail, or otherwise delivered, until they have
made fine and ransom to the King at his will, and satisfaction to the party who shall be aggrieved.

And none the less, before they be delivered, they shall
make full renunciation and find sufficient surety that they
will not attempt such thing in time to come, nor sue any
process against any person, by themselves or by others, in
the Court of Rome or elsewhere, for any such imprisonment or renunciation, nor any other thing dependent on
them.

7.

[The first Statute of Præmunire, 1353. "Statutes," i. 329. (French.)
"A Statute against annullers of Judgments in the King's Court."]

Our lord the King, by the assent and prayer of the great
men and the commons of this realm of England, at his
great Council holden at Westminster, the Monday next
after the Feast of St. Matthew the Apostle, the twenty-
seventh year of his reign of England, and of France the
fourteenth, in amendment of his said realm, and maintenance of the laws of and usages thereof, hath ordained and
established these things underwritten.

First, because it is shewed to our lord the King, by the grievous and clamorous plaints of the great men and commons aforesaid, how that divers of the people be, and have been drawn out of the realm to answer of things whereof the cognisance pertaineth to the King's court; and also that the judgments in the same court be impeached in another court, in prejudice and disherison of our lord the King and of his crown, and of all the people of his said realm, and to the undoing and destruction of the Common law of the said realm at all times used. Whereupon, good deliberation had with the great men and other of his said council, it is assented and accorded by our lord the King and the great men and commons aforesaid, that all the people of the King's ligeance, of what condition that they be, which shall draw any out of the realm in plea whereof the cognisance pertaineth to the King's court, or of things whereof judgments be given in the King's court; or which do sue in any other court to defeat or impeach the judgments given in the King's court, shall have a day, containing the space of two months, by warning to be made to them in the place where the possessions be which be in debate, or otherwise where they have lands or other possessions, by the sheriffs or other the King's ministers, to appear before the King and his council or in his chancery, or before the King's justices in his places of the one bench or the other, or before other the King's justices which to the same shall be deputed, to answer in their proper persons to the King of the contempt done in this behalf. And if they come not at the said day in their proper persons to be at the law, they, their procurators, attorneys, executors, notaries, and maintainors, shall from that day forth be put out of the King's protection, and their lands, goods, and chattels forfeit to the King, and their bodies, wheresoever they may be found, shall be taken and imprisoned, and ransomed at the King's will. And upon the same a writ shall be made to take them by their bodies, and to seize their lands, goods, and possessions into the King's hands; and if it be returned that they be not found, they shall be put in exigent and outlawed.

8.

[Refusal of the papal demand for tribute in the Parliament of 1366. "Rolls of Parliament," ii. 290. (French.)]

The Chancellor told them how the King had heard that the Pope, by force of an oath that he said King John made to the Pope, to do him homage for the realm of England and the land of Ireland, and that by reason of the said homage, he should pay a thousand marks every year perpetually, is desirous of bringing process against the King and his realm to recover the said service and tribute. And that the King prayed the prelates, dukes, earls, and barons for their advice and good council upon this, as to what he should do in case the Pope should wish to proceed against him or his realm of England for this cause.

The prelates requested the King that they might take counsel upon this separately, and give their answer on the next day. And on this next day first they by themselves, and then the other dukes, earls, barons, and great men replied—that neither the said King John nor any other could put him nor his realm nor his people in such subjection without their assent and accord.

And the commons having been asked about this, and having taken counsel replied in the same manner.

And beyond this, the dukes, earls, barons, great men, and commons agreed and granted, that in case the Pope should strive or attempt anything by process or in any other manner, to constrain the King or his subjects what it is said that he wishes to claim, that they will resist and oppose it with all their might.

9.

[For John de Wyclif, professor of theology, and others, to treat with the papal nuncios. (Latin.) "Foedera," III. ii. 1007.]

The King to all to whose notice these present letters shall come, greeting—Know that we, having full confidence in their loyalty and discretion, have appointed the venerable father John Bishop of Bangor, and our beloved lieges Master John Wyclif, professor of theology and [5 others] our special ambassadors, nuncios, and procurators to parts abroad, giving them, five, or six of them, of whom we wish the aforesaid bishop to be one, authority, power and special mandate to treat and take friendly counsel with the ambassadors of the Supreme Pontiff upon certain business for which we lately sent the aforesaid bishop [and others] to the Apostolic See; and to make full report as to those matters which shall have been treated and agreed upon among them to us and our council. That those things which may concern the honour of Holy Church and the preservation of the rights of our crown, and of our realm of England in this matter may by the guidance of God and the Holy Apostolic See, be despatched. and brought to a favourable conclusion.

Given at London, on the 26th day of July (1374).

10.

[From a complaint against the Pope and cardinals, 1376. "Rolls of Parliament," ii. 337. (French.) The following extracts are taken from a long statement covering the whole ground of the disputes, and urging a remedy. It was presented in the "Good Parliament".]

There is no man that loves God and Holy Church, the King and the realm of England that has not matter for thought, sorrow, and tears, inasmuch as the court of Rome, that ought to be the fountain and source of holiness, and the uprooter of all covetousness and simony, has

so subtly, little by little, by the sufferance and connivance
of evil persons now more excessively than ever before
drawn to itself the collations of bishoprics and other benefices of Holy Church in England, whereof the tax amounts
to more than five times the amount of all the profits pertaining to the King each year throughout the realm. And
of each bishopric and all the other benefices that the Pope
gives, he will have the tax . . . and of one voidance he
makes two or three by way of translations. And when a
bishop has obtained his bulls, he will be so indebted to the
court of Rome for the tax and other payments and costs,
that he must needs sell the woods of his bishopric, borrow
from his friends, and have aid from his poor tenants and
subsidy from his clergy. . . . Also, there are many persons
who, when they have purchased a benefice, and made payment of the tax, and to the "brocours" of benefices dwelling
in the sinful city of Avignon, they make them let their
benefices to farm, which farm will be sent to the "brocours" to purchase more benefices therewith . . . . And
thus by way of simony and brocage, an ignorant good-for-
nothing shall be advanced to churches and prebends worth
1000 marks, while a Doctor and master of divinity will be
glad to get a little benefice of 20 marks.

And thus clerks lose all hope of being advanced by their
clergy, and all inclination to learn ; and for the same cause,
parents cease to send their children to the schools. . . .

Be it considered, that God has committed His sheep to
our Holy Father to be fed, not to be shorn. . . .

And be it remembered for the common profit that the
Pope's collector, who is an alien, and of the obedience of
France, and also many other open enemies, and spies of
the secret matters of this realm, stay continually in the
City of London, and have their procurators and spies,
Englishmen, Lombards, and others, throughout the
country to spy out the vacancies of benefices, sending

word thereof continually by letter to the court of Rome ;
. . . and also they send certain intelligence of the secrets
of the realm.

. . . And the said collector is receiver of the Pope's
money, keeping a great household in London, with clerks
and officials, just as though it were the dwelling of a prince
or duke.

11.

[The great Statute of Præmunire, 1393. "Statutes," ii. 84-85. (French.)
The statute opens with a long preamble reciting the abuses, and
continues :—]

. . . Our said lord the King, by the assent aforesaid, and
at the request of his Commons, hath ordained and established,   That if any purchase or pursue, or cause to be
purchased or pursued in the court of Rome or elsewhere,
by any such translations, processes, or sentences of excommunication, bulls, instruments, or any other things whatsoever which touch our lord the King, against him and his
crown, and his regalty or his realm . . . or receive them,
or make thereof notification, or any other execution whatsoever within the realm or without—that they, their
notaries, procurators, maintainers, abettors, fautours and
counsellors shall be put out of the King's protection, and
their lands and tenements, goods and chattels forfeit to our
lord the King.   And that they be attached by their bodies,
if they can be found, and brought before the King and his
Council, there to answer to the cases aforesaid ; or that
process be made against them by "Praemunire facias," in
manner as is ordained in other Statutes of Provisors and
others who sue in any other court, in derogation of the
regalty of our lord the King.

12.

[Petition for the removal of clerical ministers in the Parliament of
February, 1371. "Rolls of Parliament," ii. 304. (French.)
The petition was the work of a party having the support of the
court and perhaps also of John of Gaunt; its leader was John
Hastings, Earl of Pembroke. Its object was secured by the resignation of the Chancellorship by William of Wykeham, and of the
office of Treasurer by Bishop Brantingham of Exeter.]

Whereas in this present Parliament it was shown to
our lord the King by all the earls, barons, and commons
of England that the government of the realm has long
been in the hands of men of Holy Church, who cannot be
brought to account for their acts, whereby great mischiefs
have happened in times past, and yet more may happen
in time to come, to the disherison of the crown, and great
prejudice of the realm, for divers causes that might be declared—therefore may it please the King that laymen of
sufficient condition be chosen, and henceforth no other
persons be made Chancellor, Treasurer, clerk of the Privy
Seal, chamberlains or controller of the Exchequer, or other
great officers and governors of the realm. And that this
matter be now established in such manner that it may by
no means be undone, and that nothing may be done to
the contrary in time to come. Saving always to the King
the right of choosing and removing such officers, provided
that they be laymen, as is aforesaid.

13.

[The arrival of the Flagellants in England. Knighton. (Latin.)]

In the year 1349, about Michaelmas, more than six
score men, natives, for the greater part, of Holland and
Zeeland, came to London from Flanders. And twice a
day, sometimes in the Church of St. Paul, sometimes in
other places of the City, in sight of all the people, covered

with a linen cloth from the thighs to the heels, the rest of
the body being bare, and each wearing a cap marked before and behind with a red cross, and holding a scourge
with three thongs having each a knot through which sharp
points were fixed, went barefoot in procession one after
another, scourging their bare and bleeding bodies. Four
of them would sing in their own tongue, all the others
making response, in the manner of litanies sung by
Christians. Three times in their procession all together .
would fling themselves upon the ground, their hands
outspread in the form of a cross, continually singing.
And beginning with the last, one after another, as they
lay, each in turn struck the man before him once with his
flail; and so from one to another, each performed the
same rite to the last. Then each resumed his usual garments, and still wearing their caps and holding their flails,
they returned to their lodging. And it was said that they
performed the same penance every evening.

14.

[Early instance of heresy. (Latin.) From the "Register" of Bishop
Grandison of Exeter (ed. Hingston-Randolph, vol. ii., 1147, 1178 ;
also vol. i., Introduction, whence the following is in part extracted).]

Ralph de Tremur . . . craftily going about as well in
our diocese as in other parts of England for a long time . . .
" a renowned Master of Arts, a learned grammarian, able
to speak fluently in four languages, Latin, French, English, and in the Cornish and Breton tongue. . . . This
man proclaims openly and teaches in secret otherwise
than the Holy Catholic and Apostolic Church believes.
. . . Worse than all, he does his best . . . not only
to lead others along with himself to destruction, but to
secure the secret support of simple and unlearned folk,

13

ignorant of theological verities, and already prone to
heresy; for the purpose of spreading his errors."
(From the Bishop's mandate concerning the matter.)

15.

[Mandate of the Archbishop of Canterbury concerning John Ball's
preaching, 1366. Wilkins, iii. 64. Addressed to the Dean of
Bocking ; from the Archbishop's register. (Latin.)]

It has come to our hearing by common report that one
John Ball, pretending to be a priest, is preaching manifold
errors and scandals within our said jurisdiction, as well to
the ruin of his own soul and the souls of his adherents as
to the manifest scandal of the whole Church. Being unwilling, therefore, to tolerate this hurt, we order you to
warn all and sundry of the said deanery, peremptorily
forbidding any to be present at the preaching of the said
John, on pain of greater excommunication. . . . And de-
nouncing all who shall offend against it, . . . you shall cite
them to appear before us. . . . You shall also cite . . .
the said John to appear personally before us, to make
answer concerning certain articles and interrogations to
be put before him touching the correction and safety of
his soul.

16.

["Chronicon Angliae." Notice of Wyclif's doings about 1377-78.
(Latin.)]

Meanwhile, as men said, the Duke [1] was taking counsel
unceasingly with his accomplices, either as to how he
could render the Church subservient to himself, or else
by what means he could subject the Kingdom in some
way to himself. For he knew that so long as the Church
stood intact he would have difficulty in attaining his ends;

[1] The Duke of Lancaster.

moreover it would be most perilous openly to attempt
what he had in mind, while the might and liberties of the
City of London were inviolate.   Whence he strove first
to subvert the liberties both of the Church and of that
City.

He therefore attached to himself a certain false theo-
logian, or rather, a true enemy of God, who already for
many years in all his lectures in the Schools had been
barking against the Church, because he had been justly
deprived by the Archbishop of a benefice in the University
of Oxford to which he had wrongfully attached himself.
And he had invented many new opinions, lacking indeed
all foundation, but such as were likely to win the ear of
his listeners, inviting to hear him simple persons, who
were always seeking for some novelty, as is the way of
such men.   This man was called John, undeservedly, for
the grace that God gave him he rejected, turning from the
truth, which is God, to empty fables.   And among other
unspeakable things, he denied that the Pope is able to
excommunicate anyone . . . and said, moreover, that
neither the King nor any secular lord could give property
in perpetuity to any person or church; because if such
should habitually commit sin, temporal lords might meritoriously take away from them what they had previously
given—which, he said, was practised in the time of
William Rufus. . . . He asserted, moreover, that, if they
stood in need, temporal lords might lawfully lay claim to
the goods of possessioners to relieve their own want.

These and much more serious things, he had not only
discussed and handled in the Schools of Oxford, but had
also preached publicly in the City of London, more especially to obtain the favour of the Duke and others, whom
he knew to be inclined to pay heed to his opinions.   Then
he found certain lords of the realm who embraced his
imbecilities, and would have hardened him to blunt the

13 *

sword of Peter, protecting him with the secular arm lest
he should be publicly struck with the same. And supported by the patronage of these men, he imparted his
forbidden topics with still greater boldness and daring, so
that he drew with him into error not only the lords, but
certain plain citizens of London. To say truth, he was
not only eloquent but a thorough hypocrite, working
always to one end, namely, that he might spread abroad
report of himself and his opinions.

He made pretence of despising temporal possessions, as
vain and perishable, from love of the things which are
eternal; wherefore he had no intercourse with the possessioners, but adhered to the mendicant orders, the more to
beguile the populace, speaking with approval of their
poverty, and extolling their perfections. . . .

The Duke and the lord Henry Percy were full of praise
for his opinions, busily lauding to the skies his learning
and virtue; and so it came to pass that, puffed up by
their favour, he did not fear to spread his vain teaching
far and wide, hurrying from church to church, and instil-
ling his false ravings into the ears of great numbers of
people.

17.

[Remarks extracted from " The Answer of Master John Wyclif to the
under-written query addressed to him by the lord King of England Richard II, and his Great Council, in the first year of his
reign," 1377. "Fasciculi Zizaniorum," 258. Rolls Series.
(Latin.) A long and reasoned argument was returned to the
inquiry.]

There is a doubt as to whether the kingdom of England
may legitimately, under the urgent necessity of her defence, withhold the treasure of the realm from being
carried abroad, even though the Pope require this on
pain of censure, and by virtue of her obedience.

. . . Every natural body is given power from God of

resisting what is hostile to it, and of duly preserving itself.
. . . Since therefore the realm of England ought, in the
words of Scripture, to be one body, and the clerks, lords,
and community its members, it seems that it has such
power from God, the more clearly in that that body has
been most excellently adorned by Him with virtue and
knowledge.

.   .   .   .

It is proved by the law of conscience, for as well Kings
as lords who have received the burden of governing their
realms or lordships, are bound by the law of conscience
to defend the prosperity and estate of their realms, and
the pious intentions of their forbears, which they would
not do unless they safeguarded the alms of their forefathers
in the form wherein they are founded in their testaments.
. . . For the secular lords of this kingdom gave the
possessions wherefrom the Pope draws forth treasure, not
to the Church at large, but to the Church of England in
particular.

18.

["The manners and customs of the Lollards," c. 1382. The Continuator of Knighton, p. 197. (Latin.) The writer lived, it has
been pointed out, "in the country most affected by Wycliffism".]

So they were called by the people disciples of Wycliffe
and Wycliffites, and a very great many were thus sense-
lessly beguiled into their sect. The original false Lollards,
at the first introduction of this unspeakable sect, wore, for
the most part, russet garments, showing outwardly, as it
were, the simplicity of their hearts, the more subtly to
attract the minds of beholders, and the more securely to
set about teaching and sowing their insane doctrine. . . .
Their opinions prevailed to such an extent that the half,
or the greater part of the people were won over to them,
some sincerely, others from shame or fear; since they

extolled their adherents as worthy of all praise, immaculate, and conspicuous for their goodness, even although their public and private vices might be well known . . . while, on the other hand, those who did not join or favour them, but continued to observe the ancient and sound doctrines of the Church, they declared impious, depraved, malignant and perverse, worthy of all censure, and opponents of the law of God. They asserted that only those turned from them who were malignant and confirmed sinners, not keeping the law of God which they themselves preached; and constantly in all their sayings they made use of this same ending, always alleging " Goddis lawe ". . . .

In all their discourses, their doctrine appeared at first to be devout and full of sweetness, but declining towards the end it became abundant in subtle malice and slander. And although newly converted, and but lately imitators of that sect, all their disciples at once adopted in extraordinary fashion the same manner of speech . . .; and suddenly changing their natural phrase, both men and women became teachers of the evangelic doctrine. . . .

Thus from the day of their coming into the kingdom there has been violent dissension, because they stirred up son against father, the mother against her son's wife, the servants of a household against their master, and, as it were, every man against his neighbour. . . . Never, probably, since the foundation of the Church, were such suspicion, discord, and dissension to be seen. They adopted fittingly enough the name of "Wycliffe's disciples," applied to them everywhere by others; for just as Master John Wycliffe was powerful beyond others in disputation, being held second to none in argument, so these people, even when newly attracted to the sect, became surpassingly eloquent, getting the better of others in all subtleties and wordy encounters, mighty in words and prating. So that what they might not achieve by reason-ing, they made up for by quarrelsome violence, with angry shouting and bombastic words. . . .

These Wycliffites incited both men and women to reject the teaching of all others, instructing them on no account to listen to the mendicant friars, whom they dubbed "false preachers"; they constantly plotted against them, and clamorously proclaimed themselves true and evangelical preachers, in that they had the Gospel translated into the English language. . . . And as a result of their exhorta-tions, the mendicant friars were looked upon with hatred by many in those days, whereby the Wycliffites, em-boldened, strove the more to turn the people's hearts from them, and to hinder them from preaching and asking alms.

19.

["Rolls of Parliament," iii. 124. May, 1382. (French.) Also
"Statutes of the Realm". (Cf. "Chronicon Angliae," 1382,.
"Another Parliament was held in London, wherein there was
granted to the King . . . a tenth from the clergy of the realm,
on condition that he should apply himself to the defence of the
Church, and give assistance in the suppression of the Wycliffite
heretics, who with their corrupt doctrine had polluted nearly the
whole realm".)]

Whereas it is notorious that there are many wretched persons within the realm, going from county to county and from town to town, in certain habits under pretence of great holiness, without license of our Holy Father the Pope, or of the ordinaries, or other sufficient authority; and they preach daily, not only in churches and cemeteries, but in markets, fairs, and other public places where there is great concourse of people, divers sermons containing heresy and notorious errors, to the injury of faith, the destruction of the laws and estate of Holy Church, and the great peril of the people's souls and of all the realm.

The which has been sufficiently found and proved by the reverend father in God the Archbishop of Canterbury, and other prelates, masters of divinity, doctors of canon and civil law, and great part of the clergy of the realm especially summoned for the purpose. And the same persons preach also divers matters of slander, to make discord and dissension between divers estates of the realm, as well temporal as spiritual. . . .

And these preachers, when cited or summoned before the ordinaries, will not obey their mandates, paying no heed to the censures of Holy Church, but expressly despising them. Further, by many subtle words they entice the people in great multitudes to listen to their sermons, and to maintain them in their errors :—

Therefore it is ordained in this Parliament, that after, and according to, the certifications of the prelates, thereon to be made into the Chancery, the King's commissions shall from time to time be issued to the sheriffs and other his officers . . . to arrest all such preachers, their fautors and abettors, and keep them in close prison until they will submit according to reason and the laws of Holy Church.

And the King wishes and commands that the Chancellor shall issue such commissions whenever he shall be certified by the prelates . . . as is aforesaid.

20.

[Wyclif. ("Select English Works," ed. Arnold, iii. 324. From a tract "against worldly clergy," c. 1382.)]

. . . Also they cursen all hem that ben necligent to prison cursed men, but here they cursen hem that God blisseth many times, for oft they cursen wrongfully true men, for prechynge of the Gospel. . . . And God blisseth these true prechours and all that faveren hem in this ; then these worldly clerkis cursen the Kyng and his justices and officeris, for they meyntenen the Gospel and true prechours thereof, and wolen not prison hem for wrongful command-ment of Anticrist and his clerkis. But where ben fouler heretics than these worldly clerkis? . . .

And many times they maken the Kyng and his lordis sue trewe men and the Gospel, when they wenen to sue heretics hardid in their error, and to distroie hem and meynteyne Goddis worship. . . .

Then worldly clerkis maken the Kyng and lordis . . . to tormente his body as he were a stronge thief, and cast him in a deep prisone . . . and thus they betraien our Kyng and lordis, and rob hem of right bileve and rightful doom, and workis of mercy, and stopen Goddis word.

["Rolls of Parliament," iii. 141. Parliament of October, 1382.]

The commons pray that whereas a statute was made in the last Parliament in these words [the ordinance in No. 19 is quoted] . . . the which was never granted by the com-mons, what was said upon this matter being without their assent—that this statute be annulled; for it was not their intent to be made subject to jurisdiction, nor to bind them-selves nor their successors to the prelates more than their ancestors have been bound in times past.

21.

[Continuator of Knighton, 1388. (Latin.)]

The lords and commons of the realm, seeing that the ship of the church was daily being endangered by the in-cessant force of these and innumerable other errors and unspeakable opinions, asked the King for a remedy in the present Parliament. . . . And he, taking the wholesome counsel of the whole Parliament upon the point, ordered the Archbishop of Canterbury and other bishops that each should do his duty more zealously within his diocese, and

punish delinquents, more carefully examine their English
books, uproot error, and study to preserve the unity of the
orthodox faith. . . .

And without delay the King ordered his letters patent to
be sent at once into all counties of the realm, appointing
certain persons in each county to examine such books and
their possessors and speedily to apply remedy, sending
any persons offering resistance to the nearest gaol. . . .
But this was tardily executed, and of little help.

22.

[From the oath of recantation for a Lollard, 1396. Wilkins, iii.
225. From an entry on the "Close Roll".]

I; William Dynot, before yow worshipfull fader and
lord archbishop of Yhork and your clergie, with my fre will
and full avysed, swere to God and to all His seyntes upon
this holy gospell. . . .

. . . And also I shall be buxom to the laws of holy
Church and to yhowe as myn archbishop, and to the laws
upon my power and meyntein them; and also I shall
never more meyntein, ne techen, ne defend errours, conclusions, no teching of the Lollards, ne swych conclusions
and techings that men clopith Lollards doctrin. Ne I shall
her books ne swych books, ne hem or any suspect or
diffamed of Lollardery receyve or company withall wittyn-
glye, or defend in tho maters; and if I knowe ony swiche,
I shall withall the haste that I may do yhowe or els your
ner officers to wyten, and of ther bokes. And also I shall
excite and stirre al tho to good doctrin that I have hindred
with myn doctryne up to my power.

BOOK IV. POLITICAL AND CONSTITUTIONAL.

A. PARLIAMENTARY PROCEEDINGS, 1340-1378.

1.

[In the Parliament held in April, 1340, since the King was in extreme
financial difficulties, an unusually generous grant was made, in a
new form ; the magnates and knights of the shires granted " the
9th sheaf, fleece, and lamb," and the citizens and burgesses " the
very ninth of all their goods ". In return for this, and to allay the
uneasiness caused by his unusual demands of the last three years,
the following Statute was accorded. (" Statutes of the Realm," i.
290 ; 14 Ed. III, Stat. 2, cc. 1 and 4. French.)]

. . . We, wishing to provide for the indemnity of the
said prelates, earls, barons, and others of the community,
and also of the citizens, burgesses, and merchants . . .
will and grant . . . that this same grant which is so
chargeable shall not another time be had in example, nor
fall to their prejudice in time to come ; nor that they be
henceforth charged or grieved to make common aid or to
sustain charge if it be not by common assent of the prelates,
earls, barons, and other magnates and commons of our
realm of England, and that in Parliament.

2.

[After abandoning the Siege of Tournai, Edward, finding that no supplies reached him from England, and that his financial difficulties
were now acute, returned unexpectedly on 30 November, 1340,

prepared to make sweeping inquiries into the management of affairs. Murimuth. (Latin.)]

Soon after his arrival in this manner, the King removed all the sheriffs and other ministers, and put others, even unwillingly, in their places. And he made a knight Chancellor of England, to wit, Sir Robert Bourchier, and another, Treasurer, Sir Robert Sadington (and afterwards Sir Robert Parning), and took counsel of young men, despising that of the old. And he ordained that in each county Justices should sit to inquire concerning the collectors of the "tenths" and "fifteenths" and of wools, and concerning all other officers. And in each county he appointed a chief Justice, an earl, or a great baron, with whom he associated others of middle condition; and these Justices proceeded so rigorously and in such arbitrary fashion, that none escaped unpunished. . . .

And in the quinzaine of Easter, to wit, in the year 1341, . . . the King held a Parliament in London, wherein the prelates, lords and magnates, that is, the peers and community of the realm, with one accord made many good petitions for the community of the realm, and especially that the Great Charter and the Charter of the Forest, and other liberties of the Church should be preserved to the quick. And that those who infringed them, even though it were the King's officers, should be punished; and that the greater officers of the King should be chosen by the peers of the realm in Parliament. And these the King opposed for a long time, according to his private counsel. Thus the Parliament lasted until the eve of Whitsun. Finally the King granted the greater part of the said petitions, but concerning the appointment and election of his officers he would not yield. He agreed however at length that his officers should swear in Parliament that in performing their offices they would do justice to all; and if they did not do so, in every Parliament, on the third day after its opening, they should resign their offices, and make answer to all persons complaining of them; and that the guilty should be punished by the judgment of the peers. Upon this and other matters a statute was made and sealed with the King's seal.

3.

[The statutes, which were drawn up by the Parliamentary opposition, contained concessions greater than any the King had been willing to grant. On 1 October, 1341, Edward definitely revoked these. "Statutes of the Realm," i. 297.]

. . . Whereas in our Parliament summoned at Westminster in the Quinzaine of Easter last past certain articles expressly contrary to the laws and customs of our realm of England and to our prerogatives and royal rights were pretended to be granted by us in the manner of a statute— We, considering that we are bound by our oath to the observance of such laws, customs, rights, and prerogatives, and providently desiring to recall such things to their due state which be so improvidently done; upon conference and treaty had thereupon with the earls, barons, and other wise men of our realm, and because we never consented to the making of the said statute, but, to avoid the dangers which we feared by denying the same (forasmuch as the said Parliament otherwise had been dissolved in discord, without despatching anything, and our urgent business would most probably have been ruined) we dissembled herein, and allowed the same statute to be sealed; it seemed to the earls, barons and other wise men that, since the said statute did not proceed from our free will, it was void, and ought not to have the name of a statute—

And therefore, with their counsel and assent, we have decreed the said statute to be annulled. . . .

Desiring, however, that the articles contained therein

which . . . have before been approved by other statutes of
us or our progenitors . . . shall be observed. . . .

And this we do only for the conservation and reintegra-
tion of the rights of our crown.

4.

[Complaint concerning the demand for hobblers and archers, 1346.
"Rolls of Parliament," ii. 160.   (French.)]

To our lord the king and his Council pray the people of
his commons, for the common profit, that the ordinances,
promises, and grants made in Parliament to the commons
be henceforth held and kept, in ease of the commons against
the great charges and oppressions which they have suffered
for a long time—so that henceforth commissions to the
contrary may not issue out of the Chancery, as charging
the people with Array, men-at-arms, hobelours, archers, and
victuals ; or in any other manner charging the commons
without the assent and grant of Parliament.   And if by
chance commissions to the contrary be sent, that the people
be not bound to obey, nor be charged by them.

Answer—As to the first point of this article,—it is our
pleasure that they be kept and guarded in manner as they
ask.   As to the second point of the same article,—it is well
known that in many Parliaments hitherto, the magnates
and commons have promised our lord the King, to assist
with body and goods so far as they are able, in aid of his
quarrel with France, and the safety of the realm of England.
Therefore the magnates, seeing the necessity that the King
had, before his passage, of men-at-arms, hobelours, and
archers . . . advised that those who had a hundred
shillings' worth of land, and beyond, South of the Trent,
should find men-at-arms, hobelours and archers, according
to the rate of their holding, to go with the King at the
King's wages.   And then those who did not wish to go in

their own person, nor find others, should willingly suffer that they should make contribution, so that the King might hire others in their place. And so it was done, and not otherwise. And the King wills that what was done in this necessity shall not in future be had in example.

5.

[Declaration as to what offences shall be judged treason. 25 Ed. III, Stat. 5, c. 2 (1352) ; "Statutes of the Realm," i. 319. (French.)]

Whereas divers opinions have been before this time, in what case treason shall be held, and in what case not, the King, at the request of the lords and the commons has made the following declaration; namely, that when any compass or imagine the death of our lord the King or our Lady his queen or of their eldest son; or if any violate the King's wife, or his eldest daughter unmarried, or the wife of the King's eldest son and heir; or if any do levy war against our lord the King, or be adherent to the King's enemies in his realm, giving them aid and comfort in the realm or elsewhere, and thereof be provably attainted of open deed by people of their own condition ; and if any counterfeit the King's Great Seal or Privy Seal, or his money, and if any bring false money into the realm . . . knowing it to be false, to merchandise or make payment, in deceit of our lord the King and of his people; and if any slay the Chancellor or Treasurer, or the King's Justices of the one Bench or the other, Justice in Eyre, or of Assize, and any other Justices assigned to hear and determine, being in their places and doing their offices— be it understood that in the above cases, that ought to be judged Treason, which extends to our lord the King and to his royal majesty. And of such Treason the forfeiture of the escheats pertains to the King, as well of the lands and tenements held of others as of himself.

6.

[Appointment of Lords to treat with the Commons in 1373. "Rolls of Parliament," ii. 316. (French.) The causes of summons were first explained by Sir John Knyvett, the Chancellor.]

. . . And he commanded the commons to take thought as to giving good counsel and advice upon the above points; and that they should depart for that day, and return into the said chamber[1] on the morrow, so that they might be near the magnates, who would be in the White Chamber, in case they should desire to have their advice and counsel upon the matter, and upon other matters put before them.

And on that day some of the commons came into the White Chamber in the name of them all, and prayed the lords there present for certain bishops, earls, and barons, with whom they might treat, discuss and debate, the better to accomplish the matters wherewith they were charged; asking for the bishops of London, Winchester, and Bath and Wells, the earls of Arundel, March, Salisbury, Sir Guy Brian, and Sir Henry le Scrope. And it was granted that these should go to the commons and treat with them upon the aforesaid points in the Chamberlain's chamber. Thus deliberation was had between the said magnates and commons until Tuesday, the eve of St. Andrew.[2]

7.

["The Good Parliament," 28 April, 1376. "Rolls of Parliament," ii. 321. (French.)]

On the Monday next after the Feast of St. George, in the 50th year of the reign of our lord King Edward III, that was the first day of the present Parliament, the

___

[1] The Painted Chamber.   [2] Five days later.

greater part of the prelates and lords, and some of the commons were assembled at Westminster before the King himself in his chamber.   But because some of the sheriffs had not then returned their writs of Parliament, and also because some of the prelates, earls, barons, knights of the shires, citizens of the cities, and burgesses of the boroughs were not yet come, the King decided to wait until the following day to declare the causes of this Parliament; and so this was done.   And proclamation was made in the Great Hall at Westminster that all those who were summoned to Parliament should be there the next morning at eight of the clock ; and that all sheriffs should make return there of their writs of Parliament, under heavy penalty.

On this next day the prelates, duke, earls, and barons assembled, with the other magnates and the commons, Justices, and Serjeants-at-law and others, in the Painted Chamber; and there before the King himself and all the rest, Sir John Knyvett, knight, Chancellor of England, by the King's command, pronounced the causes of the summons of the present Parliament—Saying, that the Parliament was held especially for three causes ; The first and principal cause was to make ordinance, by the good counsel of them all, for the maintaining of the peace of his realm of England ; the second was to ordain as to the defence and salvation of the realm externally; and the third, to arrange for carrying on the war that the King must needs wage in pursuit of his quarrel with France, and elsewhere, and in what manner this can be done most speedily, and to the greatest profit and honour of the King and the realm ; asserting expressly that the King had always acted with their good counsel, comfort, and aid, wherefore, praised be God, he had hitherto had good issue ; for the which aids, counsel and comfort he thanked the prelates, lords, and commons heartily, desiring their good

14

continuance henceforth. Therefore the Chancellor prayed
them in the King's name diligently to take counsel, to wit,
the prelates and lords by themselves, and the commons by
themselves, and to make favourable answer as soon as they
well could, for the speedy issue of the Parliament.

[As in 1373, the commons asked for the help of the lords ; the bishops
of London, Norwich, Carlisle and St. Davids ; the earls of March,
Stafford, Warwick and Suffolk ; and the lords Henry Percy, Guy
Brian, Henry le Scrope, and Richard Stafford were chosen.]

(*Chronicon Angliae.*)   When therefore these lords had
had deliberation with the Knights concerning the royal
request, it was agreed among them that they would unanimously refuse what the King asked until certain abuses
and defaults should be corrected, and certain persons, who
were seen to have impoverished the King and the realm,
besmirched his household, and enfeebled his power, should
be removed, and their misdeeds suitably punished. In
these circumstances the question arose as to who among
the knights should speak on behalf of the King, the realm
and the people ; for they feared certain among the King's
confidants who had completely won his goodwill and
favour, and would, as they knew, lay snares for them,
because the commons intended to expose their shortcomings. But in the midst of their anxiety, God en-
kindled the mind of a certain knight called Peter de la
Mare, filling him with abounding wisdom and unlooked-
for eloquence. . . . He showed himself formidable to all
opponents ; by no gifts could he be mollified, by no threats
of the magnates could he be turned from the path of
justice.

(*Rolls of Parliament.*)   Then afterwards the commons
came into Parliament, making open protestation that
they were of as good will and firm purpose to aid their
noble liege lord with their bodies and goods as ever any

others were in times past, and always would be according
to their power. But they said that it seemed to them
certain, that if their liege lord had had loyal counsellors
and good officers about him, he would have been rich in
treasure, and so would have no great need to charge his
commons by way of subsidy, tallage, or otherwise ; having
regard to the great sums of gold that have been brought
into the realm by the ransoms of the Kings of France and
Scotland, and other prisoners. . . . And they said further,
that it appeared to them that, for the singular profit and
advantage of certain privy persons about the King, and
others of their covyne, the King and the realm are greatly
impoverished, and many merchants almost ruined and undone. Wherefore they thought it would be profitable . . .
to apply due correction with all possible speed.

And the commons promised the King that if he would
execute justice and hasty judgment upon those who should
be found guilty, and take from them what law and reason
should give him, they would undertake that with what
they have granted him in this Parliament, he would be
rich enough to maintain his wars and other business for
a long term, without greatly burdening his commons in
any manner in future. Moreover they said that herein
our lord the King would be acting right meritoriously, giving satisfaction to God, and great ease and profit to all his
commons of England ; whereby they would be of better
heart and goodwill to help their liege lord with all their
might, if occasion befel that he needed greater aid from
them. . . .

[They proceeded to make detailed charges against persons employed by
    the Government, involving frauds in connection with the Staple at
    Calais, fraudulent purchase of Government debts from private
    creditors, and the engineering of loans to the King among their
    friends at exorbitant interest. Richard Lyons, a financial agent
    of the Government, and the Chamberlain, Lord Latimer, were

14 *

especially attacked, in spite of the Duke of Lancaster's opposition to the whole proceedings.]

(*Chronicon Angliae.*)   The Duke with feigned mildness, deceitfully seemed to encourage them, saying that he well knew how excellent were the intentions of these knights who were thus labouring for the good estate of the realm ; and therefore they were to make known whatever they thought ought to be corrected, and he would apply the desired remedy.   The knights returned thanks to him, although they knew that he was treacherous.   Then, entering Parliament, and standing around in their places, they deposed against Lord Latimer, the King's Chamberlain, that he was unprofitable to the King and Kingdom, requiring upon this with great urgency that he should be deprived of his office, for that it was said he had often deceived the King and been false to him, not to say a traitor.

Meanwhile Richard Lyons, hearing that he was accused in the same way, and fearing for his skin, sent £1000 to the lord Prince Edward, with other gifts ; for he thought by no means to save himself from peril of death, unless by the Prince's intervention while he was alive.   But in truth, if the lord Prince had lived, without doubt he would have received sentence of death as he deserved.   But the Prince, weighing his villainy in the scales of justice, refused his gold, and sent back everything the said Richard had offered him, charging him to reap the fruits of his ways. . . . But Richard, seeing that the Prince rejected his bribes, sent them, and more copious ones, to the King, imploring his good favour, the which the King graciously accepted, saying in jest that he took them in part payment of the money owing to him—" Since," he said, " this and much more is due to us from him, and he offers us nothing but what is our own ".

Lord Latimer went about among his friends seeking by prayers and gifts for some who should speak in his favour.

Whence the lord Nevill, coveting his goodwill and his money, haughtily challenged Sir Peter de la Mare and his friends as to their charges against Lord Latimer, saying that it was unseemly for so great a peer to be accused by such persons —for, in spite of their accusations, he would remain Lord Latimer, and a peer of the realm. And he added that perchance they might fall into the pit which they had digged. But Sir Peter replied, "Cease, my lord, to intercede for others, since it may be that you will shortly have difficulty in answering for yourself; for we have not yet had discussion concerning your person, nor have we yet touched upon your misdeeds. I assure you that you will soon have enough to do in your own case." At these words, as though thunderstruck, Lord Nevill said no more, but silently awaited his own examination. And soon afterwards he was accused and removed from his office (for he was the King's seneschal), being justly compelled to pay 1000 marks.

[The coming of the Heir Apparent into Parliament. (The Prince of Wales died on 8 June.)]

(*Rolls of Parliament*, ii. 330.) The commons humbly prayed our lord the King that it might please him, for the great comfort of the whole realm, to cause the noble boy Richard of Bordeaux, son and heir of the lord Edward, late the King's son, and Prince of Wales, to come into Parliament, so that the lords and commons of the realm might see and honour him as very heir apparent of the realm. Which being granted, the said Richard came into Parliament before all the lords and commons on the Wednesday the morrow of St. John. . . .

And the Archbishop of Canterbury spoke by the King's desire, saying that although the right noble and puissant Prince the lord Edward was departed . . . none the less the said Prince was as it were present and not absent, in leaving behind him such a fair and noble son, who is his right image and very likeness. . . . And he said that this Richard, who was very heir apparent of the realm, as was his noble father the Prince, ought to be held among them, and all other the King's lieges, in great honour and reverence. . . .

[Petitions in the Parliament. *Ibid.* ii. 333, 355. There were some 140 petitions in all.]

The commons pray that if any officer or other of the King's Council be found in default, and be convicted thereof, or of deceit done to the King or his realm, he may be removed from office and from the King's Council, without at any time being restored; for if any such officer be restored, he will oppress and ruin those who thus impeached him with all his power. . . .

Answer. Defaults shall henceforth be shown to the King and to the lords of his Great Council, and if they seem to them such as to demand it, the King shall, with the advice of his Council, do such judgment as shall seem to him best to be done in such case.

Also, the commons pray that it may please him to establish by statute in this Parliament, that a Parliament shall be held every year, for the correction of errors and deceits, if any be found in the realm—

And that the knights of the shires for these Parliaments be chosen by common election, from the best people of the shires, and not returned by the sheriff alone without due election; upon a certain penalty—

And that in the same manner, the sheriffs of the shires be chosen from year to year, and not appointed by brocage in the King's court, as they are wont, for their singular profit, and by procurement of maintainers of the district, to maintain their deceit and malice, and their false quarrels, as they have commonly done hitherto. . . .

Answer. Touching a Parliament every year, there are

statute and ordinances made upon this point, and be these
duly held and kept; and as to the sheriffs, there is a bill
already answered; and as to the article touching the election of knights to come to Parliament, the King wills that
they be chosen by the common assent of the whole county.

[The Commons ask for the appointment of a Continual Council.
Ibid. ii. 322.]

"The commons, considering the mischiefs of the land
. . ., which is now burdened in divers manners by many
adversities, as well by the wars of France, Spain, Ireland,
Guienne, Brittany, and elsewhere, as otherwise; and that
the officers who are accustomed to be near the King do
not suffice, without others, for such great business of
government—pray therefore that the King's Council be
afforced with lords of the land, prelates and others, to the
number of 10 or 12, according to the King's will, to remain
there continually. In such manner that no important
business pass through or be discharged without the assent
and advice of all, and other lesser business be treated by
the advice of 6 or 4 at least, according as the case require;
so that at least 6 or 4 such councillors be continually
resident at the King's Council."

And the King, understanding this request to be honourable and profitable to himself and the whole realm, granted
it; provided always that the Chancellor, Treasurer, and
all other the King's officers may perform and finish the
business touching their office without the presence of the
said councillors, whom the King has appointed and will
appoint from time to time of such as it shall please him.
And it is ordained and agreed that the councillors now
assigned, and to be assigned in future, shall be sworn to
keep this ordinance, and to do justice to all according to
their power. . . .

Also, . . . that whatever shall be counselled or ordained
whereof report must needs be made to the King, to have

his advice or assent, that such report shall be made by the said councillors, or by two of them chosen by their common consent, and by no others.

And . . . that the Chancellor and Treasurer . . . and all other officers and ministers to whom its execution shall belong, shall make good and hasty execution . . . of each ordinance that shall be ordained by the counsel and advice of the King and the aforesaid councillors. . . . And if default be found in any of them, they shall incur the pain that shall be adjudged by the King and the continual councillors. . . .

(*Ibid.* ii. 330, 6 July, 1376.) Also be it remembered that our lord the King, being at his manor of Eltham, in part in disease of his body, whereby he could not well travel in his own person, sent for the prelates, lords, and commons who were summoned to this Parliament to come to him . . . to hear the answers to the common petitions, and make an end of this present Parliament. And so the same prelates, lords, and commons came, and there were heard, for the greater part, the answers to their common petitions. . . . And also the judgments of persons, and the ordinances made, as well of councillors, as others. . . . Wherefore they all heartily returned thanks to our lord the King.

[The work of this Parliament was immediately undone by John of Gaunt, the Duke of Lancaster, who dismissed the newly-appointed councillors, and restored to favour all those who had been impeached. Edward III died on 21 June, 1377.]

8.

[The Duke of Lancaster's protest in the first Parliament of Richard II, October, 1377. "Rolls of Parliament," iii. 5. (French.) A committee of lords had again been appointed at the commons' request, to advise them, of which the Duke of Lancaster was chosen a member.]

But the Duke, being in his place in Parliament, at once rose, and after bowing low to our lord the King, very humbly prayed that he would hear him a little, for urgent cause touching himself and his own person. And he said that although the commons had thus chosen him for one of the lords to commune with them upon the aforesaid matters, none the less, if it pleased the King, he would not do so until he was excused of that which the commons had evilly spoken about him. For although he were unworthy, yet he was a King's son, and one of the greatest lords of the realm after the King; and they had in such evil wise said that of his person, which, if it were true, which God forbid! would rightfully be held clear treason, that he would never care to do anything until the truth was distinctly known. And he said further, that none of his ancestors, of the one side or the other, was ever a traitor, but they were all good and loyal, and it would be a wondrous thing if he desired to turn aside from the line of his ancestors, as well by reason of nature as otherwise, for he had more to lose than any other in the realm. And that if any man, of whatever estate or condition were so bold as to wish to charge treason or other disloyalty upon him, he would be ready to defend himself by his body or otherwise, by the award of the King and the lords, as readily as the poorest batchelor of the realm.

Upon this all the prelates and lords rose and with one voice excused themselves, entreating the Duke to cease, for they thought there was no man living who would say such a thing; and the commons said that it was evident and notorious that they held him excused of all reproach and ill report, since they had thus chosen him to be their principal aid, comforter, and counsellor in this Parliament, all with one accord entreating him to hold them clear thereof.

The Duke replied that since such words had for a long time been falsely flying about the realm, he marvelled how that any man would begin or carry on such a thing, for shame and peril that might arise thereby; for the man who first invented these tales, whereby debate might easily be provoked among the lords of the realm, was a very traitor, since such debate might turn to the destruction of the realm for ever. And he prayed for good ordinance and just and severe punishment to be ordained in this Parliament against such inventors of lies, to escape the aforesaid mischiefs in time to come; but that it be pardoned for time past, as for his own person.

9.

[Speech of Sir Peter de la Mare. *Ibid.* iii. 5. (French.)]

Then afterwards the commons came into Parliament before the King, and there Sir Peter de la Mare, knight, who spoke for the commons,[1] made his protestation, that what he had to say he should not say of his own motion, but by the motion, assent, and express will of all the commons there present; and if it should happen that he erred in any point, or perchance said aught that was not with the assent of his companions, that it might at once be amended there by them, before they departed from that place—

[Sir Peter first complained of the decay of chivalry, the falling-off in military glory and success, and the general misgovernment, and continued :—]

. . . And because our lord the King, whom God preserve, is at present innocent and of tender age, the commons, for the amendment of the aforesaid mischiefs and the salvation of the realm, that is now in great peril, more than ever it was before, make prayer to the King and the lords of three things in especial—First, that it may please them to appoint in this present Parliament eight sufficient persons . . . to be continually in attendance at

[1] "Avait les paroles de par la commune."

the council with the King's officers, upon the business of
the King and the realm; of such as have best knowledge,
and are willing and able to labour most diligently for the
amendment of these mischiefs, and the good government
and salvation of the realm; in such wise that the commons
may be distinctly certified of the names of these councillors,
who shall have the spending and ordaining of what they
will grant for the wars, and so the commons may have the
better heart to do . . . that wherewith they are charged.

Also that it may please them to appoint in this present
Parliament those who shall be about the King's own
person . . . and that these be of the most virtuous, up-
right, and sufficient in the realm, so that our lord the
King, who is a person sacred and anointed, may be guided
nobly and nurtured in good virtues. . . .

And that it may be ordained that our lord the King's
household be governed with good moderation, in expend-
ing only of the revenues of the realm and the other rights
of his crown and lordships.

And that what shall now be granted for the maintenance
of his war be expended upon the war, and not otherwise,
in aid and discharge of his said commons.

Also that the common law, and the particular laws,
statutes, and ordinances made before this time, for the
common profit and good governance of the realm, be
entirely ratified and confirmed, that by these they may
be honestly governed. . . .

—Entreating the lords of the realm that whatever shall
be ordained in this Parliament be not repealed without
Parliament; and that,—having consideration that the
days are now short, and time is rapidly passing, and
there must be speedy travail about the ordinance of the
realm and the wars, or otherwise the Kingdom is undone,
which God forbid! they will take counsel thereon, and give
good and speedy answer; saving in all things the King's

prerogative and dignity, whereto the commons desire not that prejudice in any wise be done, for their requests.

To this answer was given that the lords would take counsel together, the commons being commanded to return to their place, and treat of the other matters wherewith they were charged, between now and Thursday next; on which day they were commanded to return into Parliament [1] to hear the answer to their requests.

10.

[The Parliament of Gloucester, October, 1378. "Rolls of Parliament," iii. 33. (French.) No military successes were obtained during 1378, in connection either with the suggested naval operations or the expedition to Brittany; on the other hand renewed negotiations with John of Montfort and Charles of Navarre had resulted in giving the English occupation of Cherbourg and Brest. The Chancellor made a long opening speech, explaining the various dangers for which provision must be made.]

On the following Friday, that was the 22nd day of October, the prelates, lords, and commons, assembled in the Great Hall, and there Sir Richard le Scrope, Seneschal of the King's household rose to speak, saying—that although he had not knowledge or worthiness for such a business in so high and noble a place, nevertheless, the King had commanded him to say what he was about to say. And he said—that true it is and clearly evident to all men that our lord the King and his realm of England, and his other lands and lordships are everywhere beset and surrounded by our enemies, who are increasing every day, as well in the parts of Scotland as elsewhere, in manner as my lord Chancellor explained to you yesterday better than I can set it before you; and [he showed you] how that at the present time there are open to us more fair and noble ports and means of entry for harassing our said enemies

[1] "Furent comandez a retourner en Parlement."

than have been in the hands of the English for a long time past; to wit Cherbourg and Brest, to say nothing of Calais, Bordeaux, and Bayonne, which demand no small matter for their safe keeping, but a very great sum. . . . For our lord the King spends every year over £24,000 at Calais and in the marches, and at Brest full 12,000 marks; and now at Cherbourg a heavy outlay must needs be made; and at Bordeaux and Bayonne, for the safety thereof, and in the King's lands and lordships in Guienne and elsewhere across the sea; also in Ireland, for the salvation and guarding of the same, apart from what must perforce be done touching the safe-guarding of the coast, which demands a great sum of money.

But perchance some of you will be inclined to take thought and marvel as to where and in what manner the two " fifteenths " of the laity and the two " tenths " of the clergy, granted in the last Parliament . . . with the subsidy of wools, have been spent in such short time, and what has become of them—Whereto, my lords and sirs, I assure you as very truth, and call to witness the High Treasurer, and all the lords here present, that these two " fifteenths " and " tenths," with the said subsidy, have been entirely expended upon the wars, and not elsewhere, by the hands of John Philpot and William Walworth, treasurers assigned, as you well know, for the war; without a single penny thereof coming into the hands of the King or his officers for his own use.   And you must plainly know that henceforward, our lord the King cannot suffice —and no King in Christendom could suffice—to bear such heavy charges without the aid of his people.   Therefore my lords, prelates and other peers of the realm, the King prays you right earnestly that you will take counsel to-gether by yourselves; and you too,' sirs, the knights, citizens and burgesses, by yourselves—as to how best one can resist the malice and false scheming of his enemies.

. . . And as to whence what must needs be spent is to be raised with the least burden to his loyal people. . . .

Then afterwards the commons returned before the King and the lords of the realm in Parliament, and there Sir James Pickering, knight, who was spokesman on behalf of the commons, making his protestation . . . briefly rehearsed the articles and charges given them by the King [saying]

. . . "And as for that our lord the King asks aid of his commons for the expenses that must be applied for the defence of the realm and his other lordships, lands and strong places abroad, and the exploit of his wars—the commons say that at the last Parliament the same matter was shown to them clearly enough on the King's behalf, at which time the commons replied that it seemed to them, and it was indeed evident, that our lord the King was not in such great need as they were told; for since he had in his hands all the alien priories, the subsidy of wools, the revenues of the realm, the lands and lordships of his noble father the Prince, and of many other great lords of the realm by the nonage of their heirs (wherefrom great revenues arise every year) there must have been great plenty of money in the treasury. Whereto answer was then made by the King's council that, although it was true that he had these lordships in his hands, his recent coronation had been a great expense, and in any case the money . . . could not be raised speedily enough for an expedition in the coming season. But if he were then aided with a good sum, wherewith he might make a great expedition . . . in destruction of his enemies at that time, which would be his beginning in the first year of his reign, then they trusted that he would afterwards have in his hands enough money to maintain the war and defend his realm—Wherefore, say the commons of England, trusting in this promise, to wit, of being discharged of tallages for a

long time to come, the commons then granted the greatest
sum that was ever given to any King in the realm. . . .

"And it seems to them, for anything that has yet been
done, that since this great sum was granted and raised,
part thereof (beyond what was spent upon the last expedition on the sea) and of the other subsidies, revenues, and
profits, should be in the King's treasury; wherefore he
should not now have need to burden his commons again,
who are now poorer than ever they were in times past.
. . . Therefore they entreat the King that he may please,
for God's sake, to hold them excused for this time; for to
say truth, even though he had in fact great need of their
aid, they could not now bear any charge, for sheer
poverty."

To this Sir Richard le Scrope replied, by the King's
command . . . protesting that he knew of no such
promise made in the last Parliament,—"that what the
commons say is not true, to wit, that great part of the
last subsidy is still in the Treasury; for it is notorious that
every penny arising therefrom . . . has been received by
the hands of William Walworth and John Philpot, citizens
of London, treasurers assigned and sworn in the last
Parliament . . . moreover, as they say, they have spent
every penny upon the wars. . . ."

Upon this the commons, having deliberated for a little,
requested the King that it might please him to let it be
shown to them how, and in what manner, the aforesaid
great sums of money . . . were spent . . . and also, that
they might be certified of the names of those who should
be the Great Officers of the realm and the King's councillors and governors of his person for the coming year, while
he is of tender age, in manner as was formerly ordained
in Parliament.

To this Sir Richard answered that although it was hitherto unknown that account should afterwards be rendered to

the commons of a subsidy or other grant made to the King in or out of Parliament by the commons, or to any save to the King and his officers; nevertheless the King willed and commanded, by his own motion, not as of right or by compulsion . . . that the said William Walworth then present, with certain others of the council, appointed for this should show them the receipts and expenses clearly in writing, on the understanding that this should not be drawn into an example or consequence in future . . . and [he said] " our lord the King commands and charges you, entreating you, as do all the lords here present, that—considering the great perils on all sides, and that the maintenance of the war outside the realm has been clearly enough proved before now, by pure reason, to be the best and necessary defence for the whole realm (the which defence touches not only our lord the King but all and each of you), and herein you cannot separate one from the other, in expenditure or otherwise—you will take counsel as to how . . , the said wars and defence can be supported, giving your favourable answer as speedily as you may, so that this Parliament may be well ended, in ease of the King and the lords and yourselves, and in discharge of the poor commons who are paying your expenses every day during this Parliament " .

And the commons . . . also prayed that five or six of the prelates and lords might come to the commons, to treat and commune with them upon the said charges. Whereto the lords made answer, that they would not and ought not to do this; for such manner was never before seen in any Parliament, save in the three Parliaments last past. But they said, and confessed, that it had been wont that the lords should choose a certain small number, six or ten, of themselves, and the commons another such small number of themselves, and that these lords and commons so chosen should talk together, in easy manner, without murmur, shouting, or noise. And thus they would soon come to some certain good purpose, by motion made among them, and this purpose would be further reported to their companions, of the one part and the other. In such manner the lords would now act, and no otherwise; for they said that if the commons wished to remain all together without separating, the lords too would act without dividing.

Whereupon the commons readily agreed to choose certain lords and commons, in small and reasonable number, in manner as had been wont in former times.

And after the commons had seen and examined the aforesaid enrolment, and the receipts and expenditure of the money arising from the subsidy . . . they returned again into Parliament, rehearsing the same matter as they had done before; and also, how that the expenditure upon the last expedition pleased them well, as a thing honourably done. . . . But they said that the war treasurers, according to their account had expended some £46,000 sterling upon the safe-keeping of certain districts, places, and fortresses, not pertaining to the charge of the commons; to wit, part in the march of Calais, part at Brest, Cherbourg, in Gascony and Ireland, and also part upon certain ambassadors to Flanders, Lombardy, Navarre, and Scotland; and part touching the bringing of the King of Scots' ransom. . . . They said that these charges did not pertain to them, nor to the defence of the realm, but were all outside it; wherefore it seemed to them that they ought not to bear or sustain these foreign charges, even if they could support any. But they were answered, "Gascony, and the other strong places that our lord the King has beyond sea are and should be, as it were, barbicans of the realm; and if these barbicans be well guarded, with the safe-keeping of the sea, it will be well enough at peace. But otherwise we shall never have quiet nor peace from our enemies, for then they would make war upon us at our very doors,

15

which God forbid.   Moreover by these barbicans, our lord
the King has good ports and good way of entry upon his
enemies to harass them.   Therefore in all reason you
should cease such words."

[Eventually a subsidy on wool was granted for three years, with a
further increase of 13s. 4d. per sack ; and an additional subsidy on
imports and exports.]

B. The Poll-Tax and the Peasants' Revolt.

11.

[A Parliament had been held in 1379 in which a new form of tax was
adopted, the first Poll-tax—a graduated payment, to which every
person was to contribute.   This, however, Parliament was told in
January, 1380, only produced £22,000, and the commons made
another grant in the usual form of "fifteenths" and "tenths,"
and continued the subsidy on wool.   In spite of this, in November another Parliament had to be called.   "Rolls of Parliament,"
iii. 88. 5 November, 1380. (French.)]

Speech by the Chancellor, Archbishop Simon Sudbury.
"Sirs, it should not be unknown to you how that the
noble lord the Earl of Buckingham, with many other great
lords, knights, and squires, archers and other good men of
the realm—whom may God save in His mercy—are now in
the parts of France in the service of the King and his
realm.   Upon the which expedition the King has spent
more than whatever you gave him at the last Parliament,
and beyond this largely of his own.   And what is more,
by a loan that he has raised—as well for the expedition to
Scotland as for the defence and succour of his lieges in
Guienne, and for the money due to the Earl of March for
the land of Ireland, and in other manner—he has pledged
the greater part of his great jewels, that are on the point
of being forfeited.   And true it is that, by reason of the
present riot in Flanders, nothing has been received from
the subsidy of wools.   And therefore the wages of the

soldiers in the Calais March, Brest, and Cherbourg are now more than a quarter and a half in arrears, whereby the King's castles and fortresses are in great peril, because the soldiers are in point of departing. . . . And you know well that neither our lord the King nor any other King in Christendom could endure such charges without the aid of his commons. Therefore, considering that the King is thus outrageously in debt, and his jewels on the point of being forfeited . . .; and he is bound by covenant . . . to make payment to the Earl of Buckingham and his companions, for the other half year next coming, and to refresh them with men and horses . . .; and also that one must needs make very heavy expenditure for the safe-keeping of the coast against the galleys, this next season, so that the enemy may be better resisted in their malice than they were in the season last past, when, as you know, they did great mischief and villainy in the realm—please you to advise the King, and show, as best you can, wherewith it seems to you that these charges may be borne, with the least trouble to yourselves, and the community, and the realm best defended against all enemies. . . ."

Then afterwards the Chancellor said to the commons . . . that they should depart to their lodging, to ease them, for that day, and return betimes on the morrow. And that for God's sake they should leave all alien matters, whereby rancour or intrigue might arise, and treat to some purpose upon this their charge, and other matters necessary and profitable. . . .

And afterwards, when the commons had talked together and treated for a day upon their charge, they returned into Parliament in the presence of the King and the prelates and lords, and Sir John Gildesburgh, knight, who spoke for the commons, asked in their name to have clearer declaration as to their charge, and in particular of the sum total that it was desired to ask of them . . . praying

15

that this sum might be so modified that no more should be asked than behoved of necessity. . . . Whereupon a schedule previously made by the great officers of the King's Council, was delivered to them, containing divers sums necessary, as was said; the which sums extended to £160,000 sterling. . . .

And upon this they returned again into Parliament, entreating our lord the King and the lords of Parliament, because it seemed to the commons that the sum now asked was very outrageous, and utterly unsupportable, that it might please them to make such moderation therein, that nothing might be asked save what was bearable for them, and necessary to be had now for the above causes. . . .

[They asked the lords to consult together and make suggestions as to possible expedients for raising the money. They did so, and suggested (1) a grant of "fifteenths" in the usual manner; (2) a "poundage" on all merchandise, or (3) another Poll-tax. The commons chose the Poll-tax.]

The grant of the Tax—" First the lords and commons have agreed that, for the aforesaid necessities, there shall be given from every lay person in the realm, male or female, of whatever estate or condition, above the age of fifteen years, three groats; save very beggars, who shall not be charged. . . .

So always that the levy be made in such ordinance and form, that every lay person be charged . . . in manner as follows, to wit, that towards the sum total accounted in each township, the richer shall aid the poorer, in such wise that the richest shall not pay beyond the sum of 60 groats for himself and his wife, and none shall pay less than one groat for himself and his wife. And that no person be charged to pay save where he and his wife and children dwell, or where he resides in service. And that all artificers, labourers, servants, and other lay persons . . . shall be each assessed and tallaged according to the rate of his condition. And that commissions be made to certain persons, to be collectors and controllers of the aforesaid sum. . . .

So that two parts of the grant be paid on the quinzaine of Hilary next coming, and the third at the following Whitsun. So always that no knight, citizen, or burgess who has come to this Parliament be made collector or controller of this levy."

12.

[From a petition of 1377. " Rolls of Parliament," iii. 21. (French.)]

To our lord the King and his Parliament, the commons of the realm show that in many parts of England the villeins and tenants of land in villeinage, who owe services and customs to the lords in various lordships . . . have by the advice, procurement, maintenance and abetting of certain persons, for profit taken from the said villeins and tenants, purchased in the King's court exemplifications from the Book of Domesday, of the manors and townships wherein they dwell. And by colour of these, and through misunderstanding of them, by the evil interpretation of the said counsellors . . . they have withdrawn, and are withdrawing the customs and services due to their lords, holding that they are fully discharged of all manner of service due both from their body and their holdings. And they have refused to permit the servants of their lords to make distraint upon them for the said customs and services, but have made confederation and alliance together to resist their lords and their servants by force, and so that each shall be aiding the other whenever they be distrained for this cause. And they threaten to kill their lords' servants if they make distraint upon them. . . .

And it is feared, if hasty remedy be not applied, that war might easily break out in the realm, because of their said rebellion, or that they will adhere to foreign enemies

. . . if there should be a sudden coming of them. And to maintain these errors and rebellions they have collected among themselves a great sum of money, to pay their costs and expenses.

13.

[The Peasants' Rising of 1381. "Chronicon Angliae." (Latin.)]

The peasants, whom we call villeins or bondsmen, with the rural inhabitants in Essex, coveting greater things, and in hopes of reducing everything into subjection to themselves, came. together in a great multitude and began to make great tumult, demanding their liberty; and they intended in future to be bound to pay service to no man. The men of two villages, who were the authors and prime movers in this mischief, sent word to each village that all, old and young, should flock to them, furnished with such arms as they could get; and that those who did not come, or despised this warning would have their goods destroyed, their houses set on fire or pulled down, and their heads cut off. These terrible threats made all hasten to them, so that in a short time so great a number was assembled that it was estimated at some 5000, of the meanest common people and peasants. . . .

[They sent messengers to the people of Kent.]

When the men of Kent heard news of what they had long hoped for, they too without delay gathered together a large band of commons and peasants, by the same devices wherewith the Essex men had collected their bands, and in a short time stirred up the whole of their county to a similar tumult. And soon they besieged all the roads by which pilgrims go to Canterbury, and stopping all the pilgrims they compelled them to swear; first to be faithful to King Richard and the commons, and to accept no King called John (from hatred of John, Duke of Lancaster, who, on account of his marriage with the daughter

and heiress of Peter, formerly King of Castile, called himself King of Castile); then that they would be ready to
come and join them whenever they should please to
send for them; that they would persuade all their fellow-
citizens and neighbours to hold with them, and would
consent to the raising of no taxes in the realm in future
save the " fifteenths " which alone their fathers and forefathers knew and submitted to.

And so it came to pass that report of this swiftly spread
into Sussex, the counties of Hertford and Cambridge, to
Suffolk and Norfolk. And the whole people waited, and
wondered as to the meaning of these things, and whither
such rash enterprises were tending, many speculating
about a better future, some fearing that they would end
in the ruin of the whole Kingdom ; for they argued that
division would result from these wild attempts, and con-
sequently its desolation and destruction. . . .

And when these great gatherings increased daily, and
already their numbers had become almost infinite, so that
they feared resistance from none, they began to show
what were their designs, and to punish all and sundry
learned in the law, both apprentices and justices, and all
jurors of the countryside whom they could lay hands upon,
by beheading them, declaring that the land could not enjoy her natural liberty until these men were slain. These
sayings mightily pleased the peasants, and conceiving still
greater designs, they resolved to consign to the flames all
court rolls and ancient muniments, so that, when the
record of ancient things had been destroyed, their lords
would not be able to claim any rights against them in
future. And thus it was done. And the lords would not
keep watch to prevent these infamous doings, but remained motionless at home as though' sleeping, until the
men of Kent and Essex were drawing near, having gathered
to them an army of 100,000 common people and peasants.

14.

[John Ball and his preaching.   "Chronicon Angliae."   (Latin.)]

For twenty years and more this man had been preaching continually in different places such things as he knew were pleasing to the people, speaking ill of both ecclesiastics and secular lords, and had rather won the goodwill of the common people than merit in the sight of God.   For he taught the people that tithes ought not to be paid unless he who should give them were richer than the rector or vicar who received them; and that tithes and offerings ought to be withheld if the parishioner were known to be a man of better life than his curate; and also that none were fit for the Kingdom of God who were not born in matrimony.   He taught, moreover, the perverted doctrines of the perfidious John Wycliffe, and the opinions that he held, with many more that it would be tedious to recite. Wherefore, being prohibited by the bishops from preaching in churches, he took to speaking in streets and villages and in the open fields.   Nor did he lack hearers among the common people, whom he always strove to entice to his sermons by pleasing words, and slander of the prelates. At last, having been excommunicated, yet not desisting, he was thrown into prison, where he predicted that he would be set free by 20,000 of his friends—which afterwards happened in the great disturbances, when the commons broke open all the prisons, and made the prisoners depart.

And when he had thus been set free, he followed them, egging them on to commit greater mischiefs, and saying that such things must surely be done.   And, to corrupt the more with his doctrine, at Blackheath, where 20,000 of the commons were gathered together, he began a discourse in this fashion :—

" Whanne Adam dalfe and Eve span
Who was thanne a gentil man ? "

And continuing his sermon, he strove to prove by the
words of the proverb that he had taken for his text, that
from the beginning all men were created equal by nature,
and that servitude had been introduced by the unjust op-
pression of evil men, against the will of God, who, if it had
pleased Him to create serfs, surely in the beginning of
the world would have appointed who should be a serf
and who a lord. Let them consider, therefore, that He
had now given them the hour wherein, laying aside the
yoke of long servitude, they might, if they wished enjoy
their liberty. Wherefore they must be prudent, hasten-
ing to act after the manner of a good husbandman, tilling
his field, and uprooting the tares that are wont to destroy
the grain; first killing the great lords of the realm, then
slaying the lawyers, justices and jurors, and finally root-
ing out everyone whom they knew to be harmful to the
community in future. Thus at last they would obtain
peace and security, if, when the great ones had been removed, there were among them equality of liberty and
nobility, and like dignity and power.

And when he had preached these and many other ravings, he was in such high favour with the people that they
cried out that he should be Archbishop and Chancellor,
and that he alone was worthy of the office, for the present
Archbishop was a traitor to the realm and the commons,
and should be beheaded wherever he could be found.

Moreover, he sent a letter to the leaders of the commons
in Essex, full of dark sayings, and exhorting them to
finish what they had taken in hand; this was afterwards
found upon a man who was to be hanged for taking part
in the disturbance, and ran as follows :—" John Schepe,
summe tyme Seynt Marye preest of Yorke, and now of
Colchestre, gretith wel Jon Nameles, and Jon the mellere,

and Jon Karter, and biddeth them that they be ware of gyle in bourghe, and stondith togidre in Goddes name; and biddeth Piers Plougheman go to his werk, and chastise wel Hob the robbere, and taketh with you Jon Trewman and alle his felawes, and no mo, and loke ye shape you to oon hed and no mo.

Jon the Mellere hath y grounden smal, smalle, smalle:
The Kingis son of hevene shal paye for alle;
Be ware or ye be wo,
Knoweth youre frer   your fo;
Haveth ynowe, and say th ho
And do wel and betre and fleth synne
And seketh pees, and holde yow ther inne,
And so biddeth Jon Treweman and alle his felawes."

The said John Ball confessed that he had written this letter and sent it to the commons, and admitted that he had written many more. Wherefore he was hanged at St. Albans on the 15th of July, in the King's presence.

15.

[An illustration of the charges against some of the rebels, printed from the official records, in "Archæologia Cantiana," vol. xviii. p. 88, in the translation given. 1381.]

Hundred of Boughton. "The jurors say on their oath that Roger Boldwyn of Boughton-under-Blean raised insurrection with other malefactors on the Wednesday next after the feast of the Holy Trinity in the 4th year of the reign of the King that now is, and was aiding and abetting when Simon, Archbishop of Canterbury was feloniously killed, and was there and then present. . . .

Also they say that John Hales . . . and other unknown malefactors made insurrection on Monday next after the feast of Holy Trinity by force and arms, and feloniously broke into the castle of our lord the King in Canterbury, and carried away divers felons that were in the said

castle and prison, and took William Septvanz, the sheriff
of Kent and dragged him away with them, and compelled
him to deliver to them the books and writs of our lord the
King; and immediately that they were delivered they
burnt them, to the prejudice of our lord the King and his
crown. Also they say that James Grene, and Richard
Daly feloniously broke into the gaol of Maidstone, and
took away the prisoners that were in the said gaol, to the
prejudice of our lord the King and his crown."

16.

[Letters Patent addressed to the authorities and townspeople of various
important towns, 23 June, 1381.   "Foedera," IV, i. 125.   (Latin.)]

We think it is well enough known to you and other
our lieges how that many malefactors have lately risen
in hostile manner against our peace, in congregations and
unlawful assemblies, in divers counties of our realm, to
the great disturbance of our faithful lieges ; cruelly putting
to death the venerable father Simon, late Archbishop of
Canterbury . . . our Chancellor, and brother Robert de
Hales, late Prior of the Hospital of St. John of Jerusalem
in England, our Treasurer, John Cavendish, our late Chief
Justice, and many other our faithful servants and lieges ;
and monstrously perpetrating homicides, burnings, wast-
ings, and various other destruction of churches, manors,
houses, property and other possessions of our faithful
lieges. But because the aforesaid malefactors, in order
that they may be able to continue their malice, and . . .
be excused of all the foregoing, have falsely and mendaci-
ously asserted that they perpetrated these same evils,
homicides, and mischiefs, by our will and authority, we
desire it to come to your knowledge, and to that of all our
faithful lieges, that the aforesaid mischiefs . . . were in
no wise committed by our authority, but, right sorely

grieved, we hold that they redound to the great slander of ourself, the prejudice of our crown, and the damage and no small disturbance of our whole realm. Therefore we command you . . . to cause public proclamation of this present mandate to be made in our name. . . . And further you shall forbid any . . . within the said city or elsewhere, to make such congregations or assemblies, or to attempt or procure anything whereby our peace may be broken, or our people disquieted or disturbed, on pain of forfeit of life and limb.

17.

[Letters Patent revoking the charters of manumission, 2 July, 1381. Writs addressed to the sheriffs of all counties. "Foedera," IV, i. 126. (Latin.)]

Although lately in the abominable disturbance horribly made by some of our liege subjects who made insurrection against our peace, certain our letters patent were made at the importunate demand of these same insurgents, to the effect that we enfranchised all our liege subjects . . . of certain counties, freeing and quitting them of all bondage and service, and also that we pardoned them for all insurrection made against us . . . granting each and all of them our firm peace; that we willed that they should be free to buy and sell in all cities, boroughs, market towns and other places within the realm ; and that no acre of land in the aforesaid counties held in service or bondage should be held at more than 4d. the acre. . . . Because, however, the said letters were issued unduly, and without mature consideration, we, considering the grant of the aforesaid liberties highly prejudicial . . . tending manifestly to the disherison of the prelates, lords and magnates, and the Holy Church of England, and to the loss and damage of the state, with the advice of our council we have . . . recalled and annulled the said letters.

18.

[The Parliament of 9 November, 1381.   Speech by the Treasurer, Sir
Hugh Segrave, on the 5th day of Parliament.   "Rolls of Parliament," iii. 99.   (French.)]

"My Lords and Sirs, you are aware how that the honourable father in God, the lord William, Archbishop-elect of
Canterbury, appointed Chancellor of England by our lord
the King, lately explained to you in part the causes of
summons of this Parliament in a general manner, telling
you . . . that the same causes would afterwards be declared
to you more fully in particular.   For this reason, our lord
the King here present, whom may God save, has commanded me to make the said declaration to you, which is
as follows—First, our lord the King, desiring above all things
that the liberty of Holy Church be entirely preserved without blemish, and the estate, peace, and good government
of his realm be maintained and preserved as best it was in
the time of any of his noble ancestors . . . [wishes] that
if default be found in any part, it may now be amended
by the advice of the prelates and lords in this Parliament.

"And . . . [he desires] especially to make good ordinance
for restoring the King and the realm to peace and quiet
after the great disturbance and rumour lately stirred up
in divers parts through the rising and insurrection of certain of the lesser commons and others, and their horrible
and contemptuous trespass against God, the peace, and the
King's prerogative, estate, dignity and crown ; although
these same commons coloured their misdeeds otherwise,
saying that they desired to have no King save our lord
King Richard. . . . And to seek out, and touch upon the
means whereby the said malefactors may be chastised,
and the disturbance entirely removed and ended ; and to
inquire and seek out the causes and principal occasions

thereof, so that when these have been found and known, and completely removed, we may more surely trust in the remedy to be ordained, if the commons should again wish or make ready to do evil in the same way.

"Also, it is not unknown to you, how that our lord the King, during the said rumour, was constrained to grant his letters of liberty, franchise and manumission . . . to his villeins and others, well knowing at the time that he could not do this in good faith, and by the law of his land ; but he did it for the best, as not then being in his rightful power as King. But as soon as God by His grace had restored him to his power . . . by the advice of his council then near him, he caused the said grants to be repealed. . . . And therefore he would like to know your wishes, my lords, prelates, lords and commons here present—if it seem to you that he has done well by this repeal, to your pleasure, or no. For he says, that if you desire to en-franchise the said villeins by your common assent—as it has been reported to him that some of you do—the King will agree thereto with you, at your request."

And hereupon the Treasurer requested the commons from the King, to withdraw to their place in the Abbey of Westminster and take counsel well and diligently upon these matters, and as to the remedies which it seemed to them should be ordained.

19.

[The Speaker's answer, *ibid.* (French.)]

On the Monday next following, in the third week of Parliament, that was the 18th day of November, the com-mons returned into Parliament, and there Sir Richard de Waldegrave, Knight, who spoke on behalf of the commons, strove to have excused himself from this office of speaker,[1]

[1] Vant-parlour.

but the King charged him by his allegiance to perform it, since he had been chosen thereto by his companions.

Then Sir Richard, making his protestation . . . said— " My liege lord, my companions here present, and I have talked together upon our charges lately given to us by your royal majesty ; but we are in part at variance among ourselves touching the same charge. Therefore, if it please you, we will rehearse the same . . . or may it please your royal majesty to cause it again to be rehearsed before us, so that we may more clearly understand it, and so be of one accord among ourselves thereon."

The King commanded Sir Richard le Scrope, Knight, then lately made Chancellor,[1] to repeat—their said charge —and he did so clearly, especially as to the repeal of the grant of franchise and manumission to the bondsmen and villeins.   And it was again inquired in the King's name in full Parliament, of all those present, if this repeal were pleasing to them or no.   Whereto as well the prelates and temporal lords as the knights, citizens and burgesses, answered with one voice—that the repeal was well done ; adding, that such enfranchisement or manumission of the villeins could not take place without their assent, who had the greatest interest therein ; and thereto they never agreed, willingly or otherwise, nor ever would do so, if it were their dying day.

[Pardon was then granted to all persons who had executed summary punishment, without due process of law, upon any of the rebels. Also, at the request of the King's bride, Anne of Bohemia, then about to arrive in England, to all persons concerned in the disturbance—with certain important exceptions, including the townsmen of Canterbury, Bury St. Edmunds, Beverley, Scarborough, Bridgwater, and Cambridge.]

[1] During the Parliament.

20.

[The commons' complaint as to the state of the country, *ibid.*
(French.) The commons returned into Parliament, after discussion with a few of the prelates and lords, and made the following
declaration :—]

". . . That if the government be not shortly amended,
the realm will be utterly ruined and destroyed for ever, and
by consequence, our lord the King and all the lords and
commons, which God, in His mercy, forbid! For it is
true that there are very great defaults in the government
—about the King's person, and in his household, and by
the extravagant number of domestics in the said household; and in his courts, to wit, in the Chancery, King's
bench, Common Pleas, and the Exchequer; and by the
grievous oppressions throughout the country by the outrageous multitude of maintainors, and embracers of
quarrels, who are like kings in the country, so that justice
and right are scarcely done to any. And the poor commons are from time to time plundered and ruined—what
with the purveyors for the household of the King and of
others, who pay nothing to the commons for the victuals
and carriage taken from them, and what with the subsidies and tallages often raised from them, . . . and otherwise by grievous and outrageous oppressions done to them
by divers servants of the King and of other lords of the
realm, and especially by the aforesaid maintainors—so
that they are brought to great wretchedness and discomfort, more than they ever were before.

And without all this, although great treasure is continually granted and levied from them for the defence of
the realm, nevertheless, they are not thereby any better
defended or succoured, so far as they can tell; but from
year to year they suffer burning, robbery, and pillage by
land and sea, by the galleys, barges, and other ships of the
enemy, for which no remedy has been, nor ever is, pro-

vided. The which mischiefs the said poor commons, who were wont formerly to live in all honour and prosperity, cannot any longer endure. And to say truth, by these said outrages, and others such as have lately been inflicted upon the poor commons, more generally than ever before, they felt themselves so greatly burdened, that these caused the lesser commons to stir, and do the mischiefs that they did in riot. And greater mischief is to be feared if good and due remedy be not betimes provided for the above mentioned outrageous oppressions and mischiefs.

And that it may please the King and the noble lords of the realm . . . to apply such remedy and amendment to the government, that the estate and dignity of the King . . . and of the lords of the realm be entirely preserved, . . . and the commons put in quiet and peace, the evil officers and councillors being wholly removed so far as they can be known, and better, more virtuous, and sufficient put in their place; and also the evil occasions, that have thus been the moving cause of the late rumour and other mischiefs. . . . Or it is thought that this realm cannot be long without greater mischief than ever happened herein before."

21.

[Appointment of a committee of inquiry, *ibid.*, November, 1381. (French.)]

Afterwards . . . the King . . . willed and granted that certain prelates, lords, and others should be assigned to survey and examine in privy council, as well the estate and governance of our lord the King's person as of his household, and to take thought as to sufficient remedy, if need were, and make their report thereon to the King. And the lords said in Parliament that 'it seemed to them that if amendment of government should be made throughout the realm, it would be necessary to begin with the

16

principal member, which is the King himself, going from person to person, as well of Holy Church as other, and from place to place, from the highest degree to the lowest, sparing none. . . .

[A committee of eighteen bishops and lords was appointed.]

And be it remembered—that our lord the King's confessor was charged in presence of the King and lords to abstain from coming to the King's household, or staying there, save only on the four principal feasts of the year. And this was done with the assent of the lords, at the request of the commons, who had begged the King to have the said confessor utterly removed from the King and from his office.

. . . .

It was reported to the commons from the King that the Earl of Arundel and Sir Michael de la Pole were chosen, appointed and sworn to be near the King's person and in his household, to counsel and guide his person.

22.

[Grant of a subsidy, *ibid.*, November, 1381. (French.) The commons at first refused a grant, on the ground that too great resentment still existed in the country; the Government thereupon asked them to renew the subsidy on wools, then about to expire.]

When the commons had considered for a little, they returned before the lords, saying that they had heard what excessive charges the King sustained . . . and how that the subsidy of wool, wool-fells, and leather, wherefrom arises the greatest profit that the King takes in his realm . . . should expire and cease at the coming Christmas, by the last grant made at the Parliament of Northampton; and they would willingly aid the King to bear the said charges according to their small power. And considering, on the other hand, that by continual possession of the said subsidy in the King's hands, without interruption, one might easily claim for him and in his name, to have it as of right and custom, (although the King has none in the said subsidy save by their grant), the which by process of time might thus fall to the disherison and continual charge of all the commons of England . . . therefore, and to escape this mischief, the prelates, lords and commons . . . grant such subsidy . . . from the feast of the Circumcision next following. . . . So that the space of time between Christmas and the Circumcision be wholly void, in order to cause the said interruption to be had.

C. THE KING AND THE OPPOSITION.

23.

[The years 1382 and 1383 were critical ones for Richard. During 1382 he was drawing towards de la Pole, and becoming more estranged from Arundel and his party. In March, 1383, the King asserted himself, and appointed de la Pole as his Chancellor; Arundel ceased to attend the Council. Later in the year an important question arose for the Government, concerning the truce with France; discussions had been opened after the failure of Bishop Despenser's crusade, and in January, 1384, a truce was definitely signed, formal peace negotiations being suggested. The opposition was already inclined to attack de la Pole's foreign policy. "Rolls of Parliament," iii. 170. April, 1384. (French.)]

Item, touching the charge given to the commons in the Parliament as to the peace which shall be made, if it please God, between our lord the King and his adversary of France (of which certain articles newly made and appointed during the discussion about the said peace which has been held in the march of Calais . . . were delivered to the commons for their better information as to the said discussion and its effect), the commons made answer. . . . That for the outrageous perils which they see clearly on all sides, they cannot and dare not expressly advise their liege lord in one way or another, although if it should please God to grant

16 *

a peace honourable and profitable for their liege lord and
his realm, it would be the most noble and gracious aid and
comfort to them that could be devised in this world. And
it seemed to them that the King may and should act herein as shall seem best to his noble lordship, as of a matter
which is his own heritage, descended by direct royal lineage
to his noble person, and not pertaining to the realm or
crown of England. . . . And that, for the insupportable
perils and mischiefs that might happen, the poor commons
be discharged from giving their answer for the present.

Upon this they were charged by the King to say which
of the two things they desired, namely, if they wished for
peace or war with their French foes, for there was no other
middle course, because the French would not now agree to
a truce which should be good and profitable.

To this the commons replied, "that they desire very
greatly that a peace good and honourable for the King and
the realm might be made. But . . . they understand that
certain lands and lordships which our lord the King is
to have now in Guienne . . . would be held of the King of
France by homage and service; but they do not think that
their liege lord would easily be willing to hold the town of
Calais and other lands conquered by the sword . . . by such
service, nor would the commons wish it thus to be done,
if one could well do otherwise."

24.

[" Historia Vitae Ricardi II," February, 1385. (Latin.)]

Our lord the King ordained to hold a Council at Waltham after Christmas, to which the lords were summoned;
among whom the lord Duke of Lancaster, as chief of the
Council was invited to attend. But before he set out, he
was told secretly to take care if he went to the Council,
because some of those about the King were plotting his
death, that he should be suddenly slain.

When the Duke heard this, feigning some hindrance of his coming, he sent to the King, entreating that he would hold him excused, if it might please him. But the King sent again, admonishing him, by his allegiance, that he should in no wise omit to attend. Then the Duke began to take counsel as to how he might save his allegiance, and not lose his life. Wherefore he was advised, that, to save his allegiance, and preserve himself from death, he should go with a strong band of retainers. And according to this counsel, he came to the place with a large armed company, telling the King that he must not wonder at the manner of his coming, because he was in fear of being slain. The King excused himself with oaths, saying that he knew nothing of these plots. Then the Duke afterwards had the less faith in that behalf.

In the following Lent, the lord William Courtenay, Archbishop of Canterbury, urged and induced by certain lords, as it was said, rebuked the King as pertained to him, for his insolence and ill government, asserting that unless he would permit himself to be directed otherwise, this ill government would shortly tend to the subversion of himself and the realm. The King, greatly angered by this rebuke, would have struck the Archbishop, if his uncle, lord Thomas of Woodstock had not prevented it; and he addressed many scandalous reproaches to him, and conceived great indignation against him. So the Archbishop withdrew, and betook himself to a distance.

25.

[In July, 1386, Lancaster set out on his expedition to Portugal, where he remained until 1389. This gave opportunity to the Duke of Gloucester, who joined the Earl of Arundel in a definite campaign of opposition to de la Pole. During the autumn of 1386, the French were preparing an invading fleet, and the excitement prevailing in London when Parliament met on 1 October helped

to forward Gloucester's plans.   Continuator of Knighton, 1386.
(Latin.)]

The King held his Parliament at Westminster on Monday the morrow of St. Jerome, and ended it on the Feast of St. Andrew.   The Earl of Oxford, Marquis of Dublin, was made Duke of Ireland on the Feast of St. Edward the Confessor.

The King stayed for the greater part at Eltham during the Parliament; therefore the lords of the realm and the commons sent word to him, with common consent, that the Chancellor and Treasurer must be removed from their offices, because they were not profitable to the King and the realm; and also, they had such business with Michael de la Pole, as they could not transact with him so long as he remained in the Chancellor's office.   The King, in anger, commanded them to say no more about this matter, and to make haste and proceed with the business of Parliament, saying that he would not remove the meanest servant of his kitchen at their request.   (For the Chancellor had asked in the King's name for four "fifteenths" to be paid in one year, and as many "tenths" from the clergy, saying that the King was so greatly indebted that he could not otherwise be relieved from his debts and other burdens. . . .)

By common accord the lords and commons returned answer to the King that they could not, nor certainly would not, proceed in any business of Parliament, nor despatch the smallest point, until the King should come and show himself to them in his own person in Parliament, and remove Michael de la Pole from his office. But the King sent back the command that they should send forty knights to him, of the most skilled and able of the commons, to set before him the wishes of all.   Then they feared greatly for their own safety; for a dark rumour had reached their ears that he was scheming their destruction. For it was said that when they went to their interview with the King, an armed band would attack and slay them. . . .

Therefore acting upon sound advice, with the common consent of the whole Parliament they sent the lord Thomas of Woodstock, Duke of Gloucester, and Thomas Arundel, Bishop of Ely, to the King at Eltham, to greet him from the lords and commons of his Parliament, reporting their wishes in words to this effect—Lord King, the lords and all the community of your Parliament with most humble subjection, commend themselves to your royal excellency . . . and on their behalf we declare to you the following matters—We have an ancient statute and praiseworthy custom to the effect that our King is to call the lords and nobles of the realm and the commons once a year to his Parliament, as to the highest court of the whole realm, wherein all justice ought to shine without blemish as the noonday sun, where rich and poor may seek infallible refuge for the refreshment of tranquillity and peace and the removal of injuries ; where the errors of the realm may be reformed, and there may be discussion as to the state of the realm and government. . . .

They say also, that they have another ancient statute, to the effect that if the King wilfully withdraw from his Parliament without infirmity or other necessary cause, and wantonly absent himself for the space of forty days, as though heedless of the vexation and grave expense of his people, then it is lawful for all and sundry . . . to return to their own homes. . . .

And now for a long time you have absented yourself, and refused to come to them, for what cause they know not. The King replied—" Now we think indeed that our people are plotting to resist and rise up against us ; and in such case, it seems that we cannot do better than appeal to our kinsman the King of France, and ask his counsel and aid ; and rather submit ourself to him than yield to our own subjects." "That is no sound plan," they returned, "but tends rather to inevitable ruin ; for the King of France is your mortal foe, the greatest enemy of your realm, and should he set foot in your land, he would rather strive to despoil you, seize upon your Kingdom, and drive you from your throne, than lend you helping hands. . . ."

There remains one thing more for us to show you on behalf of your people. It is permitted by another ancient statute—and this was unhappily seen in very deed not so long ago—that if the King shall alienate himself from his people by malignant counsel, foolish contumacy, contempt, or wanton waywardness; and shall be unwilling to be governed and guided by the laws and statutes of the realm, with the wholesome advice of the lords and peers, but stubbornly, in his evil counsels, exercise his own singular will—then it shall be lawful for them, with the common consent of the people of the realm, to depose him, and place on the throne some near kinsman of the royal house. . . .

[Richard promised to yield, and return to London.]

The King therefore came to Parliament as he had promised, and then the Bishop of Durham was removed from the office of Treasurer, and the Bishop of Hereford appointed in his place. The lord Michael de la Pole was removed in dire disgrace from the Chancellor's office, and Thomas Arundel, Bishop of Ely, made Chancellor by consent of Parliament. After this, Michael de la Pole was accused of many transgressions, frauds, deceits, and treasons, that he had committed to the grave prejudice and mischief of the King and realm, and convicted upon a marvellous number of the said articles; but they were unwilling to

punish him with death, or take from him the name of Earl,
for honour of his knightly rank, but he was awarded to
prison in Windsor castle. . . .

The lords and magnates of Parliament, seeing that by
the greed of the King's officers, the goods of the realm
were wasted, that the King was very greatly deceived, the
people impoverished by heavy burdens, the revenues and
profits of the lords and magnates much shrunken, the tillage of poor tenants in many places abandoned to desolation
—and amid all this the officers immoderately enriched—
chose fourteen lords who should control the whole gover-
ment of the realm, three of them from the new ministers
chosen by Parliament . . . and they gave them power
and permission to inquire, treat, define and determine
concerning all business, and as to all causes and complaints, arising from the time of Edward III the King's
grandfather to the present, as well within the realm as
in distant parts.

26.

[From the Commission of Reform. "Statutes," ii. 39. The original
 is a long document, specifying the duties of the commissioners in
 minute detail. 19 November, 1386. Confirmed by Statute, 1
 December. (French.)]

. . . And . . . by his royal authority, certain knowledge,
goodwill and pleasure, and by the advice and assent of the
prelates, lords and commons in full Parliament, in aid of
good government in his realm, and good and due execution
of his laws, and in relief of the estate of him and his people
in time to come; upon the full trust that he has of the
good advisement, wit, and discretion of the honourable
fathers in God the Archbishop of Canterbury, and the
Archbishop of York, his dear uncles the Duke of York and
the Duke of Gloucester, the honourable fathers in God
the Bishops of Winchester and Exeter and the Abbot of

Waltham, and his well-beloved and faithful the Earl of Arundel and John lord Cobham, Sir Richard le Scrope and Sir John Devereux—has ordained, assigned and deputed them by his letters patent . . . to be of his great and continual council, from the eve of St. Edmund the Martyr for a whole year next following; to survey and examine with the great officers, to wit, the Chancellor, Treasurer, and Keeper of the Privy Seal, as well the state and governance of his household and of all his courts and places, as the estate and governance of all his realm, and all his officers and ministers. . . . And to amend and correct all faults, wastes, and excesses. . . . And to hear and receive all manner of complaints and grievances of all his lieges which will sue and complain to them, of all manner of duresses . . . which may not well be amended nor determined by the course of the common law of the land. . . .

Whereupon the King has ordained and established . . . that every one of his said lieges shall be attending and obedient in whatever touches the aforesaid articles. . . .

And that no person . . . give to our lord the King, in secret or openly, counsel . . . whereby the King should repeal their power within the time aforesaid in any point, or do anything contrary to his grant.

[The penalty for giving such advice to be forfeiture of goods and property for the first offence, and for the second, loss of life.]

27.

["Rolls of Parliament," iii. 221. (French.) Parliament made a grant of "fifteenths" and "tenths" and increased the customs.]

. . . All the which grants the lords and commons have made at this time upon the following conditions—To wit, that if the power given by the aforesaid commission to the lords ordained to be of the continual council . . . be in

any manner repealed or undone, or if the said lords . . .
be in any way disturbed, so that they cannot freely use or
fully execute the power committed to them . . . whereby
they cease utterly to do so, from that time the levy and
collection of all that then shall remain to be raised, by
colour of the said grants, shall cease utterly for ever.

(*Ibid.* p. 224.) Be it remembered that the King, in
full Parliament, before the ending thereof, made public
protestation by his own mouth, that, for anything that
was done in the said Parliament, he would not that
prejudice should come to himself or his crown; but that
his prerogative and the liberties of his crown should be
preserved and kept.

28.

[Richard determined at once to reverse the triumph of the opposition,
  releasing de la Pole, and gathering round him a band of supporters whom he could trust. He made what preparations he
  could to resist the commissioners, and approached the Justices to
  secure opinions that might justify him in this. At Nottingham,
  in August, 1387, he obtained from five Justices the following
  opinion touching the behaviour of the opposition in 1386. Continuator of Knighton. "Rolls of Parliament," iii. 233, 357.
  "Statutes," ii. 102. (Latin.)]

Questions addressed by the King to the Justices, at
Nottingham Castle, on 25 August, 1387.

First they were asked, Whether the new statute, ordinance, and commission made and issued in the last Parliament at Westminster are derogatory to the royal power
and prerogative of our lord the King? Whereto they replied with one accord—that they are derogatory, especially
in that they were made against the King's will.

Item, they were asked, How they who procured the
aforesaid statute, ordinance and commission to be made,
should be punished? To which question they replied—
that they deserve to be punished with capital penalty, to

wit, of death, unless the King shall be willing to pardon them therein.

Item, they were asked, How they should be punished, who urged the King to consent to the making of this statute, ordinance, and commission? Whereto they replied with one accord—that unless the King shall pardon them, they ought deservedly to be punished with capital penalty.

Item, they were asked, What penalty do they deserve who compelled or constrained the King to consent to the making of the aforesaid statute, ordinance, and commission? Whereto they replied with one accord—that they deserve to be punished as traitors.

Item, they were asked, How also they should be punished, who prevented the King from exercising the powers pertaining to his royal prerogative? Whereto they replied with one accord—that they also should be punished as traitors.

Item, they were asked, If, in the assembled Parliament, after that the business of the realm and the cause of the meeting of Parliament shall have been set forth and declared by the King's command, and certain points shall be defined by him, upon which the lords and commons should proceed, they shall insist upon treating of other articles, refusing in any wise to proceed upon those appointed until sufficient answer shall first have been given by the King to the points put forward by them, notwithstanding the King's command to the contrary — whether the King ought to have the rule of the Parliament therein, and indeed direct, to the end that they shall proceed upon the articles first defined by him, or whether the lords and commons first ought to have answer from him upon their articles, before proceeding further? Whereto they replied with one accord—that the King ought to have rule and control therein, and so continuously in all points touching the Parliament, until the end thereof; and if any should take action contrary to this, they should be punished as traitors.

Item, they were asked, Whether the King may dissolve Parliament whenever it shall please him, and command the lords and commons to withdraw, or no? Whereto they replied with one accord—that he may; and if any afterwards against the King's will proceed as in Parliament, he ought to be punished as a traitor.

Item, they were asked, Since that the King may remove his justices and officers whenever it please him, and judge and punish them for their offences, whether the lords and commons may, against the King's will, impeach the said justices and officers in Parliament for their offences, or no? Whereto they replied with one accord—that they may not; and if any acted to the contrary, he ought to be punished as a traitor.

Item, they were asked, In what manner ought he to be punished who moved in Parliament that the statute, whereby Edward, great grandfather of the present King was adjudged in Parliament, should be sent for, by the inspection whereof the aforesaid new statute, ordinance, and commission were contrived? Whereto they answered with one accord, that as well he who made that motion, as the other who, by pretext thereof, brought that statute to Parliament, ought deservedly to be punished as criminous and traitors.

Item, they were asked, Whether the judgment given in the last Parliament against the Earl of Suffolk was erroneous and revokable? Whereto they replied with one accord, that if that judgment were now to be given, they . . . would not give the same, because it seemed to them that the judgment might be repealed as erroneous in every part.

29.

[During September, King and commissioners were preparing for
mutual resistance. But by the middle of November, failing to
secure the armed support of the Londoners, Richard submitted
to a reconciliation with Gloucester and his friends, who had the
general support of the country. His real hope lay in the force
which the Duke of Ireland was collecting in Chester, but it was
defeated on 20 December, at Radcot Bridge. The "Appellant"
lords then summoned Parliament, and put forward the following
among other articles. The Appeal was made late in December,
1387, and Parliament met on 3 February, 1388. There were 39
articles, in most of which Tressilian and Brember were also included. "Rolls of Parliament," iii. 230. (French.)]

1. First Thomas Duke of Gloucester, Constable of England, Henry Earl of Derby, Richard Earl of Arundel and
Surrey, Thomas Earl of, Warwick, and Thomas Earl
Marshal appeal and declare, that Alexander Archbishop
of York, Robert de Vere, Duke of Ireland, and Michael de
la Pole, Earl of Suffolk, false traitors and enemies of the
King and realm, seeing our lord the King's tender years,
and the innocence of his royal person, made him to understand as truth so many false matters imagined and contrived
by them against good faith and loyalty, that they caused
him utterly to give them his affection, faith and credence,
and to hate his loyal lieges, by whom he ought rather to
have been governed. And also, accroaching to them, royal
power, depriving the King of sovereignty, impairing and
diminishing his royal prerogative and regalie, they made
him submit so far, that he was sworn to be governed,
counselled, and led by them. By virtue of the which oath,
they have so long held him in submission to their false
offences, ill-deeds and contrivings, that the mischiefs . . .
contained in the following articles have befallen. . . .

3. Item, with the assent and counsel of Robert Tressilian, false justice, and Nicholas Brember, false knight of
London, by their false covyne, they would not suffer the

great men of the realm, nor the King's good counsellors
to speak to the King nor approach him, to give him good
counsel, nor the King to speak to them, save in the presence and hearing of [themselves] or at least two of them,
and then according to their plan, and such thing as they
desired.

4. Item [1] . . . by their false covyne and accroachment,
they led and ill-counselled the King, by their false wickedness, so that whereas he ought as of duty to show his
presence to the great lords and to his liege people, and
make answer to the grace and justice that they may ask,
he did not do so, save according to their will and design,
turning the King from his duty, against his oath, and the
hearts of the great lords and the people from their liege
lord ; compassing to withdraw his heart from the peers
of the land, to have the government of the realm among
themselves alone. . . .

7. Item . . . by the assent and counsel of the said
Nicholas Brember, false knight of London, accroaching
to them royal power, they caused the King to give them
great sums of gold and silver, as well of his own goods
and jewels, and of the goods and treasure of the realm, as
"fifteenths" and "tenths" and other taxes granted in
divers Parliaments to be spent for the safeguard of the
realm and otherwise, which sum amounts to 100,000 marks
and more ; as to the said Robert de Vere, Duke of Ireland,
and others in divers ways.   And beyond this, they have
hindered many good ordinances and purposes made and
ordained in Parliament, as well for the wars, as for the
defence of the realm. . . .

14. Item . . . they have caused that whereas some of
the lords and other loyal lieges of our lord the King, having great fear and dread for the ruin of the realm, by

[1] Here, and in Nos. 14 and 21, Tressilian and Brember are also
specified.

reason of the said mischiefs, moved in divers Parliaments
for good governance to be had about the King . . . our
lord the King was so sorely stirred against them that he
commanded some to depart from his council, and from
Parliament, so that they dared not speak of the matter,
nor touch upon good governance of the King and realm,
for fear of death. . . .

[The Appellants give their version of the Parliament of 1386, and mention a plot, according to which the Mayor of London was to raise
a force in the City, fall upon the Parliament, and kill the members;
upon his refusal the King was withdrawn to Eltham. From this
time, they say, the accused determined to pursue the commissioners as traitors.]

19. Item . . . with the assent and counsel of the said
Robert Tressilian and Nicholas Brember . . . they caused
the King to go with some of them throughout his realm,
for the greater part, and into the parts of Wales; and to
summon before him the magnates, knights, squires, and
other good men of the said parts, as well of the cities and
boroughs as of other places, and caused them to be bound,
some by their obligations, and some by their oaths, to our
lord the King, to be with him against all men, and to
accomplish his purpose; which purpose was at that time
to carry out the will and designs of the aforesaid malefactors and traitors. . . . The which sureties and oaths
were made contrary to the good laws and customs of the
land, and to the King's oath. . . .

20. Item, by force of such bonds and oaths, the whole
realm was stirred to great murmur and disturbance, . . .
and in peril of suffering divers unbearable mischiefs.

21. Item, to afforce their said traitorous purpose [they]
often caused the King to withdraw himself into the most
distant parts of the realm, in order that the lords assigned
by the aforesaid ordinance, statute, and commission might
not take counsel with him upon the business of the realm,

to the hindering and undoing of the purport and effect of
the said ordinance. . . .

24. Item, the said traitors . . . caused the King newly
to make great retinue of divers people, and to give them
divers signs, otherwise than was wont to be done in
former times by any of the King's his forefathers, to the
end that they might have power to perform their aforesaid
false treason. . . .

[They assure him that the opposition meant to depose him.]

28. Item, after this false and traitorous information . . .
the said malefactors and traitors counselled him to
strengthen himself by all possible means, as well by the
power of his French enemies and others, to destroy and
put to death the aforesaid lords and all others consenting
to the making of the said ordinance. . . .

30. Item . . . to accomplish this high treason of
treachery and murder, they made the King promise the
French King to give up and surrender . . . the town and
Castle of Calais, and all other castles and fortresses in the
March of Picardy and Artois, and the castles and towns
of Cherbourg and Brest. . . .

33. Item, the said Nicholas Brember, false knight of
London, with the assent and counsel of the aforesaid . . .
caused that some of them should come to London . . .
without the knowledge and consent of the King, and there
openly, in the King's name, made all the Crafts of the City
of London to be sworn to hold and perform divers dis-
honourable matters, as is contained in the said oath, that
is of record in the Chancery. And among others, that
they would hold and maintain the King's will to their
power against all rebellious or contrary to his person or
his regalie, and be ready to live and die with our lord
King Richard, against all who have purposed . . . treason
against him in any manner. And that they would be

17

ready, and speedily come to their Mayor . . . whenever
they should be required, to resist all those who purpose
. . . against our liege lord. . . . At which time by the evil
information of the said malefactors and traitors, and by
the false answers of the justices, the King firmly held
that the said lords, and others who were of assent to make
the said ordinance . . . were rebels against him, his enemies and traitors; the which information was at that
time unknown to the people of London.   And so altogether, with such dark words in the said oath, the intent
of these malefactors and traitors was to stir up the people
of London, to do their power to destroy the aforesaid
loyal lords.

30.

[" Rolls of Parliament," iii. 236.   (French.)   February, 1388.]

At which time the justices, sergeants, and other sages of
the law of the realm, and also the sages of the Civil Law,
were charged by the King to give their loyal counsel to the
lords of Parliament, as to proceeding in due manner in the
cause of the aforesaid Appeal.   And they had deliberation,
and made answer to the said lords of Parliament, that they
had seen and well understood the tenor of the Appeal, and
that it was not made or affirmed according to the form required by the one Law or the other.   Whereupon the lords
of Parliament took counsel and deliberated, and it was declared, with the assent of our lord the King, and by their
common accord,—that in such high crime as is alleged in
this Appeal, that touches the King's person, and the estate
of his whole realm, committed by persons who are peers
of the realm, with others, the cause shall not be prosecuted
elsewhere than in Parliament, nor by other law than the
law and course of Parliament.   And that it pertains to the
lords of Parliament, and to their franchise and liberty, by
ancient custom of Parliament, to be judges in such case,

and to adjudge such case, by the King's consent.   And
that thus it shall be done in this case, by the award of
Parliament; because the realm of England was not before
this time, nor, according to the intent of the King and the
laws of Parliament, ever shall be, ruled or governed by
the Civil Law; and also their intent is not to rule or
govern such high cause as this Appeal . . . by course,
process, and order used in any lower court or place within
the realm, which courts and places are but executors of
the ancient laws and customs of the realm, and of the
ordinances and establishments of Parliament.   And it was
the opinion of the same lords of Parliament, with the assent of our lord the King, that this appeal was well and
duly made and affirmed, and the process thereof good and
effectual, according to the laws and course of Parliament. . . .

[The appellants proceeded to pass judgment of execution or exile
  upon the accused, and upon others among the King's supporters.
  The "Merciless Parliament" lasted until 4 June.]

D. RICHARD II's PERSONAL RULE.

31.

[Richard's self-assertion.   Continuator of Knighton, 1389.   (Latin.)]

In the month of May the King held a council at Westminster, and on the Feast of the Invention of the Cross,
coming into the council, he unexpectedly removed all the
great officers, and appointed others whom he chose in their
places.

The Earl of Arundel, to whom was entrusted the direction of Parliament, and the keeping of the sea, and who
had been Admiral, was also removed from his office in the
same way.   The King did this moreover, in the case of
other officers, saying, that he ought not to be of inferior
condition to any other heir in the realm, since the law

and custom of England affirm that every heir . . . when
he has reached his 21st year, shall at once enjoy his
father's inheritance, and lawfully have liberty of disposing
of his wealth and property. "It has befallen that now for
several years we have remained under your counsel and
control, and we render thanks many times, first to God,
and then to yourselves, in that you have directed and
guided us, our inheritance and our realm . . . especially
against our enemies on all sides. . . .

"But now . . . we have attained our majority, and are
at present in our 22nd year; therefore we request henceforth full liberty of ruling and controlling ourselves and
our inheritance, and we desire to possess our realm, and to
choose our officers and ministers at pleasure . . . and appoint them to any offices, remove those now in office at
our will, and appoint others in their places."

There was none who strove to infringe the King's will,
but all glorified God who had ordained that they should
have a King of such wisdom.

32.

In August, 1389, a truce for three years was made with France and
Scotland. Lancaster had previously come to an agreement with
Castile, abandoning his own claim to the throne. In November,
1389, he returned to England, and early in 1390 Richard invested
him with the whole of the Duchy of Guienne for life. The Order
of Proceeding in Council, 1390; Nicolas, "Proceedings and
Ordinances of the Privy Council," i. 18. (French.)]

First, that the lords of the Council be prepared to be at
the Council between eight and nine of the clock at latest.

Item, that the business of the King and the realm be
examined first before all others, when the greatest of the
Council and other officers shall be present.

Item, that business touching the Common Law be sent
to be determined before the justices.

Item, that business touching the office of Chancellor be sent to be determined before him in the Chancery.

Item, that business touching the office of Treasurer be sent to be determined before him in the Exchequer.

Item, that all other matters which cannot be despatched without special grace and permission of the King, be laid before him, to have his opinion and his wishes.

Item, that no gift or grant that may turn to the decrease of the King's profit pass without the advice of the Council, and the assent of the Dukes of Guienne, York, and Gloucester, and of the Chancellor, or two of them.

Item, that all business sent to the Council to have their advice, and other business of great charge, be determined by those of the Council who shall be present, with the officers.

Item, that all other bills of the people, of lesser charge be examined and despatched before the keeper of the Privy Seal, and others of the Council who shall be present at the time.

Item, that the ordinances touching office to be given by the King, formerly made by the assent of himself and his Council, be held and kept.

Item, that no seneschals or justices be henceforth appointed for term of life.

Item, that the batchelors being of the King's Council shall have reasonable wages for the time that they shall be at work about the Council.

Item, that the lords being at the Council shall have reward for their labour and expenses by the advice of the King and his Council.

Item, after that any matter be broached in the Council, they shall pass on to no other matter until answer be given to the matter first broached.

On the 8th day of March, in the 13th year, this ordinance was made at Westminster in the King's presence,

the Duke of Guienne, the Duke of York, the Earl of Salisbury, the Earl of Northumberland, the Earl of Huntingdon, the Chancellor, the Treasurer, the Privy Seal, the
Seneschal, Lovete, Stury, and Dalingrugg being present.

33.

[Letter from the Council to the King in Ireland; Nicolas, "Privy
  Council," i. 50. (French.) About October, 1394. The Parliament referred to eventually met at Westminster. Richard had
  crossed to Ireland in September.]

Right dread and sovereign lord, We your humble and
faithful lieges commend us very humbly to your royal
majesty. Whom may it please to know that we have heard
and understood through the report of the right reverend
father in God the Archbishop of York, your Chancellor,
right pleasant news, as well of your gracious passage to
your land of Ireland, as of your good estate and health of
body, to the great joy and comfort of us your said lieges.
And how also at the departing of your said Chancellor
from your right noble presence, it pleased your royal
majesty, for certain causes then moving you, that your
Parliament should be held at Nottingham at the octaves
of St. Hilary next ensuing. For the accomplishment
whereof, and of all other your pleasure and commands,
we and all your other lieges are and shall be always ready
and prepared with all our power, if it please God. But,
right dread and sovereign lord, saving always the most
high and wise advice and command of your said royal
majesty, all things being considered, and in particular the
winter weather, and how that to many magnates of your
realm who dwell here about, and might do much profit in
this case, it would be too grievous to travel to so distant
parts—both for the infirmities and feebleness of some of
them and for fear of the floods and heavy roads, that
might put them in peril, and your people in great discom-

fort, and peradventure hinder their coming to the same
Parliament, and so prevent the good profit of you and
your whole realm, which God forbid !—(And consider also,
right dread lord, that in the Parliament thus to be held in
your absence, no other matter will be touched upon or
despatched for the profit or ease of your people, save
touching the grant that shall be made in your aid);—it
seems to us, according to our small and simple opinion,
that it would be expedient that your said Parliament be
held in some other fitting place to be appointed by your
most wise discretion. The which may be more ease for
the lords and great men of your realm, and also for your
people, who, by reason of their ease would be more ready
and of better will to aid you in your need than they would
be in case of their grievance and discomfort. Whereon
may it please your royal majesty to acquaint us as to your
will and command, between this and the Saturday next
after the Feast of Our Lady's Conception next ensuing, to
the end that we may then perform your pleasure and
command. Understanding, right dread lord, that in case
that within this time no answer come from you to your
Chancellor, he will cause your writs to be made to hold
your Parliament at Nottingham according to your first
desire. And do not marvel, right dread lord, for that your
Chancellor has not given his advice with us in this part;
for as he said, he dared not do so, by reason that he was
fully informed of your will touching the place and time
of your Parliament, according as he reported to us from
you, as above.

34.

[Letter from the King in Ireland to the Council; *ibid.* i. 55. (French.)
1 February, 1395.]

Right dear and entirely well-beloved uncle, right reverend fathers in God, and our beloved and faithful lieges—

we greet you right heartily, doing you to wit that at the making of these our letters we were in good and perfect health, our Lord be thanked. And right entirely with all our heart we desire continually to have good and gracious news from you of your well-being and estate, and especially of the good governance and prosperity of our realm. May God of His high puissance continually grant us thereof good and pleasant tidings. And touching news from here, be pleased to know, that for great and notable causes moving us thereto, we have, with the advice of our Council, ordained to hold our Parliament in our city of Dublin on Monday the morrow of the Octaves of Easter next, and the writs for the said Parliament will be made in all haste. For that in our land of Ireland there are three manner of people, to wit, wild Irish, our enemies, Irish rebels, and obedient English, it seems to us and to our Council about us, considering that the said rebellious Irish have perchance rebelled for griefs and wrongs done to them on the one part, and by default of remedy being given them on the other; and that thus if they were not prudently treated, and put in good hope of pardon they would probably join our enemies, which we would not have by our default,—that general pardon should be granted them, by fine and fee of our seal to be paid by each who shall have the pardon; whereby it seems to us and our said Council that in many ways great benefit would come to us and our said land. But inasmuch as we do not think of doing such, or so weighty a thing without your counsel and assent, we have taken generally all the said rebel Irish into our especial protection until the quinzaine of Easter next, to the end that betwixt now and then, those who will may come and show the causes of their rebellion, and especially that in the meantime we may have your full counsel and advice, if the said pardon should be granted or no. Thus we will and command, firmly charg-

ing you, that having had communication among you upon
the said matter, with good deliberation, you send us clearly
your counsel and advice as soon as in any way you can,
by the entire confidence that we have in you; For love of
us acquainting us fully with news of you at all times when
you shall be able. Our Lord have you in His keeping.
Given under our signet in our city of Dublin on the first
day of February.

35.

[In the summer of 1396 peace negotiations were suggested by the
French Government; discussions were followed by formal inter-
views between the two kings in October. It had been agreed
that Richard should marry the French princess, then a child
of seven, and a truce for twenty years was signed. "Annales
Ricardi II." (Latin.)]

[On October 26th.] The new queen was led to the
pavilion of the French Council, and with her there came
the Duchesses of Lancaster and Gloucester, and the
Countess of Huntingdon, with their ladies. The Dukes of
Berry and Burgundy, clad in crimson velvet brought the
Queen to the place appointed for the interview; she was
dressed in a close garment, after the older fashion, of red
velvet powdered with lilies, wearing on her head a costly
crown. And the King of France gave her to the King of
England with these words—"I commend to you, dearest
son, the creature whom I love best in the world, save the
Dauphin, my son, and my wife". King Richard took her
by the hand, thanking the King for so honourable and
gracious a gift, and promised to receive her upon the conditions agreed between them.

36.

[The incident of Thomas Haxey; "Rolls of Parliament," iii. 338, Parliament of January, 1397. (French.)]

On Friday the feast of Candlemas the King caused the lords spiritual and temporal to come before him at Westminster in the said Parliament, and showed them how he had heard that on the preceding Thursday they were with the commons, and that the commons had shown them and touched upon certain matters whereof it seemed to him that some were contrary to his prerogative, estate, and royal liberty ; commanding the Chancellor to set forth and repeat the said matters.

Whereupon the Chancellor made report to him of the said matters, that were in four points. . . .

And the fourth point was, that the great and excessive charge of the King's household should be amended and diminished ; to wit, as to the multitude of bishops having lordships, who are promoted by the King, and their retinues ; and also as to many ladies and their retinues, who dwell in the King's household, and are at his cost.

. . . Upon which report the King himself declared his will to the lords; how that, " by the gift of God he is by line and right of inheritance the inheritor of the realm of England, and will have his prerogative and the royal liberty of his crown." . . .

. . . And as to the fourth article, touching the charge of the King's household, and the staying of bishops and ladies in his company,—the King was greatly grieved and offended that the commons, who were his lieges should misprise and take upon themselves any ordinance or governance of the King's person, or of his household, or of any persons of estate whom he might please to have in his company. And it seemed to him that the commons com-

mitted great offence herein, against his prerogative and
royal majesty, his liberty and that of his royal ancestors,
which he is bound, and desires, to maintain with the help
of God.   Wherefore the King commanded the lords . . .
that on the following Saturday morning they should plainly
show and declare to the commons the King's will in this
matter.

And on Saturday . . . the lords . . . were with the
commons, and showed them the King's command; and
the commons delivered the said bill to the lords, with the
name of him who gave it them, to wit Sir Thomas
Haxey. . . . .

And afterwards the commons came before our lord the
King in Parliament by his command, and there with all the
humility and obeisance that they could, greatly grieving,
as appeared by their countenance, for that the King should
have conceived such thought against them, humbly entreated the King to accept their excuse, that it was never
their will or intent to say, show, or do anything that might
be offence or displeasure to the King's royal majesty, or
against his royal estate or liberty, and especially in this
matter touching his own person . . . well knowing and
recognising that such things pertained not to them, but
only to the King himself and his ordinance.   But that
their intent was . . . that the lords should entreat the
King to consider his honourable estate, and do what should
please him therein. . . .

And upon this the commons humbly submitted themselves to the King's will and grace, entreating his royal
majesty to hold them graciously excused. . . . Whereupon
the Chancellor said to them, by the King's command, that
of his royal benignity and gracious lordship the King held
them fully excused, and promised' them good lordship.

37.

[*Ibid.* iii. 341.]

Be it remembered that . . . after the judgment given against Thomas Haxey, clerk, who was condemned to death in Parliament, as a traitor, there came before the King in Parliament the Archbishop of Canterbury and all the other prelates, making . . . protestation that their entire and full intent was, and always would be, that the King's royal estate and prerogative might be always saved and guarded without blemish; And they humbly entreated the King that it might please him of his grace to have pity and mercy upon the said Thomas, and of his royal dignity to remit and release the execution of his death, and grant him his life. And upon this . . . the King of his royal pity and especial grace, remitted and released the execution of the death of said Thomas and granted him his life.

Whereon the prelates, returning thanks to the King for his great benignity and mercy, humbly entreated him that it might please him, of his abundant grace, to the reverence of God and the honour of Holy Church, to grant them the guard of the body of the said Thomas. . . .

Whereupon the King . . . granted them the keeping of his body.

E. THE FALL OF RICHARD II.

38.

[From the Chancellor's Speech in Parliament, 1397. (French.) "Rolls of Parliament," iii. 347.]

" He took for his theme the words of Ezekiel the Prophet, There shall be one King over all; alleging upon this various authorities of Holy Scripture that there shall be one King and one governor, and that by other manner no Kingdom can be governed. And that to the good government of any King three things are necessary—first, that

the King be puissant to govern, secondly that the laws
whereby he should govern be justly kept and executed;
thirdly that the subjects of the realm be duly obedient to
the King and his laws.   And by this cause, first so that
Kings may be powerful to govern their subjects they have
of right several privileges given to them, as 'Regalies,'
Prerogatives, and many other rights annexed to the crown,
which they are obliged in their coronation oath to guard and
sustain.   And these they may not alienate nor transfer to
other use, so that if alienation be affirmed by oath, the law
repeals such alienation, and releases the oath. . . .'

39.

[Gower, "Confessio Amantis," Book VII.]

What is a lond wher men ben none?
What ben the men whiche are al one
Withoute a kinges governance?
What is a king in his ligance,
Wher that ther is no lawe in londe?
What is to take lawe on honde,
Bot if the jugges weren trewe?
These olde worldes with the newe
Who that wol take in evidence,
Ther mai he se thexperience,
What thing it is to kepe lawe,
Thurgh which the wronges ben withdrawe
And rihtwisnesse stant commended,
Whereof the regnes ben amended.
For wher the lawe mai comune
The lordes forth with the commune,
Ech hath his propre duete;
And ek the kinges realte
Of bothe his worschipe under fongeth,
To his astat as it belongeth,

Which of his hihe worthinesse
Hath to governe riht wisnesse,
As he which schal the lawe guide,
And natheles upon som side
His pouer stant above the lawe,
To give both and to withdrawe
The forfet of a mannes lif;
But things which are excessif
Agein the lawe, he schal noght do
For love ne for hate also.
    The myhtes of a king ben grete
Bot yit a worthi king shal lete
Of wrong to don, al that he myhte;
For he which schal the people ryhte
It sit wel to his regalie
That he himself first justifie
Towardes god in his degre;
For his estat is elles fre
Toward alle othre in his persone
Save only to the god al one
Which wol himself a king chastise
Wher that non other mai suffise.
    So were it good to taken hiede
That first a king his oghne dede
Betwen the vertu and the vice
Redresce, and thanne of his justice
So sette in evene the balance
Towards othre in governance,
That to the povere and to the riche
Hise lawes myhten stonde liche,
He schal excepte no persone.
Bot for he mai not noght al him one
In sondri places do justice,
He schal of his real office
With wys consideracion

Ordeigne his deputacion
Of suche jugges as ben lerned,
So that his poeple be governed
Be hem that trewe ben and wise.
For if the lawe of covoitise
Be set upon a jugges hond,
Wo is the poeple of thilke lond,
For wrong mai noght himselven hyde:
But alles on that other side,
If lawe stonde with the riht,
The poeple is glad and stant upriht
Wher as the lawe is resonable
The comun poeple stant menable,
And if the lawe torne amis,
The poeple also mistorned is.

40.

[Early in July, 1397, Richard felt strong enough to make his long-projected attack upon the Earls of Gloucester, Warwick, and Arundel; he alleged that new plots had been discovered in which they were concerned, and proceeded to arrest them. Gloucester was sent off at once to Calais; "Annales Ricardi". (Latin.) September, 1397.]

In order that the King might carry out his designs, and take vengeance upon the said lords, he summoned all the estates of the realm to a Parliament . . . whereto he commanded all the lords who were his adherents to come with armed men and archers, as though to war, and they were about to proceed against his enemies.[1] The King himself, so that he might the more effectively carry out his infamous scheme, caused malefactors in excessive numbers to be gathered together from the county of Chester to guard his person, to whose protection he wholly committed

[1] Lancaster, Derby, and York were empowered to bring, between them, 600 men-at-arms and 1100 archers. ("Foedera," ed. 1741, III, iv. 135.)

himself. And these men, being naturally fierce, were prepared to perpetrate any wickedness; so that their insolence increased to such an extent that they looked upon the King as their comrade, and held all others in contempt, even powerful lords. These men were not drawn from the gentlemen of their country, but from the peasants, cobblers and other craftsmen; so it befell that they who at home had scarce been held worthy to take off their masters' shoes, here considered themselves the peers and comrades of lords. Their importunity, haughtiness, and cruel boldness increased so greatly that afterwards, when travelling with the King through the country, they beat, wounded, and slew his faithful lieges with great cruelty, and plundered the people's goods, paying nothing for their victuals. . . . Nor was it expedient for any to resist these evils and oppressions, for if anyone protested that he would complain to the King, he was mercilessly slain without delay. If any prepared to resist, a number of them fell upon him and overpowered him. . . . In truth their position became such that they dared not meet the least of men alone, but when they wanted to do evil, and take vengeance upon any one, they went in whole bands to attack him.

41.

["Rolls of Parliament," ii. 354. September, 1397. (French.)]

The commons entreat the King to consider how that it was formerly ordained that those who should be put in the office of sergeant-at-arms should be chosen of good, worthy, and sufficient persons, and such as would duly and honestly perform their office; and in a certain number. And now, because there is great outcry in divers districts that the number of such sergeants is excessive, that they do not know how to perform their office as they should, and are not persons noble and worthy of such estate, nor

for the King's honour, but commit oppressions and excesses against the people by colour of their office—may it
please our lord the King to be informed of the number
and condition of such sergeants, and to appoint from
them or others such persons as shall be able and sufficient,
. . . for the King's honour, and the quiet of the people.

42.

[The Parliament of 1397-8; "Rolls of Parliament," iii. 349.   17
September, 1397.   The King had secured the appointment of
his agent, Sir John Bussy, as Speaker.]

The said Sir John Bussy . . . showed to the King, for
the commons, how, in the Parliament held at Westminster
on the first day of October, in the tenth year of the reign
of our lord the King, Thomas, Duke of Gloucester and
Richard, Earl of Arundel, traitors to the King and the
realm, by false imagination and compassing caused to be
made by statute a commission directed to themselves and
other persons nominated by them, to have the governance
of the King and the realm, as well in the King's household
as without, and in his lordships beyond the sea, as is contained in the said commission. . . .

. . . Which commission, and the statute touching it
seemed to the said commons to be prejudicial to the King
and his crown, and usurpation of his prerogative and royal
power.   And the said Duke of Gloucester and Earl of
Arundel sent a great personage, a peer of the realm, as
messenger to our lord the King, who told him on their
behalf that if he would not grant . . . the said commission and statute, he would be in great peril of his life;
and thus both the commission and the statute touching
it were made by constraint and compulsion, against the
King's will and pleasure.   The commons begged the King
that the commission and the statute . . . might be repealed in this present Parliament, and be utterly annulled,

18

as a thing done traitorously against his Regalie, his crown and his dignity.

Whereupon our lord the King, with the assent of all the lords spiritual and temporal, and the procurators of the clergy assembled in this present Parliament, and at the request of the commons, repealed and utterly annulled for ever the said statute in this point, and the commission. . . . And beyond this, the King, with the assent of all the said lords and commons, ordained . . . " that no such commission, or other like it, shall be ever henceforth pursued or made ; and that any who in time to come shall secretly or openly . . . procure such a commission to be made, or use jurisdiction and power by virtue of such commission, and be duly convicted thereof in Parliament, shall be adjudged a traitor, and this for high treason committed against the King and his crown ".[1]

43.

[Declaration of the Four Points of Treason ; *ibid.* iii. 351. Statutes, 21 Rich. II, c. 3.]

. . . Also the King, with the assent of all the lords of Parliament . . . and the commons, ordained . . . that any who shall compass and purpose the King's death, or to depose him, or to surrender his liege homage, or who shall raise the people and ride against him, to make war in his realm, and of this be duly attainted and convicted in Parliament shall be adjudged a traitor, for high treason against the crown ; and shall forfeit for himself and his heirs all his lands tenements . . . and all other inheritance that he has . . . to the King and his heirs.

And that this statute shall extend and hold as well in the case of those who are adjudged or attainted of any of the four points of the said treasons in this Parliament, as

[1] Cf. Statutes, 21 Rich. II. c. 2.

of those who shall be adjudged or attainted . . . in Parliament in time to come.

44.

[The pardons granted to the appellants of 1388 were expressly revoked. Then the commons proceeded to impeach the Archbishop of Canterbury, Arundel, who was banished; and the King's appellants brought their charges against the Earl of Arundel, who was immediately executed, and the Earl of Warwick, whose confession secured him sentence of imprisonment instead of death. When Gloucester was appealed, it was announced that he had died at Calais, and a confession made by him was produced, upon which sentence of treason was based. "Rolls of Parliament," iii. 352.]

Our lord the King, at the request of the commons and with the assent of all the lords assembled in this Parliament, has ordained and established, that if any, of whatsoever estate or condition shall pursue, procure, or advise, to repeal or annul any judgments given against any persons adjudged in this Parliament, or any statute or ordinance made in the same Parliament, or any part of them in any manner, and this be duly proved in Parliament, that he shall be adjudged and have execution as a traitor to the King and realm.[1]

45.

[Gloucester's Confession; "Rolls of Parliament," iii. 378. Professor Tait has shown, in "Owens College Historical Essays," 1902, that this was tampered with by Richard, being read to the Parliament in a brief and mutilated form.]

Thomas duk of Gloucestre, be the name Thomas of Wodestoke, the viii day of Septembre the yer of the Kyng

---

[1] Statutes, 21 Rich. II, c. 4. Extreme precautions were taken to secure this; at Westminster and again at Shrewsbury the lords were sworn on the Cross of Canterbury to uphold it, and similar declaration was obtained from the commons. On 29 September, Parliament was adjourned to meet at Shrewsbury on 28 January.

Richard on and twenty, in the Castel of Caleys be vertu of a Commission of the Kyng, as it is more pleynleche declared in the same Commission directyd to William Rikhill Justice, hathe iknowe and confessyd tofore the same William alle the matires and poyntz iwrete in this grete roule annexid to this sedule the weche cedule and grete roule beth asselid undir the sele of the forseyd William. Ande the same day of Septembre alle the matires and pointz before iknowe and confessid be the foreseyd duk in the Castel of Caleys, the forssaide duk be his owne honde fully and pleynly iwrete delyverid it to the same William Rikhill in presence of Johan Lancastre and Johan Lovetot. And al that evere the forseyd William Rikhill dede touching thys matire, it was ido in the presence of the forseyde Johan and Johan, and in none other manere.

I Thomas of Wodestok the viii day of Septembre, the yeer of my Lord the Kyng on and twenty, be the vertue of a Commission of my Lord the King the same yeer direktid to William Rykhill Justice, the which is comprehendid more pleynly in the forseid Commission, knowleche, that I was on wyth steryng of other men to assente to the makyng of a Commission; in the which Commission I amonges other restreyned my lord of his freedom, and toke upon me amonge other power reall trewly naght knowing ne wyting that tyme that I dede ayens his estate ne his realte, as I dede after and do now. And for as much as I knew afterward that I hadde do wronge, and taken upon me more than me owght to do, I submettede me to my Lord, and cryed him mercy and grace, and yet do als lowlych and as mekely as any man may, and putte me heygh and lowe in his mercy and in his grace, as he that always hath ben ful of mercy and of grace to all other.

Also, in that tyme that I came armed into my lordes presence, and into his Palais, howsoever that I dede it for drede of my lyf, I knowleche for certain that I dede evyll, and ayeyns his Regalie and his Estate; wherfor I submett me lowly and mekely into his mercy and to his grace.

Also, in that I toke my lordes lettres of his messagers and opened hem ayeyns his leve, I knowleche that I dede evyll: wherfor I putt me lowly in his grace.

Also, in that I sclaundred my lord, I knowleche that I dede evyll and wykkedly, in that, that I spake it unto hym in sclaunderouse wyse in audience of other folk. But by the wey that my sowle schall to, I mente none evyll therein. Nevertheles I wote and I knowleche that I dede evyll and unkunnyngelych: wherfor I submett me heghe and lowe in his grace.

Also, in that I among other communed for feer of my lyf to geve up myn hommage to my lord, I knowleche wel, that for certain that I among other communed and asked of certeins clercs, whethir that we myght yeve up our homage for drede of our lyves, or non; and whethir that we assentyd therto for to do it, trewlich and by my trowth I ne have now none full mynde therof, but I trowe rather ye than nay: wherfor I submett me heygh and lowe evermore in his grace.

Also, in that, that I was in place ther it was communed and spoken in manere of deposal of my liege loord trewly I knowleche wele, that we were assented therto for two days or three, and than we for to have done our homage and our oothes, and putt hem as heyly in hys estate as ever he was. But forsothe then I knowleche, that I dede untrewly and unkyndely as to hym that is my lyege loord, and hath bene so gode and kynde loord to me. Wherfor I beseche to hym noughtwythstondyng myn unkyndenesse, I beseche hym evermore of his mercy and of his grace, as lowly as any creature may beseche it unto his lyege loord.

And as of any newe thyng or ordenannce that ever

I shuld have wyten or knowen, ordeyned or assentyd, pryve or apert, that schuld have bene ageyns my loordys estate, or his luste, or ony that longeth abowte hym, syth that day that I swore unto hym at Langeley on Goddys body; trewly, and be that oothe that I ther made, I never knew of gaderyng ayeyns hym, ne none other that longeth unto hym.

And as touching all this poyntes that I have made confession of tofore William Rykhill Justice, in the which I wot wele that I have offendyd my loord unkyndely and untrewly, as I have seyde befor how that I have in all this poyntes offendid hym, and done ayeyns hym; trewly, and as I wyll answere before Godd, it was my menyng and my wenyng for to have do the best for his persone and for his estate. Nevertheles I wote wel, and know wele nowe, that my dedes and my werchynges were ayeyns myn entente. Bot, be the wey that my sowle schall to, of this poyntes and of all othir the which that I have done of neclygence and of unkunnyng, It was never myn entent, ne my wyll, ne my thoght, for to do thynge that schuld have bene distresse or harmyng ayeyns the salvation of my lyege loordy's persone, as I wyll answer tofor Godd at the day of Jugement.

And therefor I beseche my lyege and souverayn loord the Kyng, that he wyll of his heygh grace and benyngnytee accepte me to his mercy and his grace, as I that putt my lyf, my body, and my goode holy at his wyll, as lowlych as mekelych as any creature kan do or may do to his lyege loord. Besechyng to his heygh lordeschipp, that he wyll, for the passion that God soffred for all mankynde, and the compassion that he hadde of his moder on the Cros, and the pytee that he hadde of Marye Maudeleyne, that he wyll vouchesauf for to have compassion and pytee; and to accepte me unto his mercy and to his grace, as he that hath ever bene ful of mercy and of grace to all

his lyeges, and to all other that have noght been so neygh
unto hym as I have bene, thogh I be unworthy.

46.

[*Ibid.* iii. 357. The Session of 1398, at Shrewsbury, 28 January.
The King's appellants recalled the events of the Merciless
Parliament :—]

. . . Whereon the said appellants, considering the
summons of the said Parliament to have been expressly
against the rights of his person and royal estate, desiring
to acquit themselves towards the King as his loyal lieges,
entreated him, that the said Parliament might be annulled
. . . and that all the judgments, ordinances, and statutes
made and rendered therein . . . be annulled, revoked, repealed, and held for null, as thing done without the King's
authority, and against his will and liberty and the rights
of his crown. . . . And also the commons prayed the
King, . . . saying that their intent was to have entreated
likewise. And upon this, the lords spiritual and temporal
and the procurators of the clergy, severally examined, expressly assented, that the said Parliament, and all the
statutes, judgments, ordinances, and all other matters
done therein . . . be annulled and of no force and
effect. . . .

And also, as well the lords spiritual and temporal and
the procurators of the clergy, as the commons, were severally examined upon the aforesaid questions and the answers
of the Justices. . . . The which questions, and the replies
thereto were read and understood, and it was asked of all
the estates of Parliament, what they thought of the aforesaid answers?

And they said that it seemed to them that the Justices
gave their answers duly and loyally, as good and loyal
lieges of the King were bound to do.

47.

[*Ibid.* iii. 368.]

Item . . . the commons of the realm, with the assent of the lords spiritual and temporal, granted the King the subsidy on wool, wool-fells, and leather for the term of his life. . . .[1]

(*Ibid.*) Item, the commons prayed the King, " since they have by them divers petitions . . . not yet read or answered, and also, many other matters have been moved in the King's presence, the which for shortness of time cannot well be determined at present—that it may please him to commit to certain lords and others whom it shall please him, full power to examine, answer, and determine the aforesaid petitions and matters." . . .

To the which prayer the King assented. And thereupon with the authority and consent of Parliament he assigned—[the dukes of Lancaster, York, Aumale, Surrey, and Exeter, the marquess of Dorset, the earls of March, Salisbury, Northumberland, Gloucester, Worcester, and Wiltshire, or six of them ; and John Bussy, Henry Green, John Russel, Richard Chelmswyk, Robert Teye, and John Golafre or three of them for the commons] to examine, answer, and fully determine, as well all the aforesaid petitions and the matters contained in them, as all other matters moved in the presence of the King, and all the dependences of matters undetermined, as shall seem best to them according to their good advice and discretion, by authority of Parliament.[2]

---

[1] Also a "fifteenth" and a "tenth," and half a "fifteenth" and "tenth" for the coming year.

[2] The Parliament was dismissed on 31 January.

48.

[The affair of Norfolk and Hereford. At Westminster, 22 September ;
"Rolls of Parliament," iii. 353. (French.)]

. . . The commons rehearsing how that our lord the
King, graciously considering that certain great persons
named in the said commission made in the 10th year were
innocent of malice, therefore pardoned them, and bore
witness to their good report and bearing towards him in
that case—therefore humbly prayed our lord the King
that it might please him to consider, How that at the
time when Thomas Duke of Gloucester, Richard Earl of
Arundel, and Thomas Earl of Warwick, rose up and rode
against him contrary to their allegiance, the said duke
and earls would have ridden to seek our lord the King
wherever he might be found within the realm, and to kill
great number of his lieges, for the accomplishing of their
evil purpose and intent, if they had not been hindered by
the honourable persons of the King's blood, Henry of Lancaster, Earl of Derby and Thomas Mowbray, Earl of
Nottingham.[1] Who, knowing and understanding that the
deed of the said duke and earls was notoriously contrary
to their allegiance and the estate of our lord the King and
desiring to do their duty towards him, departed from the
company of the said duke and earls and came to the King's
honourable presence.   And because it is to the King's
honour to cherish good and worthy persons according to
their merit and deserts, that it might please him to hold
especially commended the said Earls of Derby and Nottingham, and openly to declare in this present Parliament
their estate, good name and fame, and loyal bearing.

Whereupon the King, sitting in his royal dignity in
Parliament, answered—that this matter was better known
to him than to any other; and he bore testimony . . . to

[1] Created Dukes of Hereford and Norfolk, 29 September.

their good port and loyalty . . . and that he well knew
that they loyally did their duty towards their King, and
came to him as loyal lieges from the company of the said
duke, and the Earls of Arundel and Warwick, and since
have remained with him. . . . And he willed and granted
that as well they as those who were in their company when
the duke and earls . . . thus rode against him . . . should
be utterly pardoned; without being impeached, molested,
or grieved for the aforesaid cause at any time to come.
And beyond this the King, with the assent and advice of
all the lords of Parliament, and at the prayer of the commons, ordained that this declaration and grant should have
force and virtue of a statute, and be held for a statute.

49.

[At Shrewsbury, 30 January, *ibid.* iii. 360, 382.]

Be it remembered that Henry of Lancaster, Duke of
Hereford came before our lord the King in his Parliament
held at Shrewsbury, . . . bearing in his hand a schedule;
and said to the King, that by his command he came into
his honourable presence at Hawood, and after his coming
there the King told him how he had heard that Thomas
Mowbray, Duke of Norfolk, had spoken many dishonour-
able words in slander of his person; the which words as
the King had heard, were addressed to the said Duke of
Hereford.   Whereupon the King charged the Duke, on his
allegiance, loyally to repeat these words as they were said
to him.   The Duke of Hereford, not from malice, enmity
or other cause, but solely to comply with the King's command, as he was bound, wrote down the words in substance,
in the said schedule so far as he had understood them and
borne them in his memory.   The which schedule the said
Duke delivered to the King, with his protestation upon
this, in the following terms:—

Making protestation, that I may add to or diminish all
the matters herein . . . as I shall please, or need shall
be, saving always the substance of my libel—Sire, in the
month of December in the 21st year of your reign, as the
Duke of Hereford was riding between Brentford and London, the Duke of Norfolk overtook him in great haste, and
spoke with him upon divers matters, among which he said
"We are in point to be undone!" And the Duke of
Hereford asked "Why?" He replied, that it was for the
deed of Radcot Bridge. And the Duke of Hereford said
"How should this be? for he pardoned us, and declared
for us in the Parliament, saying that we have been good
and loyal towards him". The Duke of Norfolk replied,
"Notwithstanding this, it will be done with us as it has
been done with others before, for he would annul this
record". And the Duke of Hereford said that it would be
great marvel, since the King had said it before the people,
that afterwards he should have it annulled. The Duke of
Norfolk said further, that it was a wondrous world and
false, "For I know," said he, "that if it had not been for
some persons, my lord your father of Lancaster and you
would have been seized or slain when you came to Windsor
after the Parliament". And he said that the Dukes of
Aumale and Exeter, the Earl of Worcester and he were
pledged that they would never agree to undo any lord without just and reasonable cause; and that the malice of this
deed was in the Duke of Surrey, the Earl of Wiltshire, and
the Earl of Salisbury, drawing to them the Earl of
Gloucester; and they had sworn to undo other lords, namely
the Dukes of Lancaster, Hereford, Aumale, and Exeter,
the Marquis and he. Also the Duke of Norfolk said that
they were of purpose to reverse the judgment of Earl
Thomas of Lancaster, "and this would be disherison to
you, and many others". The Duke of Hereford replied
"God forbid, for it would be great marvel if the King

should agree to that " ; for he had made him, as he thought, such good cheer, and promised him to be good lord to him. And he himself knew well how that he had sworn by St. Edward to be good lord to him, and to all the others.

The Duke of Norfolk answered, saying that so had he done to him many times, on the Body of Christ, and in spite of that he did not trust him the better. And he said further, that the King was for drawing the Earl of March and others with the assent and purpose of the said four lords, to destroy those aforesaid. The Duke of Hereford answered " If it be so, we can never trust him ". And the Duke of Norfolk replied " For certain, no ; for although they may not accomplish their purpose at present, they will destroy us in our houses ten years hence ".

50.

[The matter led to a quarrel between the two dukes, and in the following March, Richard's parliamentary committee referred the matter to a court of Chivalry, to be held at Windsor in April ; this court appointed a day for the settlement of the dispute by combat, but on 16 September, as the duel was about to begin, Richard intervened, imposing sentence of banishment upon the dukes—Norfolk's for life, Hereford's for ten—then six—years. "Annales Ricardi," 1399. (Latin.)]

There were some flatterers who told the King that he deserved to be called a glorious conqueror, because thus without war, fire or slaughter of his commons, by his own wisdom he had crushed his mortal enemies ; in that he had slain the Duke of Gloucester and the Earl of Arundel, and flung the rest into prison. (And these were of the mendicant orders, who offered this adulation in hope of advancement.) Spurred on by these falsehoods, he borrowed great sums of money from many lords and other persons, promising them faithfully by his Letters Patent that he would repay the money at an appointed time. But he never afterwards restored it. Soon after

Easter, he invented other almost incredible pretexts whereby he might injure his subjects yet more grievously, and exact great sums of money by fear of death. He charged the people of seventeen counties with having joined the Duke of Gloucester against him, wherefore he was prepared to raid them as his public enemies. And first he took security from them, as though he dared not enter them without an army unless first he had received surety that they would contrive no ill against him or his friends. Then he sent certain bishops, with other worshipful persons to these counties, to warn all spiritual and temporal lords, and those of the middle sort to submit to the King and confess that they had been traitors to him; whereas they had never harmed him by word or deed. By which pretext both clergy and laity were compelled to grant him insupportable sums of money, to recover his good will. And so this money required from different counties was called " Le Plesaunce," because it was raised to please the King.[1]

51.

["Rolls of Parliament," iii. 372.   (French.)   John of Gaunt died on 3 February, 1399.]

Be it remembered that on Monday the 18th day of March in the 22nd year of the reign of our lord the King, at Westminster in the King's presence, it was shown by the Chancellor of England, before many lords spiritual and temporal present there at the King's command, how that after the judgment given againt Henry Duke of Hereford at Coventry, by authority of Parliament, he had made suit to our lord the King by petition concerning divers matters . . .; and among other things especially, that in case any succession or heritage should descend to

[1] Richard kept the letters of obligation, but actually for the time remitted the payments.

him in his absence, for which he should do homage, he might by his attornies sue and have livery of such succession or heritage . . . and that his homage and fealty might be respited—as fully appears by the Letters Patent made thereon.

These letters having then been seen and diligently examined, with all the circumstances and dependencies thereof, it was found that they were plainly contrary to the judgments given at Coventry, because the Duke, after this judgment, was not a person able to have or accept the benefit of the said letters.

And therefore it was adjudged by our lord the King, and by [the Dukes of York, Aumale, and Exeter, the Marquis of Dorset, the Earls of Salisbury, Northumberland, Gloucester, Worcester, and Wiltshire] and John Bussy, Henry Green, John Russell, and Robert Teye, knights coming for the Parliament, having power for this by virtue and authority of Parliament, with the assent of the lords spiritual and temporal, that the said Letters Patent . . . be utterly revoked and annulled . . . and that the enrolment in the Chancery be cancelled.

52.

[News of Richard's decision determined Lancaster to return at the first opportunity. On 29 May Richard left for Ireland, leaving the Duke of York as Regent in England. On 4 July Lancaster landed at Ravenspur, was rapidly joined by the northern lords, and marched on Bristol; before the end of July the Regent had abandoned resistance. Richard landed in Wales before the end of July, but became discouraged, and fled to the North, where he remained until his submission to Lancaster on 19 August. "Rolls of Parliament," iii. 416, translated from the Latin.]

Be it remembered that on Monday, the Feast of St. Michael, in the 23rd year of the reign of King Richard II, the lords spiritual and temporal and other considerable persons first deputed . . . to perform the following act, being gathered at Westminster in the accustomed place of the Council, went into the presence of King Richard, then within the Tower of London, at about nine of the clock.

And when the Earl of Northumberland, in place of all those associated with him, had rehearsed how that the King at another time, at Conway in North Wales, being in his full liberty, promised the lord Thomas Archbishop of Canterbury, and the said Earl of Northumberland that he would resign and renounce the crown of England and France and his royal majesty, for the causes there admitted by him, touching his unfitness and insufficiency; and this in the best manner and form in which he could do so, as by the counsel of skilled persons should be thought best to be ordained—The King readily replied that he was willing to carry out what he had formerly promised. He desired, however, to have speech with Henry Duke of Lancaster, and the aforesaid Bishop, his kinsmen, before he should fulfil his promise. And he asked for a copy of the resignation that he should make to be given him, so that he might in the meantime deliberate upon it. The copy having been given him, the Duke and the others returned to their lodging.

Afterwards, on the same day after dinner, the King greatly desiring the coming of the Duke of Lancaster, who tarried a long time, at length the Duke, and the aforesaid lords and others, and also the Archbishop of Canterbury, came into the King's presence in the Tower, the lords Roos, Willoughby, and Abergavenny and many others being present.

After the King had spoken apart with the said Duke and the Archbishop, looking from one to the other with a cheerful countenance, as it seemed to those standing round, calling all those present to him, he said openly before them that he was ready to make renunciation and resignation according to his promise. And although, to avoid the labour of such lengthy reading, he might, as he was told, have read the renunciation (that was contained in a parchment schedule) by deputy, the King, holding the schedule in his hand said at once willingly, as it seemed, and with cheerful looks, that he would read it himself. And he read it through distinctly, absolving his lieges, and making renunciation, oath, and declaration, as is fully contained in the said schedule, and signed it with his own hand.

And immediately he added thereto by his own words—that if it were in his power, the Duke of Hereford should succeed him. But because this in no wise depended upon his authority, as he said, he asked the said Archbishop of York and the Bishop of Hereford, whom he appointed as his procurators to declare and intimate his renunciation and resignation to all the estates of the realm, to declare to the people his intent and will in this matter. And in token of his intention, he thereupon drew from his finger the gold ring with his signet, and placed it on the Duke's finger, desiring the same, as he affirmed, to be known to all the estates.

And when this was done, mutual farewells having been taken, they left the Tower to return to their lodging.

On the morrow, to wit, Tuesday, the Feast of St. Jerome, in the Great Hall at Westminster, in a place honourably prepared for the holding of Parliament, the Archbishops of Canterbury and York, the Duke of Lancaster, and other lords spiritual and temporal being present, and a great multitude of the people of the realm being gathered there on account of the Parliament, the Duke of Lancaster occupying his accustomed place, and the royal throne, prepared with cloth of gold, being vacant—the Archbishop of York . . . according to the King's injunction, publicly declared the resignation to have been made by him, with the delivery of his seal, and caused the said resignation to be read in Latin and in English. . . .

[The estates and people being then asked whether they accepted the resignation, unanimously did so; the articles of accusation were read, and it was agreed that Richard should be formally deposed. Seven persons were appointed to draw up a formal sentence of deposition, which was then read by the Bishop of St. Asaph.]

And forthwith, it being manifest from the foregoing that the realm of England . . . was vacant, Henry Duke of Lancaster, rising from his place and standing erect so that he might be seen by the people, signing himself with the cross on his forehead and breast, claimed the kingdom of England, the crown and all its members, in the mother tongue, in the following words :—

"In the name of Fadir, Son, and Holy Gost, I Henry of Lancastre challenge this Rewme of Ynglond and the Corone with all the membres and the appurtenances als I yt am disendit be right lyne of the Blode comyng fro the gude lorde Kyng Henry therde, and thorghe that ryght that God of his grace hath sent me, with helpe of my kyn and of my Frendes to recover it; the whiche Rewme was in poynt to be undone for defaut of Governance and un-doying of the gode lawes."

After the which claim, the lords spiritual and temporal, and all the estates of the realm being asked generally and separately, What they thought of that claim? the said estates, and the whole people without any delay or diffi-culty, unanimously consented that the Duke should reign over them.

[The Duke showed Richard's signet to the assembled people, and was then led to the throne by the Archbishop of Canterbury, where he prayed for a short time. Both Archbishops then seated him upon the throne, amid loud acclamations, and the Archbishop gave a short address.]

And when the address was finished, the said lord King Henry, to set at rest the minds of his subjects, thereupon publicly said these words:— "Sires, I thank God and yowe Spirituel and Temporal, and all the astates of the lond; and do yowe to wyte, it es noght my will that no man thynk it be waye of Conquest I wold disherit any man of his heritage, franches, or other ryghtes that hym aght to have, no put hym out of that that he has and has had by the gude lawes and custumes of the Rewme; except thos persons that has ben agan the gude purpose and the comune profyt of the Rewme."

53.

[From the charges against Richard; "Rolls of Parliament," iii. 424. (Latin.)   There were thirty-three articles, those of a political character being mainly concerned with his proceedings in 1387 and 1397-98.]

Item, when the King asked and received many sums by way of loan from many lords and others of the realm, to be repaid at a certain term, notwithstanding that he had promised each individual from whom he received these loans, by his letters patent that he would repay them at the time appointed, he did not fulfil his promise, nor has satisfaction yet been made for the money, whence the creditors are greatly distressed. . . .

Item, whereas the King of England is able to live becomingly upon the issues of his realm and the estates belonging to the crown, without burdening his people, when that the realm be not charged with the expenses of war, the same King, although during almost the whole of his time there were truces between the realm of England and its enemies, not only gave away the greater part of his patrimony to unworthy persons, but on account of this every year charged his people with so many burdensome grants that they were sorely and excessively oppressed, to the impoverishment of his realm; not applying the money so raised to the common profit and advantage of his realm, but lavishly dissipating it upon his own pomp, display, and vain glory. And great sums of money are still owing for provisions for his household, and for his other purchases, although he had wealth and treasure more than any of his predecessors within memory.

Item, being unwilling to protect and preserve the just laws and customs of the realm . . . frequently, from time to time, when the laws were declared and set forth to him by the Justices and others of his Council, and he should have done justice to those who sought it according to those laws—he said expressly, with harsh and insolent looks, that his laws were in his own mouth, and sometimes, within his breast; and that he alone could change or establish the laws of his realm. Deceived by which opinion, he would not allow justice to be done to many of his lieges, but compelled numbers of persons to desist from suing common right by threats and fear.

Item, after that certain statutes were established in his Parliament, which were binding until they should be especially repealed by the authority of another Parliament, the King, desiring to enjoy such liberty that no such statutes might restrain him . . . cunningly procured petition to be put forward in Parliament on behalf of the community of the realm, and to be granted him in general—that he might be as free as any of his predecessors; by colour of which petition and concession the King frequently caused and commanded many things to be done contrary to such statutes then unrepealed.

Item, although by statute and custom of the realm, upon the summons of Parliament the people of each county ought to be free to choose and depute knights for the county to be present in Parliament, set forth their grievances, and sue for remedy . . . yet, the more freely to carry out his rash designs, the King frequently commanded the sheriffs to cause certain persons nominated by himself to come to his Parliament; and the knights thus favourable to him he could, and frequently did, induce, sometimes by fear, and divers threats, sometimes by gifts, to consent to measures prejudicial to the realm and excessively burdensome to the people; and especially he induced them to grant him the subsidy of wools for the term of his life, and another subsidy for a term of years, greatly oppressing the people.

Item . . . he unlawfully commanded that the sheriffs throughout the kingdom, should swear, beyond their ancient and accustomed oath, to obey all mandates under his signet, whenever they should be addressed to them; and in case . . . they should hear of any persons . . . saying or repeating in public or in private anything tending to the discredit or slander of his person, to arrest them . . . and cause them to be imprisoned . . . until they should have further command from the King; as may be found by record. . . .

Item, in many Great Councils, when the lords of the realm, Justices and others were charged faithfully to counsel the King in matters touching the estate of himself and the realm, the said lords, . . . when they gave counsel according to their discretion were often suddenly and so sharply rebuked and censured by him, that they dared not . . . speak the truth in giving their advice.

Item, the King was wont almost continually to be so variable and dissembling in his words and writings, and so utterly contradictory, especially in writing to the Pope and to Kings, and other lords within and without the realm, and to his other subjects, that scarcely any living man, being acquainted with his ways, could or would trust him. Indeed, he was held so faithless and inconstant that it gave ground for scandal not only as to his own person, but to the whole realm, and especially among foreigners throughout the world who became aware of it.

54.

[The formal renunciation of allegiance addressed to Richard in the Tower by Sir W. Thirning; "Rolls of Parliament," iii. 424.]

Sir it is welle knowe to yowe, that ther was a Parlement somond of all the States of the Reaume for to be at Westmynstre, and to begynne on the Tuesday in the morwe of the fest of St. Michall the Archaungell that was yesterday, by cause of the whiche somons, all the States of this Londe were ther gadyrd, the whiche States hole made the same persones that ben comen here to yowe nowe her Procuratours, and gafen hem full auctorite and power, and charged hem, for to say the wordes that we sall say to yowe in her name and on their behalve; that is to wytten, the Byshop of Seint Assa for Ersbishoppes and Byshoppes, the Abbot of Glastenbery for Abbotes and Priours, and all other men of Holy Chirche, Seculers and Rewelers; the Erle of Gloucestre for Dukes and Erles; the Lord of Berkeley for Barones and Banerettes, Sir Thomas Irpyngham Chaumberleyn, for all the Bachileers and Commons of this lond be southe; Sire Thomas Grey for all the Bachileers and Commons by North; and my felawe Johan Markham and me, for to come wyth hem for all thes States. And so, Sire, thes wordes and the doying that we sall say to yowe is not onlych our wordes, bot the wordes and the doynges of all the States of this lond and our charge and in her name. And he answerd and sayd, that he wyst well that we wold noght say bot as we were charged. Sire, ye remembre yowe well, that on Moneday in the fest of Seint Michele the Archaungell, ryght here in this Chaumbre, and in what presence, ye renounsed and cessed of the State of Kyng, and of Lordesship and of all the Dignite and Wirsship that longed therto, and assoiled all your lieges of her ligeance, and obeisance that longed to yowe, uppe the fourme that is contened in the same Renunciation and

Cession, which ye redde your self by your mouth, and affermed it by youre othe and by your owne writyng.   Opon
whiche ye made and ordeyned your Procuratures the Ers-
byshopp of York and the Bysshop of Hereford, for to notifie
and declare in your name thes renunciation and Cession at
Westmynstre to all the States and all the poeple that was
ther gadyrd by cause of the sommons forsayd; the which
thus don yesterday by thes Lordes your Procuratures, and
welle herde and understonden, thes Renunciation and
Cession ware pleinelich and frelich accepted and fullich
agreed by all the States and Poeple forseide.   And over this
Sire, at the instance of all thes States and Poeple ther
ware certein articles of Defautes in your governance redde
there; and tho well herd and pleinelich understonden to all
the States forseide, hem thoght hem so trewe, and so
notorie and knowen, that by the Causes and by mowe other
as thei sayd, and havyng consideration to your owne
wordes in your owne Renunciation and Cession, that ye
were not worthy, no sufficeant ne able for to governe for
your owne demerites, as it is more pleinerlych contened
therin, hem thoght that was resonable and Cause for to
depose yowe, and her Commissaries that thei made and or-
deined, as it is of record ther, declared and decreed, and
ajugged yowe for to be deposed and pryved, and in dede
deposed yowe and pryved yowe of the State of Kyng, and
of the Lordesship contened in the Renunciation and Cession
forsayd, and of all the Dignite and Wyrsshipp, and of all the
Administration that longed therto.   And we, Procuratours
to all thes States and Poeple forsayd, os we be charged by
hem, and by hir autorite gyffen us, and in her name, yeld
yowe uppe, for all the States and Poeple forsayd, homage
liege and feaute, and all Ligeance, and all other bondes,
charges, and services that longe therto.   And that non of
all these States and Poeple fro thys time forward ne bere
yowe feyth, ne do yowe obeisance os to that Kynge.

And he answerd and seyd, That he loked not ther after;
Bot he sayde, that after all this he hoped that is Cosyn
wolde be goode Lord to hym.

55.

[The following are the opening stanzas of a poem addressed to Henry
IV on his accession, by John Gower ("English Works," ed.
Macaulay, ii. 483).]

O worthi noble kyng, Henry the ferthe
In whom the glade fortune is befalle
The poeple to governe uppon this erthe,
God hath the chose in comfort of us alle ;
The worschipe of this lond, which was doun falle,
Now stant upriht thurgh grace of thi goodnesse
Which every man is holde for to blesse.

The highe god of his justice allone
The right which longeth to thi regalie
Declared hath to stonde in thi persone,
And more than god may no man justifie,
Thi title is knowe uppon thin ancestrie,
The londes folk hath ek thy riht affermed ;
So stant the regne of God and man confermed.

Ther is no man mai seie in other wise
That god himself ne hath thi riht declared,
Whereof the lond is boun to thi servise,
Which for difalte of helpe hath longe cared :[1]
But now ther is no mannes herte spared
To love and serve and wirche thi plesance,
And al is this thurgh godes purveiance.

[1] Been troubled, distressed.

INDEX

ADMIRAL, duties of, 116-19.
Aiguillon, siege of, 57.
Anjou, county of, 97.
"Annales Ricardi II," extracts from, 265, 271, 284.
Antwerp, council at, 7.
Appellant, the Lords, articles drawn up by, 254.
Aquitaine, duchy of, 42, 69.
Archers, English, 48-50; on ships, 117, 120-21, 127, 130, 138; and hobblers, 29, 206.
Arundel, Richard Earl of, 242, 243, 245, 250, 254, 259, 271, 273, 275, 281.
Athol, Earl of, 3.
Avesbury, Robert of, extracts from his "Chronicle," 4, 15, 36, 41, 43, 57, 59, 61, 64, 70, 74, 150.
Avignon, 10, 69, 72, 73, 76, 181, 190.

BAKER, Geoffrey le, extracts from his "Chronicle," 149, 183.
Ball, John, cited by Archbishop of Canterbury, 194; his preaching, 232-34.
Balliol, Edward of, 24.
Barfleur, capture of, 31, 34.
Beacons, to be kindled, 111.
Beggars, able-bodied, 152, 154, 163.
Bells, church, used as warning, 112.
Benedict XII, see Pope.
Bible, in English, arguments for, 167.
Black Death, the, 145-52; "firste deth," 168.
— Prince, see Edward.
Blois, Charles of, 15, 64, 65.
Bologna, Cardinal of, 70.
Bradwardine, Thomas, death of, during pestilence, 147.
Brember, Nicholas, 254-58.
Bristol, French pirates towards, 115; pestilence at, 145, 149.

Brittany, expedition to (1342), 15, 18, 21; campaign in (1347), 64.
Burghersh, Sir Bartholomew, 18, 46 (note), 62; Chamberlain, 67, 68; letters of, 34-36.

CAEN, siege of, 33, 35, 38.
Calais, siege of, 45; Captain of, letter from, 61; failure to relieve, 59, 61-64; truce of, 65; agreements at, 69; treaty of, 88; cession of (1360), 90; Bishop of Norwich at, 107; English outside, in 1383, 110; expenditure upon, 221; conferences at, 243; restoration of, suggested, 257; Duke of Gloucester at, 271, 276.
Canterbury, Archbishop of, John Stratford, 4, 17, 20; letters to, 34-36, 62.
— — Simon Islip, 66, 159.
— — Simon Langham, mandate of, 194.
— — Simon Sudbury, Chancellor, 226; murdered, 234, 235.
— — William Courtenay, deals with heresy, 200, 201; Chancellor, 237; quarrels with Richard II, 245, 249.
— — Thomas Arundel, 268; banished, 275; supports Henry of Lancaster, 287-89.
— pilgrims to, 230; rebels in, 234.
Cardinal, of Bologna, 70.
— of Périgord, 78-79, 178, 182.
Cardinals, at Malestroit, 16-17; at Lisieux, 42; at Calais, 62; at Avignon, 181; English, not created, 183; complaint against Pope and, 189.
Chandos, Sir John, 49, 75, 126.
Chaplains, to be compelled to serve, 159.

PRINTED IN GREAT BRITAIN BY THE UNIVERSITY PRESS, ABERDEEN

H)